The Battle of Sekigahara

The Battle of Sekigahara

The Greatest, Bloodiest, Most Decisive Samurai Battle Ever

Chris Glenn

FRONTLINE
BOOKS

An imprint of
Pen & Sword Books Ltd

FRONTLINE
BOOKS

First published in Great Britain in 2021 by

FRONTLINE BOOKS
an imprint of Pen & Sword Books Ltd,
47 Church Street, Barnsley, S. Yorkshire, S70 2AS

ISBN: 978 1 399014 137

CIP data records for this title are available from the British Library

For more information on our books, please visit www.frontline-books.com, email info@frontline-books.com or write to us at the above address.

Printed and bound by CPI Group (UK) Ltd, Croydon, CR0 4YY
Typeset by Concept, Huddersfield, West Yorkshire

Pen & Sword Books Ltd incorporates the imprints of Pen & Sword Archaeology, Atlas, Aviation, Battleground, Discovery, Family History, History, Maritime, Military, Naval, Politics, Social History, Transport, True Crime, Claymore Press, Frontline Books, Praetorian Press, Seaforth Publishing and White Owl

For a complete list of Pen and Sword titles please contact
PEN & SWORD LTD
47 Church Street, Barnsley, South Yorkshire, S70 2AS, England
E-mail: enquiries@pen-and-sword.co.uk

Or

PEN AND SWORD BOOKS
1950 Lawrence Rd, Havertown, PA 19083, USA
E-mail: Uspen-and-sword@casematepublishers.com

For Toshiro and Leia.

With special thanks to Yuka.

SEKIGAHARA

泣かぬなら殺してしまえホトトギス

Nakanu nara koroshite shimae, hototogisu.

If the cuckoo won't sing, I'll kill it.

– Oda Nobunaga

泣かぬなら泣かせてみようホトトギス

Nakanu nara nakasete miseyo, hototogisu.

If the cuckoo won't sing, I'll make it want to sing.

– Toyotomi Hideyoshi

泣かぬなら泣くまでまとうホトトギス

Nakanu nara naku made matou, hototogisu.

If the cuckoo won't sing, I'll wait for it to sing.

– Tokugawa Ieyasu

Contents

List of Illustrations

can be seen below the red and white power pylon bottom left of Mt. Nangu. Ieyasu's second command post was positioned within the clump of pine trees, at the very centre of the photograph. The Eastern forces' front lines were where the houses border the rice fields.

features were recreated by Dr Nagayasu Shuichi, former Chief of Engineering, Tokyo National Research Institute of Police Sciences at the request of photographer and descendant of Mitsunari, Mr. Ishida Takayuki. It appears that Mitsunari had a pronounced defect in his teeth that caused them to bow outwards. The rest of his skeleton was later studied by Dr. Ishida Tetsuro (no relation) of the Kansai Idai Medical University.

32–33. The forensically-recreated face of Ishida Mitsunari. (Ishida family collection)

List of Maps

Acknowledgments

I am profoundly grateful to my parents, John and Val Glenn, and to the members of the Encounter Bay (South Australia) and Sapporo Teine (Hokkaido, Japan) Rotary Clubs for giving me the life-changing opportunity to come to Japan all those years ago. My deepest gratitude also goes to the staff and students of Sapporo Seiryo High School (1985) and to the Yamamoto, Yamagishi and Watanabe families.

I am indebted to Kato Yuka for helping to source materials, checking details and following me countless times to the battlefield and most grateful to David White for his valued friendship, advice and tireless support while fine-tuning my manuscript.

To traditional armourer Ogawa Nobuo Sensei for allowing this foreigner the honour of being your first apprentice and for that very first trip together to Sekigahara. To my fellow members of the Japan Armor and Weapons Research and Preservation Society. Thank you Yamauchi Naomi Sensei for the cover calligraphy, Ito Hironobu for the maps and graphics, Ishida Takayuki (15th descendant of Ishida Mitsunari) and to the Town of Sekigahara, Department of Education and the Gifu Sekigahara Battlefield Memorial Museum. Thanks also to the team at Frontline for getting it all together.

And to the samurai, East and West, who fought and died for peace at Sekigahara.

Preface

I first came across the name Sekigahara in April 1985. As a Rotary exchange student based in Sapporo, Hokkaido, I had been given a copy of Japanese writer Yoshikawa Eiji's *Musashi*, brilliantly translated by Charles S. Terry. The book opens with a description of Musashi lying amongst the corpses at the end of what would become recognised as Japan's biggest, bloodiest and most decisive of all samurai battles, the Battle of Sekigahara, which took place on 21 October 1600.

Musashi proved to be a major turning point in my life for not only having introduced me to the life and works of the master swordsman Miyamoto Musashi, but also to the first battle he was said to have taken part in as a 17-year-old adventurer. Since that time, for me, the name Sekigahara has had a magical connotation.

Even though there is so much interest in the samurai worldwide, the Battle of Sekigahara is still relatively unknown outside of Japan. Compared with other great battles throughout world history, it remains markedly over-looked. Looking at some of the greatest battles in history and the number of participants killed, we find:

> The Battle of Culloden (16 April 1746)...............2,000 killed
> The Battle of Hastings (14 October 1066) ....6,000 killed
> The Battle of Gettysburg (1–3 July 1863) ....7,863 killed
> The Battle of Agincourt (25 October 1415) ....10,000 killed
> The Battle of Sekigahara (21 October 1600) ......30,000 killed
> The Battle of Waterloo (18 June 1815) ....47,000 killed

Comparing Gettysburg to Sekigahara, both civil war battles, the number of deaths at Sekigahara was more than four times that of Gettysburg, which was fought over three days, not six hours. Sekigahara saw the deaths of an estimated 30,000 samurai and many noble clans destroyed in those six hours of battle alone, as well as many more deaths in the other engagements leading up to the great battle.

Sekigahara was a major turning point in Japanese history. It signified an end to over 200 years of civil unrest and brought about the political unification of Japan. Victory for Tokugawa Ieyasu at Sekigahara led to the revival of the dormant position of shogun and opened the doors to the Tokugawa clan's 260-year hold on the nation, ushering in a relatively calm period in Japanese history. It was the decisive battle that would forge the Japan we know today and for these reasons alone the story of the Battle of Sekigahara should be known and remembered. It was a time of absolute horror, not just for the samurai but for the townsfolk of Sekigahara also, to have witnessed such a ferocious battle fought just prior to the autumn harvest and to then have been encumbered with the clean-up of corpses for months afterwards.

My first visit to Sekigahara was on 21 October 1994, 394 years to the day of the great battle. I had become apprenticed to Japanese armourer Ogawa Nobuo and together with his wife, we made the 50km trip from Nagoya to the battlefield in a light rain. The killing fields of Sekigahara appeared almost as I had imagined and had barely changed in the centuries since the battle was fought. Sekigahara is a small, flat plain of rich greenery, gently sloping upwards towards the surrounding lushly forested, rolling hills and mountains that seem to suddenly spring from the earth in the way Japanese mountains do. On the plain were numerous rice fields of different sizes and shapes almost ready for harvesting. Small copses of trees and clumps of houses dotted the flatland as the village of Sekigahara has slowly encroached on the actual battlefields. It was a scene of calm and serenity, with little to show for the horror and bloodshed that once and indefinitely stained this land. I was aware of how many had participated in the battle and of the huge number of casualties and was shocked to find the area was far smaller than I had imagined. The bulk of the fighting took place in a strip about 500m wide and a kilometre long. Indeed, once the fog lifted on the morning of that fateful day in 1600, the samurai who had taken their positions on the field were also surprised at the close proximity of the enemy.

In 2000, along with Ogawa *Sensei* and a few members of the Japan Armor and Weapons Research and Preservation Society, I took part in the 400th anniversary re-enactments, along with 850 others from across the nation. On the Saturday I played a role in the Western forces, who had been situated just below Mount Sasao and on the Sunday, that of an Eastern army samurai.

I commenced researching and writing for my first book on Sekigahara in 1996, dismayed at the lack of quality information in English on this vitally important turning point in Japanese history. In 2015, I was invited to become one of the committee members and advisors serving on the board of the Governor of Gifu Prefecture and Mayor of Sekigahara's 'Sekigahara Grand Vision' project. For my efforts in wanting to preserve and promote the old battlefields, in 2017, the Mayor of Sekigahara asked if I would accept the role of Sekigahara Tourism Ambassador.

This is the story of the greatest samurai field battle in history, encompassing numerous causes and a great number of smaller skirmishes that escalated into the decisive battle, a six-hour engagement that took place from 8 a.m. on the morning of Saturday, 21 October 1600. The story is long, intrinsic, filled with some fascinating characters, complex plots, politics, intrigue and conflict. *Dozo*, enjoy.

Introduction

For Japan, the sixteenth century was a period of incessant civil strife, the land wracked by war and chaos. The government of the long-ruling Ashikaga shogunate, a relatively weak and decentralised authority that had lasted for almost two and a half centuries, collapsed in 1564 following the death of the 13th shogun, Yoshiteru. Yoshiteru was called the *Kengo*, or Great Sword Shogun, as he seriously undertook sword practice and upheld the military traditions and as such was acknowledged as being more samurai-like than any of his predecessors. He negotiated peace between many of the warring *daimyo* and sought to reaffirm the authority of his position, something his handlers, the influential Miyoshi *Sanninshu* (the Triumvirs Miyoshi Masayasu, Miyoshi Nagayuki and Iwanari Tomomichi) wished to prevent. However, Yoshiteru failed to stem the Triumvirs' power and his attempt at re-establishing his authority only made them more daring – daring enough to attack and bring about Yoshiteru's forced suicide. This resulted in the installation of a powerless puppet regime, leaving various provincial warlords to fight over the divided land. Alliances of convenience were formed and broken with regularity. The *daimyo*, the mighty land-holding warlords, rose and fell from power almost overnight. It was one such warlord, Oda Nobunaga, who showed great promise in his efforts to unite the nation under a single ruler and bring peace to the country. He rose from the position of a lesser *daimyo* to become one of the most honoured men in the empire.[1]

Oda Nobunaga

Oda Nobunaga was born in 1534 during the height of the unrest that had rocked Japan for almost 400 years. The second son of Oda Nobuhide, the *daimyo* of Owari province (present-day western Aichi Prefecture), Nobunaga was entrusted with his father's ever-expanding domain, which he ruled from

---

1.   Japan at this time was fragmented into various domains called *kuni*, or countries, hence the term 'empire' is used in this context.

the clan's well-fortified castle at Nagoya. The Owari districts, held by the Oda clan, were strategically important, with ample rice-growing plains to the north and well irrigated by numerous wide rivers flowing into the rich fishing grounds and salt-producing waters of Ise Bay in the south-west. The sea also allowed for trade and transportation, altogether making the Owari districts highly desirable. These productive agricultural lands were hemmed in on all sides by the Oda clan's rivals. The young lord was well aware of his enemies' intentions and seems to have deliberately acted the fool in order to deceive them.

In 1551, when Nobunaga was 17, his father died unexpectedly following a short illness, leaving Nobunaga as the head of the Oda clan. Dressed inappropriately for his father's funeral, he stormed into the Bansho-ji Temple, threw incense at the altar and upended the offertory table in full view of his family and retainers, before departing without a word to the mourners, family, vassals or monks. Upon witnessing this rash and undisciplined conduct, many thought the noble Oda clan had reached the end of their line. Few saw much of a future under the wild son of their late lord, Nobuhide.

Nobunaga's early life is riddled with similar episodes. On a visit to Gifu Castle to meet his prospective father-in-law, Saito Dosan, Nobunaga is said to have arrived facing backwards on his horse, dressed like a peasant and eating fruit from a bag. The samurai of Gifu, a castle he would later win in battle, were horrified, as was Dosan. The scruffily-dressed Nobunaga was led into a room and left to wait for his father-in-law. When the lord of Mino finally made his appearance, he was surprised to find the young man had changed his clothes, was properly attired and well behaved throughout the interview. Dosan must then have realised that the Fool of Owari, as Nobunaga had been dubbed, was hiding a sharp mind behind the absurdity.

Oda Nobunaga's senior retainer, Hirate Masahide, also known as Kiyohide, found the motives behind such behaviour unfathomable. Appalled by the repeated and compounded disgrace his young charge was bringing on the family, he put his thoughts in writing for one last time, sent them to his lord and committed *seppuku*.[2] This act of loyalty and sacrifice shocked Nobunaga and he became increasingly serious, although no less unpredictable, pouring his energies into consolidating his power.

---

2.   *Seppuku* is the polite term for the form of ritual suicide better known as *hara-kiri* to most Western readers.

The warlord Nobunaga's opponents would also fatally misjudge him. In 1560, with an army of just 2,500 men, he defeated a force of 25,000 samurai led by Imagawa Yoshimoto (1519–12 June 1560) at the Battle of Okehazama. This victory had numerous major consequences: the powerful Yoshimoto, who could well have secured the nation for himself, was killed, Nobunaga's reputation was greatly enhanced, and the victory secured the freedom of Tokugawa Ieyasu, a long-time hostage of the Imagawa. Ieyasu would become the most influential character in the upcoming Battle of Sekigahara, as well as leaving a substantial mark on the history of Japan.

Nobunaga continued to establish himself as both cunning and merciless, attacking and claiming Gifu Castle following the defeat of his father-in-law, Saito Dosan, by Dosan's own son, Saito Yoshitatsu. The circumstances of Yoshitatsu's actions in attacking his own father remain unclear. In fact, Yoshitatsu died of illness shortly after and *his* cowardly son, Tatsuoki, was ousted in 1567 by Nobunaga, who proceeded to ensconce himself in Gifu Castle, enlarging it and making it his principal headquarters. Through political marriages he secured affiliation with surrounding warlords and potential rivals such as Azai Nagamasa, Takeda Shingen and Tokugawa Ieyasu before taking the province of Omi (now Shiga Prefecture) in his push towards Kyoto.

As further evidence of his rapidly rising influence and power, Nobunaga was approached by Emperor Ogimachi (Japan's 106th sovereign, r. 1557–86) and was secretly commissioned to quell the civil disorder that had long plagued the capital, Kyoto. In 1571 he annihilated the warrior monks of the militant Ikko-shu Buddhist sect of Mount Hiei, who had become as powerful and as daring as any provincial warlord. By burning their temples and mercilessly slaughtering some 20,000 adherents, Nobunaga soon rid the nation of one of its major concerns.

While he had been commissioned by the emperor to thwart the ambitions of the warrior monks, in 1573 he took it upon himself to put an end to the two and a half centuries of rule by the fault-ridden Ashikaga Shogunate by disposing of the 15th Ashikaga shogun, Yoshiaki. Yoshiaki had sided with Takeda Shingen in an effort to remove the Oda, who he had long considered a threat. Yoshiaki was defeated and Nobunaga exiled the former shogun to Wakae Castle in Kawachi (eastern Osaka City).

Having achieved his mission, the emperor bestowed on Nobunaga the title of *Gon-Dainagon*, Imperial Councillor of the First Rank. Had he been born to a more historically influential family, he may have accepted an offer to become shogun. Instead, in 1577, he rewarded himself by building a most magnificent castle, Azuchi, on the shores of Lake Biwa.

The Death of Nobunaga

Among the many gifted military men with whom Nobunaga had surrounded himself was Akechi Mitsuhide (1528–82). Mitsuhide began his career in the services of Saito Dosan, master of Mino. He later served Asakura Yoshikage, a militarily weak but politically and diplomatically adept *daimyo* of Ichijodani, Echizen, in modern-day Fukui Prefecture. Leaving the Asakura, he then came into the employ of the former shogun, Ashikaga Yoshiaki, as a messenger before returning to Gifu and offering his services to Nobunaga in 1566. Five years after becoming an officer in Nobunaga's army and having proved himself to be of great value, he was awarded Sakamoto Castle in Omi Province with a revenue of 100,000 *koku*. A *koku* is a unit representing the rice productivity of a domain. One *koku* is five bushels, or 180 litres of rice, equivalent to the amount of rice an adult man would consume in one year and the measurement by which lords and their fiefs were measured and valued. It was the first time Nobunaga had ever awarded an honour of such magnitude to a vassal, showing the degree to which Nobunaga both trusted and valued the man. Nobunaga's top three vassals were, in order, Akechi Mitsuhide, Shibata Katsuie and Toyotomi Hideyoshi. All had risen through the ranks on merit, rather than the traditional seniority system still practised by many of Japan's businesses today. Despite this great trust, Akechi Mitsuhide would suddenly and inexplicably turn on his liege lord and kill him in his prime.

The real reason for his treacherous actions remains one of history's greatest mysteries and a number of theories exist. These include Nobunaga having repeatedly mistreated Mitsuhide, physically and verbally abusing him in front of the other vassals to the extent that he turned. Or the story regarding Mitsuhide's mother being captured and executed by the Hatano clan samurai in revenge for having lost Yakami Castle and the Hatanao matriarch having been executed by Nobunaga upon capitulation. These often touted and much believed stories have been proven to be simply that, stories – Edo-period pulp fiction.

Yet another quite plausible theory regards the emperor. Mitsuhide was Nobunaga's most trusted vassal and confidant and as such he was privy to Nobunaga's plans, dreams and aspirations. Nobunaga had apparently been offered the position of shogun, but had refused the offer either in a show of humility or because he simply didn't want to be Number Two. Nobunaga's notes show that he had, however, considered his son for the position of shogun. That being the case, what would Nobunaga's role become? There was only one person higher in the realm than the shogun. The theory goes that Nobunaga may have wanted to topple the emperor and claim the Chrysanthemum Throne for himself. Only then would Nobunaga be supreme. On hearing this, a shocked Mitsuhide may have acted to prevent this and, to preserve the Imperial line, turned on his master. This also matches the theory that as his most trusted advisor, Nobunaga had asked the man to censure him should he ever go too far.

Another recent theory supported by the discovery of a letter in Okayama in 2014, dated the 21st day of the 5th month,[3] 1582, suggests that Akechi Mitsuhide was on friendly terms with the warlord Chosokabe Motochika of Shikoku. The previous year, Nobunaga had agreed to allow Motochika to retain his lands, yet suddenly appears to have reneged on the deal and ordered Mitsuhide to attack and oust the Chosokabe clan. In an effort to protect the Chosokabe from an Oda-led invasion of Shikoku, in anger, Mitsuhide may have turned against Nobunaga.

Yet another letter written by Mitsuhide was discovered in 2017 in a Kyoto bookstore. The letter, a confidential reply to anti-Nobunaga clique leader Tsuchihashi Shigeharu in present-day Wakayama, covers subjects including the restoration of the Muromachi shogunate and refers to communication between the 15th shogun, Ashikaga Yoshiaki – who was ousted by Nobunaga – and Mitsuhide, a former vassal of the ex-shogun.

The true story, unfortunately, has been lost to time. Either way, ordered to provide reinforcements to Toyotomi Hideyoshi in combat against the Mori forces in the Chugoku region, Mitsuhide reneged and early in the morning of 22 June 1582, he marched his 30,000 men to Kyoto where Nobunaga was lodged with just 70 guards in the temple of Honno ji and attacked. Hopelessly outnumbered and wounded by arrows in the first melee, Nobunaga retreated to the inner sanctum of the temple in anger and despair. He set the temple alight and committed *seppuku* amongst the flames. He was just days short of turning 49 years old. Records show that his remains were secretly recovered by ten of his men, taken to the nearby Amida-Jiin temple and later that day,

---

3. Japan used a lunar calendar system. Where possible, this book uses modern Gregorian calendar dating.

using timber from the Honno-ji's burned prayer hall, properly cremated in the temple's grounds. Two days after the attack his sons and most senior retainers searched the charred remains of the Honno-ji temple and recovered the scorched bowl of his helmet, which was returned to Kiyosu Castle and remains in a temple for safekeeping to this day.

Upon hearing of Nobunaga's demise, Toyotomi Hideyoshi, Nobunaga's general who had requested Akechi Mitsuhide's men as reinforcements, quickly made peace with the Mori and set out to avenge his lord's death. Within ten days, covering over 40km per day, he had moved his samurai back to Kyoto where, at Yamazaki, just outside of the capital, he met with Mitsuhide's army and a battle broke out. Unable to raise additional troops from the local peasantry or from former allies such as the Hosokawa clan who refused to participate in disgust at Mitsuhide's actions, an estimated 16,000 Akechi forces were destroyed by the 30,000 samurai under Hideyoshi and Oda Nobutaka, Nobunaga's third son. Despite the nearly two-to-one ratio, 3,000 Akechi samurai were killed, while the exhausted Toyotomi suffered 3,300 losses, proving that the Akechi army put up an extraordinarily hard fight.

Defeated, Mitsuhide fled towards his home territory, Sakamoto Castle in Omi Province. Thirteen days after having attacked Nobunaga, Mitsuhide himself came to a most inglorious end. Unlike Oda, who had died a noble samurai death by his own hand, Mitsuhide is said to have been killed by a mob of mere peasants wielding little more than bamboo staves in the village of Ogurusu in Yamashiro, south of Kyoto.

Toyotomi Hideyoshi

Toyotomi Hideyoshi was born in 1536 in the village of Nakamura, now Nakamura Ward of Nagoya City. His father died shortly after his birth and his mother remarried a lowly samurai who treated the short, wiry-limbed, monkey-faced boy harshly. At a young age he was sent to the nearby Komyo-ji temple to become a priest, but absconded at the age of 15 to join the army of Matsushita Yukitsuna as an *ashigaru* foot soldier. In 1558, at the age of 22, Hideyoshi was given six *ryo*, a fair sum of money, to purchase a coat of chain-mail armour for his master. However, the young samurai instead used the money to buy himself light armour and weapons and entered the services of Oda Nobunaga as a sandal bearer, replacing the worn straw sandals of soldiers as they marched or fought. Hideyoshi was not a physically strong man, it being his intense personality and understanding of men that allowed him to rise through the ranks.

The story is well known that one cold winter's morning, Hideyoshi put his master Nobunaga's straw sandals inside his kimono to keep them warm. Nobunaga was impressed by his attitude and rewarded him well. Nobunaga had noted Hideyoshi's intellect and promoted him as he rapidly distinguished himself in a number of campaigns, most notably those against the Azai and the Asakura. It was the phenomenal success of these campaigns for which he was awarded Nagahama Castle in Omi Province on the shores of Lake Biwa, with a revenue of 220,000 *koku*.

By this time, Mori Terumoto, one of the most powerful *daimyo* with a 1.2 million *koku* income, had annexed the ten provinces of the San-yo-do and the San-in-do ('the exposed area of the mountains' and the 'area in the shade of the mountains') that formed the western Chugoku region. Quick to assert his new status, Terumoto now refused to comply with Nobunaga's demands for submission. Nobunaga did not take this rejection of his authority well and so Hideyoshi was sent ahead, quickly taking all of the castles under Mori banners, although not entirely quashing their power. In 1580 Hideyoshi was called to Azuchi Castle and received many honours from his master. His fief was soon changed from that of Nagahama to Himeji in Harima Province (Hyogo Prefecture). Hideyoshi was not there long before resuming hostilities with the Mori. He attacked Takamatsu Castle (Okayama Prefecture.) by diverting a river, flooding the Mori's strategically important fortress and trapping its occupants. With no way for supplies or reinforcements to get to the castle, Hideyoshi hoped to win by attrition.

Upon receiving news of Nobunaga's sudden death, Hideyoshi sent Ankokuji Ekei, the wily Buddhist monk and retainer of the Mori, to Mori Terumoto to make peace. Ankokuji relayed that peace was easily obtained and all that was required was to have Shimizu Muneharu, Mori Terumoto's vassal and defender of the castle, commit ritual suicide. Muneharu bravely agreed to the conditions and cut himself open. With his sacrifice and the gift of his head (which would likely have been presented wrapped in white cloth packed in salt in a round wooden box) came a temporary peace. Hideyoshi quickly turned his men on the traitor Akechi Mitsuhide and, once he had been dispatched at the hands of lowly peasants, returned to Nobunaga's castle at Kiyosu where he met with the senior retainers of the Oda clan.

There, the majority of generals took the sides of either Nobunaga's second or third sons as his successor, while the now-influential Hideyoshi cunningly nominated Nobunaga's infant grandson, Samboshi, as heir and assigned Nobukatsu and Nobutaka, the second and third sons of Nobunaga, as the guardians of the infant until his coming of age.

However, Hideyoshi's actions in this capacity became suspect and he would be called a usurper as he governed in the name of young Samboshi. He was eventually challenged directly by Nobutaka, who called on the services of General Shibata Katsuie, who had long and loyally served Nobunaga, to oust Hideyoshi. At Hideyoshi's command, Nobukatsu defeated his sibling in a siege at Gifu Castle and then in 1583, Hideyoshi himself attacked and defeated Shibata Katsuie at the Battle of Shizugatake. Hideyoshi's lust for power was not sated and the object of his quest was becoming increasingly evident.

Despite having shown him allegiance, Nobukatsu himself soon found fault in having Hideyoshi hold the reigns of his father's hard-won estates and the following year, 1584, turned to Tokugawa Ieyasu for assistance. At Komaki, just north of Nagoya City, the Tokugawa and the Toyotomi (previously Oda) armies met. The two camps had faced off around the base of the Tokugawa–Oda joint command post on Nobunaga's former castle site of Mount Komaki for weeks, neither willing to be the first to attack. A brigade of Toyotomi troops then attempted to sneak behind the Tokugawa and attack Ieyasu's home base of Okazaki, but their plans were discovered and a battle ensued at Nagakute just east of Nagoya City. Although not recognised by the Toyotomi, the Tokugawa appear to have been victorious in this battle. Through political negotiation with Nobukatsu behind Ieyasu's back, Hideyoshi was able to sue for peace and gain the upper hand, after which he returned to Osaka to begin the building of the city's magnificent castle. There was now no one in the land more powerful than Toyotomi Hideyoshi.

Hideyoshi went further than Nobunaga had dared imagine. Unable to claim the title of shogun due to his low birth, he instead arranged to have himself adopted into the noble Fujiwara house and received the elevated imperial court title of *Kampaku*, later *Taiko*, or Great Chancellor and Regent. Hideyoshi continued to increase his control over the country, conquering the southern islands of Shikoku and Kyushu and bringing the *daimyo* of the north under his control. He surveyed the land, standardised the currency and in a measure made to cease uprisings and war, confiscated swords from the peasantry. Hideyoshi further ordered the populace – warriors, farmers, craftsmen and merchants – to remain in their respective castes.

The Korean Campaigns and the Death of the *Taiko*

Japan, now forcibly unified under one leader, was at peace for the first time in centuries. With no battles to fight, the samurai had become idle. To keep his veteran warriors busy, Hideyoshi, having pacified Japan, audaciously set his sights on conquering China via the Korean Peninsula. To this end, he launched two major campaigns, known collectively as the Seven Year War or the Korean Invasion. The first invasion took place between 1592 and 1593 with some 158,000 samurai crossing the sea to the Korean Peninsula. The second, between 1597 and 1598, involved more than 140,000 battle-hardened warriors. The result was a great loss of Korean life and infrastructure as well as enormous financial, cultural and historical destruction. So extensive was the damage that China, obliged to aid its neighbours to the north, faced such a financial burden that the invasion would greatly contribute to the downfall of the Ming Dynasty.

The samurai too suffered great losses and hardships during the ill-fated invasions of Korea and the relationships formed and broken during the campaign would eventually play an important part in the looming Battle of Sekigahara. In particular, negative comments relayed back to Hideyoshi in dispatches pertaining to a number of generals and their supposed 'reckless action and disregard for authority' by a highly-ranked samurai named Ishida Mitsunari, would become a major factor in the future of Japan. The samurai generals who would be reprimanded for these real or imagined breaches of conduct would not fail to remember Ishida Mitsunari, who was now a marked man. When these men returned to Japan, however, they found political circumstances had changed dramatically.

It was at Fushimi Castle on 18 August 1598, that Hideyoshi died at the age of 63, leaving his vast empire to his five-year-old son, Hideyori. Determined that the Toyotomi family should retain power, Hideyoshi had appointed a board of five regents, the *Go-Tairo*, to rule in his son's stead. These five included Ukita Hideie, who held domains in what is present-day Okayama Prefecture and was the husband of Hideyoshi's adopted daughter, Go-Hime. Another was Maeda Toshiie who had served Nobunaga before joining Hideyoshi. Like Nobunaga, Toshiie had been something of a delinquent in his youth, but is often depicted as a stern, reserved administrator, famed for his prowess with the spear. While Nobunaga is often falsely believed to have called Hideyoshi '*Saru*' or Monkey, a later Edo-period fiction, he called Toshiie '*Inu*' or Dog, due to his childhood name of *Inuchiyo*. Toshiie was among those at Hideyoshi's deathbed and accepted orders to take direct care of Hideyori. It had been Maeda Toshiie who had so far suppressed the growing antagonism between the warrior and administrative samurai factions and it was Toshiie who was set to take a strong stance against Ieyasu's inflammatory actions following Hideyoshi's passing, but he himself died at the age of 61 on 27 April 1599, the year before the battle at Sekigahara. Had he lived another year, his influence on the other *daimyo* may have been such that Ieyasu would have found it difficult to raise sufficient support for his cause. Toshiie's son would fill the void left by his demise.

The third regent was Mori Terumoto, the grandson of Mori Motonari. Having made peace with the Toyotomi only a year or so before, Terumoto, with a 1,200,000-*koku* income, had built Hiroshima Castle as his residence before being selected to serve on the board of regents. During the battle at Sekigahara, Terumoto would command Osaka Castle and so he would not participate directly on the field. Another of the *Go-Tairo* was Uesugi Kagekatsu of Echigo (modern-day Fukui Prefecture) who had served Nobunaga and then Hideyoshi. Appointed head of this council of regents was Lord Tokugawa Ieyasu.

On his deathbed, Hideyoshi, having ruled a unified nation for nearly 15 years, called for the then 56-year-old Ieyasu. Having done so much to unify and stabilise Japan, Hideyoshi was entrusting the most powerful of the *daimyo* to be responsible for leading the Council of Regents who would attend to his infant heir, Hideyori. Ieyasu readily agreed to the undertaking and upon the death of the *Taiko*, Ieyasu installed himself in Hideyoshi's sumptuous Fushimi Castle and immediately began to make moves to assume complete power of the country.

Enter Tokugawa Ieyasu

Tokugawa Ieyasu was the most powerful of the nearly 200 *daimyo* both militarily and financially, with an income that amounted to some 2,557,000 *koku*. Though he had been chosen to head the Council of Regents, Ieyasu wanted more than that. He wanted sole rule of the country and, in claiming descent from the ancient and noble Minamoto clan, was able to resurrect the dormant office of shogun, a position neither Nobunaga nor Hideyoshi could claim. Ieyasu's wide girth and medium stature may have provided him with a grandfatherly image, yet behind that soft exterior hid an intense intellect; once Ieyasu had his mind set, nothing could distract him from obtaining his desires.

Ieyasu's early life had not been a simple or happy one. Born on 31 January 1543 at Okazaki Castle in Mikawa Province (now eastern Aichi Prefecture), the young Ieyasu, or Matsudaira Takechiyo as he was called in his childhood, was sent as a hostage to the powerful Imagawa clan to the east by his father, Hidetada, who sought their help in the fight against the Oda. En route to his captors' castle at Suruga, the convoy was re-routed by a Matsudaira vassal who believed the future of the clan was best served through cooperation with the Oda and so the boy was taken instead to Oda Nobuhide. With the boy in his grasp, Oda Nobuhide offered the Tokugawa (Matsudaira) peace, though on such harsh terms that even at the risk of his young son's life, Hidetada refused. Ieyasu was then confined to Nagoya Castle and also kept at the home of Kato Nobumori at Tenno-bo, directly south of the Great Atsuta Shrine in Nagoya. Three years later, the Imagawa attacked an Oda-held castle where Oda Nobuhiro, an elder brother of Nobunaga, was captured. The Imagawa then offered to swap their hostage for the young Ieyasu and with the trade, the now nine-year-old was taken by the Imagawa and kept hostage at Sumpu Castle (Shizuoka). Modern-day use of the word 'hostage' has negative connotations of a captive being held against their will in harsh conditions. In the case of the samurai, Ieyasu and his minders would have been quite aware that his position of *hitojichi*, or hostage, was a political move. In both instances he was well cared for and educated with the expectation that he would be a future close ally of, in this case, the Imagawa clan.

Within the samurai caste, changing one's name at various stages of life and upon auspicious occasions was a regular custom and it was under the name Matsudaira Motoyasu that Ieyasu had taken part in commanding a corps of Imagawa-allied Mikawa troops in the 1560 battle between the Imagawa and the Oda at Okehazama, Owari Province. In this battle, the Imagawas' 25,000 men were trounced by a smaller army of around 2,500 Oda samurai. With the death of Imagawa Yoshimoto and the integration of many of the Imagawa troops into the Oda army, Ieyasu was at last free. Upon his return to Okazaki Castle he prepared for war with Oda Nobunaga, who had indirectly brought about Ieyasu's freedom and had also begun making threatening moves towards the Tokugawa-held lands at Mikawa. Ieyasu would spend the following few years reforming the Matsudaira clan and Mikawa Province. He would also arrange to ally himself with the powerful Nobunaga, thus preserving his hold on Mikawa and with help from the Oda, increasing his land-holding properties too.

Around 1566 he took the name Ieyasu[4] and received permission personally from the emperor to retain the family name of Tokugawa. By achieving this and by forging connections to the noble Minamoto clan within his family tree, he created the legitimacy he would require to eventually claim the position of shogun.

The Consolidation of Power

Politically-motivated marriages had been banned by Hideyoshi as he considered them dangerous to the peace and stability he had worked so hard to create. Invoking the ire of a number of his contemporaries, Ieyasu disregarded these laws and arranged the marriage of his sixth son, Tadateru, to the daughter of Date Masamune, the *daimyo* of the north. He wed his adopted daughter to Fukushima Masanori, the lord of Kiyosu Castle, and two of his granddaughters were married to other suitably-ranked nobles. These moves were no doubt part of a plan hatched by Ieyasu to not only strengthen his network of potential supporters, but to discover who was against him and who may be relied upon in the Tokugawa master plan.

Interestingly enough, Ieyasu's main opposition came not from one of the other regents as might have been expected, but from within the ranks of the *daimyo*. Below the *Go-Tairo* were the *Bugyo*, or commissioners, appointed by Hideyoshi, of which there were five. They included Hideyoshi's brother-in-law Asano Nagamasa, also Masuda Nagamori, who had followed Hideyoshi from his early days in Owari and the former warrior monk, Maeda Gen'i (also known as Munehisa). Cleverly, Gen'i would later feign sickness just prior to hostilities at Sekigahara, avoiding the risk of having to take sides. This enabled him to miss the war and therefore retain his domain after the battle.

---

4.   Details remaining from later in Ieyasu's life now kept in the Kunouzan Toshogu Shrine in Shizuoka show him to have stood about 1.56m tall, with girth measurements ranging from 100cm to 120cm. Order forms for split-toe tabi socks show his feet measured 22.7cm. His inside leg was about 80cm, while his leg from knee to foot was 35cm long. Handprints prove his hands were 18cm from palm base to fingertips.

Another influential lord strongly opposed to Ieyasu was Natsuka Masaie. Rounding out these five was Ishida Mitsunari, who would come to play one of the leading roles in the theatre of the coming war.

Ishida Mitsunari

Ishida Mitsunari was born in Omi Province (Shiga Prefecture) in 1560. At the age of 13 he entered the services of Toyotomi Hideyoshi. In 1585, at the age of 25, Mitsunari was appointed *Jibu-shosuke*, one of two principal commissioners below the administrator for genealogies, marriages, funeral rites, imperial tombs, theatres and music. Mitsunari was also responsible for the reception of foreigners, most notably the Spanish and Portuguese who came in growing numbers, bringing trade and proselytizing.

It is by the title *Jibu-shosuke*, or 'Gibounochio' (a mis-spelling of his title by the foreign missionaries) that Mitsunari is remembered in the journals of the international travellers of the day, in which he is described as being the ideal leader for Hideyoshi's council. In notes that still exist, the Portuguese missionaries considered Mitsunari, Maeda Toshiie, Kuroda Nagamasa and Konishi Yukinaga as the most politically astute men surrounding the *Taiko*.

Mitsunari was a gifted mathematician and was placed in charge of the famed 'sword hunt' conducted by Hideyoshi in an effort to disarm the non-military bulk of the population and thus preserve peace. Most remaining portraits of the man show him holding a manuscript rather than a sword.

He had been allocated a stipend of 186,000 *koku* and the castle of Sawayama in Omi and thus his land, wealth and power was just a fifth of that of Ieyasu. Although an able administrator, his elevated position as *Bugyo* was not awarded due to martial merit, nor for his having performed heroic deeds or services which gained him the attention of patron of the arts Hideyoshi, but was instead due to his ability in the tea ceremony.

In the warmer months of 1573, during a military exercise, Hideyoshi had come across the teenage Ishida Mitsunari not far from Hideyoshi's Nagahama Castle, where Mitsunari made three cups of tea for the thirsty lord. The first was in a big *chawan* teacup, filled with an unusually generous serving of warm green tea. For a thirsty Hideyoshi, the amount and temperature were just right and he drank it all at once. The second cup was served in the same *chawan*, but a bit hotter than the last and only about half as much. Relaxed, Hideyoshi took his time over this cup. Finally a third was brought forth, a smaller serving in a smaller bowl, but much hotter than the previous two cups. Hideyoshi, now totally composed, could enjoy this one. Perhaps the former sandal-bearer who had risen to great power saw something of himself in the 13-year-old tea server, as he appointed the boy to his staff. Mitsunari would come to serve the Toyotomi loyally and would be rewarded for it.

After Mitsunari had accompanied General Ukita Hideie on the Korean campaign, he would return to find that his position as a senior retainer had lost its power upon the creation of the *Go-Tairo*. Mitsunari soon realised that the power of his lord, the young Hideyori, was being usurped by the Tokugawa, in just the same way as Hideyoshi had usurped the power of the Oda.

The Power Game

With the backing of Maeda Toshiie, in letters sent to the various warlords before this. Ishida Mitsunari openly accused Ieyasu of taking power for himself. As the accusations flew, troops gathered around the capital, Kyoto, and the situation became volatile. Mitsunari, in the name of Hideyori, denounced Ieyasu and demanded his resignation. Ieyasu naturally refused and went on to deliberately create further controversy.

Mitsunari was aware of the difficult situation he was in. Openly opposing Ieyasu could be seen as an attempt to take power for himself and as the *daimyo* supporting Ieyasu were too powerful, he declined to wage an open war. Instead he planned an assassination.

In the early months of 1599 Ieyasu left Edo and arrived near Osaka by ship. On the docks was a palanquin waiting for him, but there was no one around it. This made Ieyasu and his men particularly uneasy. There was talk of remaining on the ship and preparing to set sail again when a giant of a man walked onto the jetty followed by a small unit of samurai. The giant himself was about to take an equally giant risk.

Standing 1.90m tall, Todo Takatora was much larger than the average man of the day. Hailing from Omi Province, he had long been loyal to the Toyotomi, in particular Hideyoshi's younger brother, Toyotomi Hidenaga and later Hideyoshi himself. The veteran of some of the fiercest battles in contemporary history, Takatora was a warrior among warriors, exceptionally skilled in weaponry and tactics, politically astute, brave beyond doubt and with an intelligence to match. Aged 44, he also had a reputation for being one of the most innovative castle designers and architects in the land.

Ieyasu had met Takatora on a number of occasions in the past and had been most impressed by his way of thinking. Some years earlier, Toyotomi Hideyoshi had set Takatora the task of designing and building a manor suitable for Ieyasu within the grounds of his sumptuous Jurakutei Mansion in Kyoto. Takatora drew up a series of layouts and architectural plans that were approved of by both Hideyoshi and Ieyasu and work proceeded on schedule. A few months later Ieyasu travelled to Kyoto to inspect his new quarters but was surprised to discover the design to be different from the original plans.

Takatora explained that having seen the surrounding area, he realised that there were possible defensive design flaws. If anything untoward were to happen to Lord Ieyasu and he and his guards were unable to defend themselves, it would reflect badly on Lord Hideyoshi for one and on himself as an architect of fortifications. 'For that reason, I took it upon myself to improve the design. If this is unacceptable', he explained pointing out the new defensive features to the touched Ieyasu, 'I shall cut myself open immediately'.

Standing at the waters' edge at Osaka, Takatora now explained Ishida Mitsunari's plan to assassinate Ieyasu somewhere along the 4km road between his estate to the north-west of Osaka Castle and Maeda Toshiie's property directly south of the castle. Takatora then suggested that he, Takatora, ride in Ieyasu's palanquin as a decoy and that Ieyasu follow some time later. Knowing that a successful attempt on Ieyasu's life would throw the nation into chaos and civil war, Todo Takatora was willing to risk his reputation, his position within the Toyotomi administration and his own life to save that of Tokugawa Ieyasu. An offer Ieyasu accepted.

By April, Ieyasu was in Fushimi Castle while Maeda Toshiie lay on his deathbed in Osaka Castle. Mitsunari travelled to the great castle at Osaka to pay his respects and it was there that a number of *daimyo*, including Ikeda Terumasa, Kato Kiyomasa, Kuroda Nagamasa, Fukushima Masanori, Hosokawa Tadaoki, Kato Yoshiaki and Asano Yoshinaga, who had learned of Mitsunari's assassination plot against Ieyasu, decided to do away with Mitsunari once and for all. Together this group planned a counter-attempt on Mitsunari's life; however, the much-despised Mitsunari learned of the plan and escaped Osaka dressed as a woman and riding in an enclosed noblewoman's litter. Surprisingly enough, he went straight to Fushimi Castle and begged the man he was trying to kill, Ieyasu, for asylum.

Ieyasu hid Mitsunari away for a few days before sending him to his home fief in Sawayama, Omi, with one of Ieyasu's sons as an escort. Despite being aware of Mitsunari's original plot against him, Ieyasu had a brilliant rationale for providing refuge to his adversary. Many of the *daimyo* disliked Mitsunari for his meddling in affairs during the Korean invasions and for his negative reports back to Hideyoshi and as long as he remained the leader of the pro-Toyotomi, or Loyalist, cause, Ieyasu could use him to complicate further opposition. Maeda Toshiie passed away on 27 April 1599, aged 61. One of the strongest gates holding Ieyasu back from his plan had now been left wide open.

The number nine is an auspicious number for samurai and in Buddhism. The 9th day of the 9th month[5] of 1599 was observed as a most auspicious day and as such, Tokugawa Ieyasu visited Toyotomi Hideyori in Osaka Castle to celebrate. While there, Ieyasu became aware of yet another assassination attempt on his life, this time by the son of the late Maeda Toshiie, Maeda Toshinaga. Gathering his allies around him and remaining within the safety of Osaka Castle, Ieyasu ordered a small tower-like defensive structure be constructed for security within the Nishi-no-maru and, no doubt, to further flaunt his authority. To subdue the cocky Toshinaga, he suddenly announced the official dispatch of the Maeda troops to Toshinaga's lands in the northern districts.

Realising he had been both exposed and endangered, Toshinaga readily complied and in an effort to seek forgiveness and express his future loyalty, he offered his own mother as a hostage to the Tokugawa. Despite her great dislike of Ieyasu, Lady Maeda Matsu, also known as Omatsu no Kata, was more than willing to volunteer as a hostage to the Tokugawa in an effort to preserve the Maeda name. Omatsu was housed within the grounds of Edo Castle for the next 14 years. She was finally allowed to leave the Tokugawa stronghold in 1615 following the destruction of Osaka Castle. She returned to the Maeda clan castle at Kanazawa, where she died two years later aged 70.

In early 1600, Tokugawa Ieyasu again went to stay with the young Toyotomi Hideyori at Osaka Castle, further upsetting his antagonists. Meanwhile, Mitsunari had assembled a faction to oppose Ieyasu. This group was composed of Mori Terumoto, the rich and powerful lord of Hiroshima, Ukita

---

5.   Early October by the modern calendar.

Hideie who controlled lands in what is now Okayama Prefecture, Shimazu Yoshihiro, a skilled military leader and the 17th head of the Shimazu clan of Satsuma (Kagoshima Prefecture), and 20-year-old Nabeshima Katsushige, who would later join Ieyasu at his father's command. Notably, the contingent also included the youngest *daimyo*, the then still 18-year-old Kobayakawa Hideaki, Toyotomi Hideyoshi's nephew, who would play a pivotal role in the outcome of the upcoming battle.

The Spectre of War

The peace that Hideyoshi had brought about was now being torn to shreds. As the spectre of war loomed, each and every *daimyo* would be faced with a difficult choice. Which side they would eventually join depended upon a variety of factors: some would choose loyalty to the Toyotomi, while others found themselves bound by an intricate web of family ties and political alliances; others believed in Ieyasu; and there were those that would make a cold calculation based on their simple desire to survive the oncoming bloodbath. These relationships and choices would prove absolutely crucial, as war appeared on the horizon.

Surprisingly, by July 1600, one of the many *daimyo* abandoning the Toyotomi cause for that of the Tokugawa was Kato Kiyomasa, born in Nakamura Ward of modern-day Nagoya City. At 38, Kiyomasa was a well-respected general who had played a major role in the invasion of Korea. He was also renowned for his sophisticated castle-building techniques, including the superb castle at Kumamoto, which he completed in 1600. Such ingenuity and innovation brought him to the attention of Ieyasu who appointed him to construct the gracefully curved stone walls defending the magnificent keep of Nagoya Castle after the latter had become shogun. However, despite being Hideyoshi's cousin and thus having blood ties to the Toyotomi, it would be his intense hatred for Ishida Mitsunari following their conflicts during the Korean campaigns that would drive Kiyomasa towards siding with the Tokugawa-led Eastern forces.

Kiyomasa was a strict adherent to the Nichiren sect of Buddhism. He was fiercely anti-Christian and his domains in Higo, Kyushu, bordered those of Konishi Yukinaga, a well-known Christian warlord loyal to the Toyotomi. His hatred for the foreign religion, for Konishi Yukinaga and in particular for Ishida Mitsunari was more than enough to drive him into the Eastern forces' camp. In mid-1600, on the instructions of Ieyasu, Kato Kiyomasa returned to his fief at Kumamoto where he stayed, missing the battle at Sekigahara. Instead of fighting in the great conflict, he aided Ieyasu by quelling the Western allies' uprisings in Kyushu.[6]

Kato Kiyomasa's sworn rival in Kyushu, Konishi Yukinaga, was born the son of a doctor and adopted into the samurai caste by a warrior in the service of Ukita Hideie and it was from there that he entered the services of Hideyoshi. Yukinaga was one of the few Christian *daimyo*, having been baptised as Augustine in 1583. He had been awarded command of the vanguard in the 1592 Korean expedition alongside Kato Kiyomasa and was the first to have landed at Pusan. There the two generals, Kiyomasa and Yukinaga, were soon unsurprisingly at loggerheads over a number of issues and cooperated only in order to complete the task of annexation as ordered by Hideyoshi.

Ties to the Toyotomi loyalist Western forces also ran strong with 39-year-old Kikkawa Hiroie. His grandfather was the great warlord Mori Motonari, his cousin was Motonari's successor, Mori Terumoto, and his wife was the sister of Ukita Hideie, all recognised as stalwarts of the Toyotomi clan. It therefore seemed obvious that Hiroie would join the Western side. However, he was also on good terms with samurai such as Kuroda Nagamasa, Fukushima Masanori and Kato Kiyomasa, all of whom would ultimately decide to fight for the East. The main problem was without doubt Ishida Mitsunari's self-appointed position as field commander of the Western forces.

Kikkawa Hiroie had come to dislike Mitsunari a long time before the country was again divided, for it was Mitsunari who had strongly suggested that the lands Hideyoshi had awarded Hiroie be redistributed to Mori Hidemoto, the adopted son of Terumoto. Another problem had arisen between the two during the Korean campaign. Hiroie had expressed a desire to lead his army on a separate expedition apart from his Mori overlord. Permission to go it

---

6.   Upon the death of Kato Kiyomasa in 1611, rumours abounded that Ieyasu had played a role in his sudden and supposedly mysterious demise. To a large extent the speculation centred on his family connections with the Toyotomi and whether he would return to support them, particularly as he had offered himself as an intermediary in an attempt to reconcile the Tokugawa and Toyotomi clans. Kiyomasa was returning from such an attempt via ship to Kumamoto when he fell ill and died shortly after arriving home. There were stories that Ieyasu had somehow poisoned the brave warrior Kiyomasa.

alone was denied; however, disobeying orders, he set off with his men on an independent camapign, which proved immensely successful. Nonetheless, due to a falling-out with Hiroie, the warrior priest Ankokuji Ekei offered a negative view of the expedition in his report to Mitsunari. This in turn was passed to Hideyoshi, who was naturally angered and Hiroie was severely reprimanded. This incident, along with a substantial number of similar confrontations, was written down in detail by Kikkawa 14 years after the battle of Sekigahara in a diary entitled 'Unforgettable reasons for having sided against Ishida Mitsunari'.

Mogami Yoshiakira was another of the *daimyo* who had initially allied himself with the Toyotomi, only to change sides and support the Tokugawa. The main reason for this defection was his hatred of the *Taiko*, Toyotomi Hideyoshi. Yoshiakira had submitted to Hideyoshi's request and married his daughter to Hideyoshi's adopted son and appointed heir, Hidetsugu. However, fearing disinheritance following the birth of Hideyoshi's natural son, Hideyori, Hidetsugu was accused of causing problems in court for which he was invited to kill himself along with his family. Despite Yoshiakira's pleas, his daughter was beheaded as was her husband-to-be – a man whom she had not yet even met – in 1595, an act for which Mogami never forgave Hideyoshi. Yoshiakira later joined the Date forces in the north, quashing the Uesugi and allowing Ieyasu to concentrate on destroying the Toyotomi loyalists.

In February 1600, Ieyasu learned that Uesugi Kagekatsu, a *daimyo* whose affluence was surpassed only by his own, had in preparation for war employed some 80,000 men to build a castle at Kazashigahara in Aizu, near the strategically-important Tsuraga Castle on the plain at Wakamatsu. Kagekatsu had been adopted by the great warlord Uesugi Kenshin, who divided his lands equally between Kagekatsu and his brother Kagetora. Upon the death of Kenshin, Kagekatsu declared war on his brother, defeated him and took his lands too. Kagekatsu had submitted and served under both Nobunaga and then Hideyoshi. Prior to the latter's death, Kagekatsu was chosen as one of the five regents to assist the young Hideyori. Uesugi Kagekatsu then exchanged his fief in Echigo for that of Aizu and increased his income to 1,200,000 *koku*. Not long afterwards, Hideyoshi was no more and so Kagekatsu rapidly started stockpiling weapons and employed labourers working around the clock on his fortress and at seven strategic positions in the vicinity, strengthening its defences.

The Rinzai sect Buddhist monk, Saisho Shotai[7] was called in to assist Ieyasu with penning the carefully-worded yet damning letter accusing the Uesugi of making preparations for war and demanding he explain himself. When he was ordered to Kyoto to face the chief counsellor Ieyasu, the greatly angered Kagekatsu made excuses not to go. In his stead he had his senior minister Naoe Kanetsugu send written communications claiming these supposedly banned strategic works were being undertaken 'through necessity since his master had taken over the lands at Aizu only recently and that they should be of no cause for alarm'. In closing he quite rudely pointed out that, 'It must be remembered, country samurai collect weapons just as those of the cities collect tea ceremony implements'.

Soon after, the Uesugi began encroaching into Tokugawa-held territory. Ishida Mitsunari had persuaded Uesugi Kagekatsu to commence waging a campaign against the Tokugawa, a campaign that Ieyasu correctly suspected was a trap to lure him out of Osaka. On 16 June 1600, Ieyasu finally left Osaka Castle and slowly, over a two-week period, made his way east along the great Tokaido road towards his own magnificent castle in Edo, arriving on 2 July.

However, the wily Ieyasu had another reason for heading eastwards. On 12 May, the Englishman William Adams[8] had been presented to him at Osaka Castle. The 37-year-old Adams was the pilot-major of the *Liefde*, a Dutch ship of 300 tons with a crew of 110. She was one of five ships that had set out two years earlier in the hopes of reaching Japan to commence trading. Only Adams's ship reached the shores of Japan, the first to do so by the Pacific route. Adams, who was then to spend the rest of his life in Japan, was fortunate enough to find a patron in the man who would become shogun and was treated as personal advisor to Ieyasu in a number of matters. Adams would later be awarded a new name, Miura Anjin and along with it the two swords of a samurai, being made a *Hatamoto*, literally a banner-man, a highly ranked and trusted vassal allowed direct access to the shogun himself. Besides the Englishman, of particular interest to Ieyasu were the ship's 18 cannons and its cargo, listed as some 500 matchlocks, 300 chain shot, 50 hundredweight (approximately 2,540kg) of gunpowder and 5,000

---

7.   Shotai would later pen a best-selling Edo-period biography of Tokugawa Ieyasu.

8   Adams would be the inspiration for the character John Blackthorn in James Clavell's novel *Shogun*.

cannonballs. Ieyasu ordered the ship be brought to Uraga, near Yokosuka in modern-day Kanagawa Prefecture, where he himself intended to inspect it. He especially wanted to see the cannon, as he had just secretly ordered some fiften of them from the famed smiths of Kunitomo Village in Omi.

After a short stay in his capital, Ieyasu ventured to Oyama in modern-day Tochigi Prefecture, where his third son and heir, Hidetada, was commanding troops in preparation for a possible war with the Uesugi. There he was joined by many of his generals including Kato Kiyomasa, Kuroda Nagamasa, Fukushima Masanori, Hosokawa Tadaoki, Ikeda Terumasa, Asano Yoshinaga and Kato Yoshiaki.

Kato Yoshiaki hailed from Nishio in Mikawa, not far from Ieyasu's ancestral lands, and had joined this force from his domain in Iyo in the northern parts of Shikoku. He was another *daimyo* who had served loyally under Hideyoshi and had taken part in the Korean expeditions. Following the death of the Taiko, Kato Yoshiaki allied himself with Kato Kiyomasa (no relation) and Fukushima Masanori and joined the Tokugawa.

When news arrived of Ishida Mitsunari's uprising in the west, Ieyasu called his staff together and offered those with family in Osaka the choice of fighting with him or, as their families were without doubt being held hostage, joining Ishida.

Ieyasu's supporters rallied to the call, with the exception of three. Satake Yoshinobu, who was once counted among the six greatest generals of the Toyotomi and was also on good terms with Ishida Mitsunari, quickly returned to the West. Maeda Toshinaga, hemmed in on all sides by the enemy, was unable to participate and the Sendai-based Date Masamune, the 'One Eyed Dragon of the North', concentrating his efforts on quelling the Uesugi on behalf of the Tokugawa, was also unable to act.

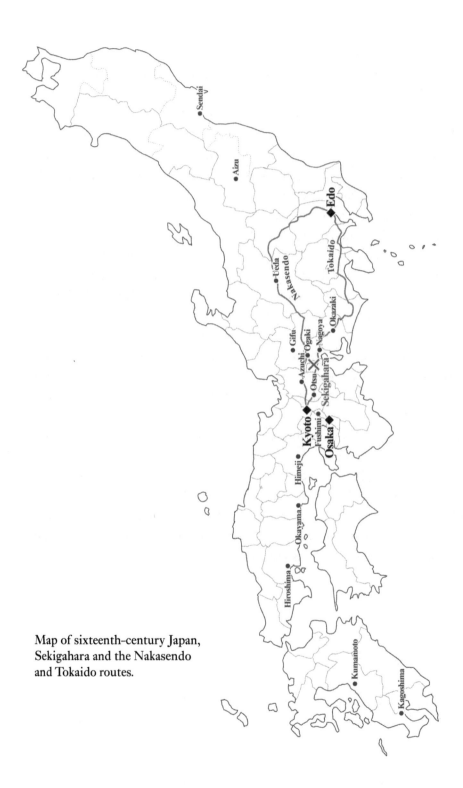

100 km

Map of sixteenth-century Japan,
Sekigahara and the Nakasendo
and Tokaido routes.

Chapter 1

The Roads East and West

Even before the Edo period (1603–1868) there were five major arterial routes linking the old capital, Kyoto, and Edo (now Tokyo). People, merchandise, communications and culture traversed these highways mostly by foot, stopping at the government-designated post towns and checkpoints along the way. Each of these post towns featured special inns, *Honjin*, *Waki-honjin* and *Hatagoya*. These establishments provided lodging, places for meals and rest and stables for horses too. *Hatagoya* were for the use of common folk, merchants, craftsmen, pilgrims and lower-ranked samurai. The *Honjin* and *Waki-honjin* were reserved for the highest-ranked samurai, the nobility and the *daimyo*.

The two most vital of these highways were the Tokaido and the Nakasendo. The Nakasendo, or Central Mountain Route, was built in 702. Connecting Kyoto and Edo, it was also known as the Kiso-kaido as it followed the route of the mighty Kiso River for much of its length. The road featured sixty-nine post towns along its 542km length. The Tokaido or Eastern Sea Route was the name given to the highway between Edo and Kyoto that traversed the Pacific Ocean side of Japan's coast, with fifty-three stations on its 514km.

The two roads came closest together about 20km west of Gifu, where the only real pass between the Suzuka mountain range spreading to the south and the Imasu mountains to the north neatly separated east and west Japan. These mountain ranges, with Mount Ibuki to the north-west and Mount Nangu to the east, formed the Sekigahara basin, some 2km by 2km in area.

Near here, a side-track from the Tokaido branched off to join the Nakasendo. The importance of these two vital arteries as military objectives cannot be overestimated. Whoever had control of these major thoroughfares and particularly at the gateway between east and west Japan had control of the country.

At this stage the Western army held a number of castles along the Nakasendo. As well as Ishida Mitsunari's fiefdom of Sawayama Castle, they now held the strategically-important Ogaki Castle, which lay just south of the Nakasendo. East of Ogaki stood Gifu Castle, overlooking the central route from high on Mount Kinkazan and Inuyama Castle a little further east along the Kiso River. Between Gifu and Inuyama lay Takehana, a small hilltop castle, more akin to a stockade than a fortress.

Further along the Nakasendo and some distance to the north, in what is now Nagano Prefecture, sat Ueda Castle, home of the Sanada clan, former vassals to the military genius and warlord Takeda Shingen. It was a humble castle, built in 1583, but well designed and strongly constructed. This was proven first in 1583 when the castle withstood an attack by a numerically superior Tokugawa force under Ieyasu. Moreover, it was the fortitude of the samurai within the fortress that saw that attack and another similar siege in 1600 repelled by the Sanada. Despite being such a distance from the battle-field of Sekigahara, events at Ueda Castle would almost destroy the plans of the Tokugawa.

The Eastern forces held most of the Tokaido from Ieyasu's base castle in Edo all the way to Kiyosu Castle north-west of modern-day Nagoya City. Behind the Western lines, Otsu Castle overlooking the southern shores of Lake Biwa was held by secret Eastern allies, as was Fushimi Castle south of Kyoto.

Ishida Mitsunari had originally planned for the battle between his Western forces and the Eastern forces led by Ieyasu to take place near the Kiso River, on what was the border between Mino and Owari Provinces (now Gifu and Aichi Prefectures), with the Uesugi entering the stage from the north, while his own army attacked from the west. Had this plan come to fruition, Ieyasu would have most likely been surrounded and possibly defeated.

Mitsunari advanced eastwards from Osaka to his own fief of Sawayama, north to the Sekigahara pass and then east again towards Ogaki Castle, which was under the command of Ito Morikage. On 6 August, his army of 6,700 passed through Sekigahara, but continued on to Tarui where they stopped for a few days. From there they continued to Ogaki, arriving on 10 August and made the castle the base for the Western army. Ogaki lay just south of the Nakasendo and thus was a strategically-important fortress.

From Ogaki, Mitsunari sent word to the keeper of Kiyosu Castle, a stronghold of equally strategic importance, to capitulate or face attack. Kiyosu was commanded by Fukushima Masanori and while he was with Ieyasu in the Kanto region, his trusted vassal Osaki Gemba was installed as caretaker.

Gemba, also known as '*Oni*' or 'Devil Gemba' thanks to his ferocity and willingness to fight on the battlefield, steadfastly refused and in defiance sent word to his master who, along with other allies, hurried back to prevent Mitsunari from taking the castle.

The nation was abuzz as warriors of all ranks rushed to take their positions, East or West, and be ready for the oncoming storm. Mitsunari was joined at Ogaki by key allies, including Ukita Hideie, Konishi Yukinaga, Shimazu Yoshihiro, Shima Sakon and Gamo Bitchu amongst others and as the number of Western troops began to swell, the small castle and surrounding areas were soon brimming with armoured soldiers.

Mitsunari Moves First

Ishida Mitsunari had been shocked at the number of his former allies defecting to the Eastern side. In an effort to prevent any more withdrawals he devised a plan to keep the various *daimyo* 'loyal'. He would take hostage the families of those he feared would turn and among the first families taken in Osaka was that of Lord Hosokawa Tadaoki, a *daimyo* with lands just outside of Kyoto worth about 230,000 *koku*.

Hosokawa Tadaoki and his father Fujitaka (or Yusai as he was known since having taken religious vows upon the death of Oda Nobunaga) had been much-valued retainers of Oda Nobunaga and at their lord's urging, Tadaoki had married the daughter of Nobunaga's most senior retainer, Akechi Mitsuhide. The lady in question was a famed beauty with intelligence to match and the marriage had been organised by Nobunaga so that ties between his close vassals might be further strengthened. When Akechi Mitsuhide turned against Nobunaga, he had first sought assistance from Hosokawa Tadaoki, who, disgusted at the actions of his father-in-law, steadfastly refused. It also caused a rift between the couple as she was torn between loyalty to both her husband and father and so for her safety, Tadaoki sent her into exile for two years.

Later, upon the intervention of Hideyoshi, husband and wife were reconciled, but relations remained partially strained, as during her exile she had converted to Christianity against his wishes, taking the name Gracia. According to the records of the Portuguese and Italian missionaries she was to associate with, Tadaoki was a jealous man and rarely allowed her to make contact with the world outside their high-walled mansion.

In fact, it had been her husband who had inadvertently introduced her to the religion. He had heard about this foreign faith from a friend, Takayama

Ukon, during a tea ceremony. Tadaoki later passed on what he had heard to his wife. She was impressed with what she heard and duly sought out the foreign religion. Ukon would fall from grace with Hideyoshi – and later be expelled from Japan by Ieyasu for his Christian beliefs – and would die in exile in Manila in 1615. Hosokawa Tadaoki never felt anything for the religion himself, but thought a great deal of his wife and refused to allow her to become a follower of Christianity. At one stage, it is said the volatile lord had even taken a dagger to his wife's throat, threatening to take her life unless she renounced her new-found faith. She refused but he still refrained from killing her.[1]

When the arresting authorities sent by Ishida Mitsunari forced their way into the Hosokawa mansion in search of potential hostages on 25 August 1600, the clan's loyal retainer, Ogasawara Shosai, approached his then 37-year-old mistress and informed her of her husband's orders that they were all to die before submitting to Mitsunari's troops. It is often incorrectly believed that Gracia then committed suicide, but being a follower of the Christian faith would have prevented her from doing so. This much is recorded in the still-existing 'Chronicles of the Hosokawa Family', a clan diary of sorts that explains that with her consent, Ogasawara Shosai drove a spear through her body, before setting fire to the mansion and disembowelling himself. Gracia's body was consumed in the flames. Tadaoki later gave her a Christian funeral at which he cried.

Despite their religious and political differences, Hosokawa Tadaoki truly loved his wife. When he died 45 years later at the age of 83, he had his tomb built next to hers at the Taisho-ji Temple in Kumamoto City, Kyushu. Another grave dedicated to the couple can be found in the Daitoku-ji Temple in Kyoto and features a stone lantern used by the great tea master Sen no Rikyu as a gravestone. Tadaoki lived his final years alone, never remarrying.

The Hosokawa family chronicles mention the defiance shown by both Tadaoki and Gracia against capitulating to Ishida Mitsunari's samurai and also records that the matter seems to have surprised and angered the samurai community. The backlash proved another setback for Mitsunari, turning many potential allies away. Realising his mistake, he then ordered his men

---

1.   It is interesting to note that the Hosokawa family long remained politically active and nearly 400 years later, in 1993, one of this couples' descendants, Hosokawa Morihiro, would become the 79th prime minister of Japan.

to simply surround the mansions of the other Tokugawa generals, including Ikeda Terumasa, Kato Kiyomasa[2] and Kuroda Nagamasa,[3] rather than try to arrest the occupants. Mitsunari then attempted to recover the ground he had through propaganda. Five days later he prepared a letter of impeachment, a list of thirteen grievances against Tokugawa Ieyasu in the hopes of spurring other *daimyo* into once again backing him against Ieyasu in battle. He distributed this list, dated the 17th day of the 7th month (30 August) 1600, amongst the *daimyo*.

Mitsunari's principal grievance focused on Ieyasu moving into the late Hideyoshi's residence at Fushimi, something he saw as a blatant usurping of the power promised to Hideyoshi's heir, Hideyori. Many of the other complaints concerned Ieyasu's being in direct contravention of laws instigated by Hideyoshi. Ieyasu's arranged marriages between his and strategically-important families and his building of and then residing in a small tower keep within the Nishi-no-maru grounds of Osaka Castle, despite a ban on all castle building and maintenance, received particular criticism. Ieyasu was also accused of purporting to have told 'lies' regarding his actions to younger members of the council and *daimyo* and making strategic promises of land and titles without the consent of the Council of Regents in an effort to gain followers.

Further scrutiny fell upon his combative behaviour, his conflict with Uesugi Kagekatsu and his taking of Maeda Toshinaga's mother as a hostage. However, perhaps most telling was that Mitsunari also accused him of usurping too much political power. Ieyasu, the letter explained, had taken it upon himself to allow the *daimyo* who had fought in Korea to return to their fiefs for 'purposes of rest' without consulting the other regents, before suggesting that Ishida Mitsunari and Maeda Toshinaga (both of whom had also made attempts on the life of Ieyasu) resign their positions as *bugyo* that Hideyoshi had appointed them to, as those, according to Ieyasu, were no longer required now that the *Taiko* was no more.

---

2. Kato's wife escaped their mansion carried out by porters hidden in a large wooden pickle barrel.
3. Kuroda's wife explained to the Ishida samurai surrounding the Kuroda property that she was sending an elderly attendant to the doctors via a closed palanquin and then she herself hid inside it with the elderly occupant to make good her escape.

Ieyasu then began to face criticism from other lords too, many of whom also demanded he resign his position. Natsuka Masaie, Mashita Nagamori and Maeda Gen'i were among those writing damning letters about the Tokugawa leader and sending them to other *daimyo*. Neither paying attention to the accusations, nor answering directly to these lords, caused further rifts between Ieyasu and the other regents.

Thus the country was immediately divided into East and West and both sides began preparations for the war that was by now inevitable. It was not a case of if, but when and where it would happen.

Hostilities Commence – The Fushimi Assault

Meanwhile, having been entrusted by Ieyasu with Fushimi Castle on the southern outskirts of Kyoto, Torii Mototada prepared to face the onslaught of the Western-allied *daimyo*. Fushimi Castle had been built by Toyotomi Hideyoshi as a southern defence for the capital and as a place for his retirement. It was elegant both inside and out, lavishly decorated with lacquer-work, gold and works of art by the leading artisans of the day. It was an exceptionally strong and well-planned castle, consisting of the central keep surrounded and protected by five smaller baileys, the Nishi-maru, the San-no-maru, the Matsu-maru, Nagoya-maru and the Jibushoyu-maru.

Sixty-one-year-old Torii Mototada was the *daimyo* of Yahagi, Shimosa, with a revenue of 40,000 *koku*. Although a little older than Tokugawa Ieyasu, they had long been close friends. Both had been born in Okazaki and as children they had been sent together as hostages to the Imagawa, during which Torii served as Ieyasu's page. On the night of 25 July Ieyasu visited Fushimi Castle and spent the night talking with Torii. This was to be the last time the two friends would spend together.

Aware of Fushimi Castle's importance, Ieyasu warned Torii of the imminent attack. Torii understood his role in the contest for the nation and that fighting to save the castle would be futile. Fushimi Castle could not withstand an assault from the combined Western forces and so he suggested Ieyasu reduce the number of troops so that he would have more men with which to fight in the field. Torii and the castle were to be sacrificed in the effort to destroy Ishida Mitsunari. For that reason alone it would have been an emotional parting between the two comrades.

Prior to hostilities breaking out, Shimazu Yoshihiro, a loyal and skilled former general of Toyotomi Hideyoshi and Kobayakawa Hideaki, Hideyoshi's nephew, had contacted Ieyasu and offered to assist in the defence of Fushimi. In Shimazu Yoshihiro's case, he had actually met with Ieyasu and confirmed verbally that he would help, but in the heat of the moment, no papers had been drawn up or signed. Ieyasu had headed north to battle the Uesugi, while the Shimazu headed south to prepare. Without this contractual proof, Torii had not trusted either of these men, especially as Shimazu Yoshihiro had such a small army of around only 200 at the time with him. Both the Shimazu and Kobayakawa would soon show their true colours by joining the enemy in the assault against Fushimi.

The expected attack came on 27 August 1600, when Fushimi was besieged by the armies of the Shimazu, Kobayakawa and the Ukita. Ten days of fierce fighting took place around the castle before Mitsunari himself arrived on 6 September to drive on the assault. Also among the attackers was Nabeshima Katsushige. He had been sent by his father with the intention of allying himself with the Tokugawa in the fight against Uesugi Kagekatsu. He arrived at Fushimi after hostilities had begun and decided somewhat strangely to join the attack on the fortress instead of defending it. After the fall of Fushimi Castle, Nabeshima Katsushige took part in the attack on Matsusaka Castle in Ise before being recalled to Kyushu for a berating by his father. Ultimately he did join the Tokugawa, but not at Sekigahara; instead he was laying siege to Otsu Castle against Tachibana Muneshige at the time of the great battle.

Back at Fushimi, the archers under the command of Kobayakawa Hideaki used flaming arrows to start a fire in one of the castle's baileys. Some damage was caused, although the blaze was soon extinguished by one of Torii's samurai, Kato Kurozaemon, at the cost of his own life. The following day, 7 September, fire broke out again in another of the baileys, the Matsu-maru keep, under the command of Koga no Goshi. Goshi's wife and children had been taken hostage by Natsuka Masaie who, via a message tied to an arrow, threatened to execute them unless Goshi turned traitor, adding that he would be well rewarded if he did. To save his family, Goshi agreed and with forty allies, broke down a section of wall and set fire to the tower. The flames soon spread to the Nagoya-maru and in the confusion the attackers broke in.

With the Matsu-maru and Nagoya-maru having been taken, Kobayakawa Hideaki offered peace terms that were quickly rejected by Torii and once again the fierce fighting resumed. In the clashes that followed, one of Ieyasu's relatives, Matsudaira Chikamasa, was cut down, as was Kambayashi

Chikuan, a tea merchant with military experience who had received permission to fight with Torii.

The attackers gained a great deal of confidence with the taking of the Matsu-maru and Nagoya-maru keeps and the fighting escalated. The commander, Matsudaira Ietada,[4] died when the Jibushoyu-maru fell. Ietada and his men were overwhelmed and realising the hopelessness of the situation, the 53-year-old samurai committed *seppuku*, cutting himself open rather than face the humiliation of capture and execution by the enemy.

With the castle burning around him, Torii personally led five counter-attacks with his last 200 samurai until just ten men remained. The castle had been overrun. The brave warrior then returned to the partially burning keep and was about to commit *seppuku* when he was confronted by the first of the attacking Western samurai forces, the spear-wielding warrior Saiga Shigetomo. Instead of fighting to the death, the exhausted Torii requested that Shigetomo wait while he and his remaining men ritually disembowelled themselves.

Torii's head was taken as a trophy and, along with those of Matsudaira Ietada and Matsudaira Chikamasa, was publicly displayed on Kyobashi Bridge in Osaka. The brave samurai's head, however, was stolen shortly afterwards by a cloth seller who had received many favours from him. In a mark of respect the merchant had it taken to a temple for a proper burial.

While the siege was declared a 'victory', an estimated 3,000 of the attackers met their death during the two-week battle, with nearly all of the 1,800 defenders of Fushimi Castle losing their lives. The castle was almost completely destroyed. With such a huge loss of life and the strategic benefits anticipated from the taking of the fortress largely gone, it is difficult to imagine the advantages that were attained from the bloody confrontation.

Although badly damaged, parts of the keep, surrounding towers and other structures within Fushimi Castle avoided complete destruction by fire. As was common practice, the sections that survived were dismantled for use in other buildings. The Zen priest Kochiin Suden (15??–1634), a former warrior who took three heads in 1573 at the Battle of Mikatagahara, was a close confidante of Ieyasu and received the floorboards from the main hall of the castle where Torii and his men had cut themselves open. Suden stored

---

4.   Ietada's diary, spanning a 17-year period from 1575, has survived and is widely recognised as an important historical source of information from this period.

the bloodstained boards for many years at the Nanzen-ji, a temple in Kyoto. From there, the floorboards were doled out to various temples around the city, including the Genko-en, Shoden-ji, Yogen-in and the Myoshin-ji in central Kyoto, and also to the Hosen-in in the Ohara region, the Jinou-ji in Yawata and the Kosho-ji in Uji, where they were used in the buildings. Even today, at the Genko-en Temple where the boards were used in the ceiling, one can discern amongst what appear to be water stains the bloody hand and footprints of Torii and his men.

In Torii Mototada's final letter, written to his son Tadamasa just prior to the attack on Fushimi, the brave samurai wrote:

> Reports have been received showing an uprising has begun in the Kamigata region. A large number of daimyo have come under the influence of the evil schemes of Ishida Mitsunari and are now preparing to attack this castle.
>
> No matter how many tens of thousands of cavalry or ranks of samurai they surround us with, I am resolved to make my final stand within this castle and hope to die a quick and glorious death.
>
> It would not be difficult to break through their troops and escape; however that is not the true way of the warrior and it would not be seen as a loyal thing to do. Instead, I will stand against the forces of the nation and even with one one-hundredth of the men required to do so, will defend this fortress with my life. This will show the enemy that to abandon a castle that must be defended, to show weakness or to avoid danger to save one's own life, are not acceptable traditions in the house of my lord, Ieyasu.
>
> I will take the initiative and encourage righteousness amongst the nation's warriors and bring a sense of resolve to Lord Ieyasu's other vassals. It goes without saying that the principle of laying down your life for your lord is the way of the warrior. This is a principle I have considered many times and so I believe that many learned warriors would find themselves envious of my position here and now.
>
> Tadamasa, I want you to never forget that our ancestors have been personal retainers of the Matsudaira clan for many generations. My late father, the Governor of Iga, served Lord Kiyoyasu well and after him, his son Lord Hirotada. My older brother

Genshichiro proved his absolute loyalty, giving his life in the Battle of Watari.

When Lord Ieyasu was sent as a child to Suruga, the governor of Iga accompanied him as a guardian and when Lord Ieyasu returned to Okazaki castle at the age of 19, the governor continued to serve him faithfully. For 80 years he served the Tokugawa house with great devotion and was regarded by our lord as a valued retainer.

I was brought before Lord Ieyasu when I was 13 and his lordship just seven years old. The many kindnesses received since that time must never be forgotten by the future generations of our house.

Lord Ieyasu has entrusted me with the important Kamigata region and as deputy of Fushimi Castle while he advances eastwards. That I should have the good fortune of being able to lay down my life for my master ahead of any other warrior across the nation is an honour long desired by our family.

After I have been killed, you must take responsibility for your younger brothers, starting with Hisagoro. Your brothers must look up to you as they would their father and must never disobey you. Ensure they remain on friendly terms with each other and remain grateful to their ancestors who established this house. As they come of age, they must present themselves and pledge their loyalty to Lord Ieyasu, using what talents they have to be of service and follow every command.

They must be determined to unwaveringly support Lord Ieyasu's clan and only his clan at all times, in its ascent and its decline, during war and during peace, when they are sleeping and when they are awake. Never have them desire land, nor forget the debt of gratitude we owe, nor feel dissatisfaction or entertain treacherous thoughts, for that is not the way.

Whatever the circumstances, should all the provinces rise up against Lord Ieyasu, our family must never waver nor serve another domain. Help each other to remain righteous. Exert yourselves in the cause of loyalty and bravery. Be careful not to sully this family name that has continued to gain fame for martial valour particularly since the time of the Governor of Iga.

Bear in mind at all times a sincerity in offering your life for your lord and by being of this thought, no fear or trembling will ever be felt, no matter the adversity.

I am now 62 years old and cannot remember the number of times I have barely escaped death since my days in Mikawa. Yet I have not once acted in a cowardly way. A man's life and death, his fortune and ruin, are subject to fate and so there is no merit in seeking the things you desire. It is important to learn from the senior retainers, to properly employ men of skill and knowledge; listen to your retainers and avoid rash acts.

The entire country will soon be in the hands of Lord Ieyasu and many men who serve him will be hoping to be appointed *daimyo* or to positions of rank. Do not expect a position or reward. If such a feeling arises, then this marks the beginning of the end of your way as a warrior. Becoming desirous of such things as rank and reward leads to valuing one's life. A man cannot perform acts of martial valour if he values his life! A samurai, born into the house of a warrior, with no loyalty in his heart, but thoughts of his fortunes and position, lacks righteousness and will stain his reputation for generations to come. This is most regrettable.

I have already spoken to you about managing the affairs of the clan and you have seen and heard about the ways of the past and so there is no need to tell you again.

Be discreet in your actions, display the correct manners always, develop harmony between the master and vassals, show no partiality between you and your retainers and have compassion for those below you. Be fair when doling out rewards and punishments. The foundation of ones' duty is truth. Beyond this, there is nothing more to be said.

The Western Forces' Three-Pronged Attack

With Fushimi Castle destroyed, the Western forces' confidence rose. The Toyotomi loyalists then commenced a three directional advance towards the Owari–Mikawa border (modern-day central Aichi Prefecture) where Ishida Mitsunari had assumed the actual battle with the Eastern forces would most likely take place. Mitsunari was no doubt aware that fighting Ieyasu in this area would give the Eastern troops the home-ground advantage and so a well-planned and decisive attack was called for.

Leading 30,000 men, Mitsunari and a number of *daimyo* took the inland mountainous Nakasendo route towards Mino, leading from the capital, Kyoto, going via Otsu to the south and then along the eastern edges of the great Lake Biwa to Mitsunari's fief of Sawayama (modern-day Hikone City) then further north through Maihara, Ibuki and crossing the border into Mino Province via Sekigahara. Another force of 40,000 under the command of Mori Hidemoto took the Pacific coastal Tokaido route via Ise (Mie Prefecture), while Otani Yoshitsugu and his retinue of around 20,000 departed Echizen (Fukui Prefecture) via the central Hokuriku highway.

Having entered Ogaki Castle and knowing Kiyosu Castle to be unobtainable, Mitsunari concentrated on obtaining other strategically-vital regional castles, including Takegahana (Gifu Prefecture) and Inuyama Castle (Aichi Prefecture) with the new intention of striking the Eastern armies along the Mino–Owari border instead. He was soon joined in Ogaki by the Konishi, Shimazu and other allies.

The *daimyo* of Ise's northern districts supported the West, while Tomita Nobuhiro, the *daimyo* of the central and southern Ise districts, had allied himself with the East. Taking a route through the friendly northern areas, a 30,000-strong force under Kikkawa Hiroie, Mori Hidemoto, Chosokabe Morichika, Natsuka Masaie and Ankokuji Ekei advanced on Tsu Castle. Tomita Nobuhiro had received Tsu from Toyotomi Hideyoshi only five years earlier. Tsu was a grand castle for its time, with an impressive five-storey main keep and a smaller secondary keep watching over three main compounds and completed around 1577 by its previous master Oda Nobukane, younger brother of Oda Nobunaga. Tsu Castle was defended by less than 1,700 troops, who put up such fierce resistance that the attacking Western forces, concerned at the loss of life and excessive damage to the castle, offered of surrender. Among the defenders and fighting as boldly as any man was Tomita's wife, Oyuki (also known as Yuki no Kata) dressed in lightweight yet strong black-lacquered leather armour and fighting with a spear. This was an unusual situation, as generally women did not take combat roles in battle, despite the wives and daughters of samurai being expected to competently wield various weapons. Unable to continue fighting and with the bulk of the castle reduced to ashes, the remaining men of Tsu capitulated.

With Tsu captured, the Western forces concentrated on the even larger Matsusaka Castle further south, before setting their sights on the more strategically-positioned Nagashima Castle further to the north, then under the control of Fukushima Masanori's younger brother, Fukushima Takaharu. Like Tsu, the defenders of Matsusaka and Nagashima Castles both put up an extraordinary defence and it was not long before orders came for the large numbers of attackers to abandon the Ise region and join the fight in Mino.

Maeda Toshinaga, Lord of Kanazawa Castle in the north-western Hokuriku region, had openly announced his support of the Tokugawa coalition. In response, Otani Yoshitsugu had led a force including the men of Hiratsuka Tamehiro, Wakisaka Yasuharu, Kutsuki Mototsuna and Akaza Naoyasu to Kitanosho Castle (currently Fukui City) to confront him. The armies of the last three lords were to later play a surprising and pivotal role in the battle at Sekigahara. The two armies faced off without fighting before Ishida Mitsunari sent an urgent message ordering them to make their way towards Sekigahara. Otani's units departed first from Kitanosho Castle, followed by the others and arrived at Sekigahara on 9 October.

Attack on Tanabe

Two days after the Siege of Fushimi had started, another began between Eastern and Western forces on 29 August 1600, when a vassal of Ieyasu, Hosokawa Yusai, was attacked by Western troops while in Tanabe Castle in Tango (the modern-day northern districts of Kyoto Prefecture). Tango Province would have posed a risk to the rear of the Western forces as they faced the Easterners and so an attack was believed to be imminent. Having been notified of the death of his daughter-in-law Gracia and of Ishida Mitsunari's moves in Osaka days before, the semi-retired lord entered his castle and prepared for a siege. He did not have to wait long.

Hosokawa Yusai was defiant in his defence of the fortress, though he had just 500 men holding the fort against a force of 15,000. Yusai was an old man of 67 and a brilliant scholar and poet. It just so happened that many of the commanders of the attacking forces were former students of the old samurai and 'attacked' only half-heartedly. Out of respect for their teacher, some deliberately failed to load projectiles into their matchlocks and cannons, firing off round after round of nothing but gunpowder. Many others in the attacking forces were in reality already considering abandoning Mitsunari and joining the Eastern army.

Yusai had a number of rare and important books of poetry in his possession at the time of the siege. One of those books was an edition of the *Kokinshu*, a 20-volume collection of 1,100 mostly *tanka* poems ordered by Emperor Daigo and completed in 922. Fearing that these and his other precious books may be damaged in the attack, Yusai sent a messenger to the younger brother of Emperor Go-Yozei, Prince Tomohito, requesting he send Maeda Gen'i to receive the books and pass them on to the Imperial family.

When this had been done, the Imperial Court, worried at the potential loss of such a distinguished scholar and noble samurai, advised Yusai to surrender. However, being the dignified, proud samurai they all knew him to be, he steadfastly refused. The resulting siege lasted two months before the Western troops disengaged. Yusai was thus successful in diverting 15,000 Western troops from joining the main battle at Sekigahara. Meanwhile, as Yusai engaged in this diversion, his son Tadaoki represented the Hosokawa clan splendidly on the battlefield.

The Siege at Ueda

It was not just the Western forces that were short of men. Some 38,000 samurai under the command of 21-year-old Tokugawa Hidetada, Ieyasu's third son and heir, were supposed to be coming southwards along the Nakasendo highway to join the Eastern forces at Sekigahara.

Hidetada had initially been ordered to assist in the campaign against Uesugi Kagekatsu and had gone as far as Utsunomiya, in present-day Tochigi Prefecture, when he received news of Mitsunari's's uprising. Turning his men around he headed south along the Tosando to Ueda where the Sanada clan resided.

Ueda Castle in Shinano Province (modern-day Nagano Prefecture) was held by Sanada Masayuki, whose wife was the sister of Ishida Mitsunari and their second son, Nobushige, better known as Yukimura,[5] who was married to the daughter of Otani Yoshitsugu, a staunch ally of Mitsunari. Sanada Masayuki's father was one of the famed twenty-four generals[6] under the warlord Takeda Shingen and had begrudgingly submitted to the Tokugawa

---

5.   Sanada Nobushige (1567–3 June 1615) remains among the most popular of all *Sengoku*-period heroes. Although better known as Yukimura, he was never known by that name during his lifetime. It appears to have been coined by an Edo-period author of action stories, using the popular image of the Sanada clan and their fictional band of ninja as the protagonists of his work.

6.   The most trusted companions and advisors to Takeda Shingen, noted for their loyalty, bravery and martial expertise. A third of them had been killed in action fighting a joint force under Oda Nobunaga and Tokugawa Ieyasu at Nagashino in 1575 that all but destroyed the mighty Takeda clan.

after the defeat of Takeda Katsuyori at the great gun-battle of Nagashino in 1575 where his elder brother was killed fighting the Oda and Tokugawa.

It was through this submission that Sanada Masayuki was forced to hand over his eldest son, Nobuyuki, as a hostage to the Tokugawa at Hamamatsu Castle, where Hidetada had been born. Further, he had refused to hand over his domains to the Tokugawa, who intended giving them to the Hojo. This led to the Tokugawa attacking Ueda Castle from August to December 1585, when 7,000 Tokugawa troops laid siege to Ueda with 2,000 Sanada troops inside.

The small but sturdy Ueda Castle was the epitome of the philosophy 'simple is best'. It made excellent use of the surrounding topography for protection, including the Chikuma River and the steep cliffs along it. Even the layout of the town below, which was cleverly intersected by well-designed waterways, all helped to hinder any attackers. The outer defences of Ueda Castle covered an area around 300m x 400m, with the central stronghold being approximately 100m x 150m in size. This main section was a square-shaped area surrounded by a moat and ringed by high earthen walls, cliffs and stone walls topped with seven defensive *yagura* watchtowers and with two large gates with watchtowers built above them.

In the first attack, known as the First Battle of Ueda, Sanada Masayuki lured the Tokugawa attackers close to the castle gates, before ambushing them from behind with a reserve army just as the Tokugawa commenced the attack. Confused and unable to recover, the Tokugawa hurriedly retreated. A second attempt was planned, but support for the Sanada from the powerful Uesugi clan of Echigo (Niigata Prefecture) forced the Tokugawa to reconsider. Victory over Ieyasu was claimed by Sanada Masayuki and his reputation was greatly enhanced. Now, the Tokugawa would face off against the Sanada for a second time, this time with 3,000 Sanada samurai defending their small castle against the 38,000 samurai of Tokugawa Hidetada.

Hidetada was accompanied by a large number of highly-trusted Tokugawa generals, many hand-picked by Ieyasu himself in an effort to provide his son with the best of counsel. Ieyasu appears to have never truly recognised Hidetada's talents, nor allowed him much of an opportunity to display them. Indeed, Hidetada was long under the shadow of his great father. Even when he was shogun, Ieyasu continued to pull the strings, manipulating Hidetada's government. In fact, Hidetada was never fully able to shine in his own right until after his father's death in 1616. Once his father had passed away, however, Hidetada would quickly and decisively step up to the mark,

relocating the various *daimyo* and their fiefs, banning Christianity and intro-
ducing the *Sakoku*, or isolationist policy, that saw Japan enter a 214-year-long
self-imposed quarantine, severely limiting foreign trade and relations, and
preventing Japanese from leaving and foreigners from entering Japan.

Among the men attending Hidetada was Aoyama Tadanari. In 1585, Ieyasu
had directly requested Aoyama Tadanari watch over Hidetada. The Aoyama
clan, former provincial lords of Nukata District in Mikawa (now part of Okazaki
City, Aichi Prefecture), had loyally attended Ieyasu's father and Tadanari himself had served Ieyasu personally for many years with the two remaining close
friends. For the last 15 years, however, he had remained at Hidetada's side,
carefully advising him on military and political affairs. Aoyama Tadanari had
been appointed one of the Magistrates of Edo and he shared his time equally
between his duties as magistrate and mentor to the future second Shogun.
Incidentally, the affluent Aoyama district of Tokyo is named after Aoyama
Tadanari, as his sprawling residence and lands were originally located there.

The ever-reliable Honda Tadamasa, Honda Masanobu, Sakai Ietsugu
and Okubo Tadasuke, all men from Mikawa, the Tokugawa homeland, were
among Hidetada's top generals, as was Asano Nagamasa, one of the original
five *bugyo* appointed by Toyotomi Hideyoshi to serve Hideyoshi's infant son.
Nagamasa had retired from public life after the death of Hideyoshi as he had
relations with both the Eastern and Western factions, but was enticed out of
retirement to join Hidetada's force.

Makino Yasunari, the *daimyo* of Ueno in Kozuke Province (Gunma
Prefecture) since 1590, was another of the able generals with Hidetada at
the time. During the early stages of the mostly uneventful Siege of Ueda,
the sound of matchlock gunfire and a roar of voices was suddenly heard as
a contingent of samurai under Makino banners stormed a section of Ueda
Castle. Not knowing what was going on put the rest of Hidetada's forces on
high alert and tensions rose as the attackers faced a heavy volley of return
matchlock fire and archery from the defenders. Many of the Makino men,
exposed and unable to take cover, were killed in the short exchange.

Makino Yasunari was soon called before Hidetada to explain. He and his
men had not received instructions nor permission from Hidetada to engage
the enemy and as the results had been disastrous, Hidetada was furious.
Although he had not personally led nor ordered the attack, Yasunari was
compelled to take responsibility and command his subordinates who organised the skirmish to commit *seppuku*. Yasunari felt that as their leader, he

should be the one to cut himself open and could not bring himself to demand the penalty on those involved. Those whose lives may have been forfeit that day included Yasunari's son, Tadanari and his vassals, who then fled the camp in fear, bringing greater disgrace to the Makino and angering Hidetada even more. Instead, the Makino's *Hata Bugyo* (battle flag commissioner) is said to have performed *seppuku* as a substitute for his lord's failures. Makino Yasunari was then sentenced to house arrest and confined to a single room in his castle at Ueno. In this second Tokugawa-led attack on Ueda Castle, Sanada Masayuki and his younger son, Nobushige, held up Hidetada's extensive forces for fifteen days until 16 October 16, resulting in Hidetada failing to arrive on the field of Sekigahara in time to support his father.

Incidentally, Sanada Masayuki had ordered his first son, Nobuyuki, who was married to a daughter of the Tokugawa General, Honda Tadakatsu, to fight for the East, while Nobushige, having ties to Otani Yoshitsugu, was to fight for the West. It seemed an ideal situation in which to preserve the family name, as a Sanada would be among the victors whatever the outcome. Following Sekigahara and as a reward for his services, the Eastern-allied Nobuyuki would receive his father's estates of Ueda and Numata Castles and later in 1622, nearby Matsushiro Castle.

Meanwhile, other minor battles between those supporting the Tokugawa and Ishida Mitsunari's Toyotomi loyalists raged across the country. In league with the Western forces, Shishido Kageyo, under the Mori clan banners, had invaded Eastern-allied Kato Yoshiaki's Misaki Castle in Shikoku Island's Iyo Domain (modern-day Ehime Prefecture) in the hopes of regaining his clan's former territory, but was defeated in a counter-attack by Yoshiaki's younger brother Tadaaki and a small defensive force. Kageyo finally retreated upon learning of the Western defeat at Sekigahara. At around the same time and upon the orders of Tokugawa Ieyasu, Kamei Korenori[7] attacked and laid siege to Tottori Castle in Inaba (Tottori Prefecture).

The majority of Kyushu's military commanders had sided with the Western army and so while their main forces were absent, Kuroda Josui, Kato Kiyomasa and other Eastern affiliates took advantage of the situation

---

7.   Kamei Korenori (1557–27 February 1612) served Toyotomi Hideyoshi and played an important role in the annexation of Kyushu. After Hideyoshi's death, he served Tokukawa Ieyasu. For his services to the Eastern war efforts, his income was raised from 13,000 to 43,000 *koku*.

by attacking the now-vulnerable castles of the Western-affiliated *daimyo*. To achieve this, Kuroda Josui opened his domain's coffers and using the stored gold and silver, hired 3,600 *ronin*, masterless and now freelance samurai, and enhanced their numbers further by mobilising an army consisting of local farmers and even merchants to make up for the absent samurai now with his son in the central districts.

Two days before Sekigahara, the Battle of Ishigakibaru took place near Kyushu's north-eastern hot springs resort city of Beppu, in which Otomo Yoshimune (1558–2 September 1610) attempted to regain his former territory by invading Kuroda Josui's Bungo Province (Oita Prefecture). The Otomo had been deprived of their lands in 1587 by Toyotomi Hideyoshi for their cowardice at the Battle of Pyongyang in Korea. Discovering a large Chinese army was advancing to defend the city, Otomo Yoshimune quickly retreated, leaving his commander, Konoshi Yukinaga and his troops exposed. Upon hearing of Yoshimune's actions, Hideyoshi confiscated his lands and in turn presented them to the Kuroda clan. The battle at Ishigakibaru commenced around midday with the Otomo gaining much ground and confidence as the Kuroda were pushed back. The Kuroda feigned a retreat at one stage and as the Otomo forces moved in for the kill, they were routed by an ambush of Kuroda reinforcements. The Battle of Ishigakibaru ended early evening of 19 October when the encroaching Otomo were forced to surrender as the make-shift Kuroda army had defended their lands superbly. Otomo Yoshimune was captured and later exiled. The lords of Kyushu, Kuroda Josui, Kato Kiyomasa et al, continued their attacks and sieges of Western castles until as late as December 1600 when Tokugawa Ieyasu ordered a ceasefire.

The Assembly of Forces

Fukushima Masanori (1561–1624) was a samurai of the Owari districts serving under Hideyoshi, who had awarded him Kiyosu Castle, Oda Nobunaga's former formidable fortress and a revenue of 20,000 *koku*. After Hideyoshi's death, Ieyasu had cleverly orchestrated the marriage of his adopted daughter to the son of Masanori, Masayuki, thus creating a highly strategic alliance.

Anecdotally, Fukushima Masanori was said to have been something of an alcoholic, drinking from early morning until late at night. He also had a reputation for a quick temper, especially when under the influence of sake. Not only was he quick to anger, but he was just as quick to forget the consequences of his drunken fury. An incident that has since passed into legend occurred some years earlier during his return from the Korean Peninsula en route to Edo. As the ship stopped at Tomonoura in Hiroshima Prefecture, Fukushima was drunk as usual and forgetting that he had not ordered a change of clothes, began berating his clothing coordinator, a close aide called Tsuge Kiyoemon, for not having his attire prepared. When Tsuge mentioned that Fukushima had not yet asked to be changed, the lord was sent into a howling rage, claiming belligerently that he had and then demanded Kiyoemon's head. The unfortunate samurai went off to another part of the ship and committed *seppuku*. Later, when the boat docked and Fukushima was preparing to alight, he asked his staff where Tsuge Kiyoemon was. His men looked at each other astonished, before one bravely informed his lord in a hushed voice, 'He is no longer with us, he has committed *seppuku*'. Fukushima was shocked. '*Seppuku*? But why?' Once again his men looked at one another nervously. 'Because you demanded it, my lord'. Realising what he'd done, Fukushima broke down and cried out in sorrow.

At the outbreak of hostilities, Fukushima had quickly returned to his fief with 16,000 of his samurai. The armies of Kuroda Nagamasa and then Ikeda Terumasa followed with a combined total of 18,000 men. All came together on 11 August at Fukushima's stronghold and with Kiyosu Castle once again firmly established as a secure base, the armies prepared for battle. Over the next few days, other Eastern-allied *daimyo* and their troops arrived in Owari and were billeted to various temples and houses in the region.

All the armies were then engaged in the undoubtedly tedious but vitally important task of preparing themselves for war. Besides weapons, gunpowder and ammunition, preparations for all forces included the packaging of utensils and foodstuffs to feed a mobile army. Foods such as rice, pickled plums, miso (fermented bean paste) and other foodstuffs that were long-lasting, nutritious and easily carried, including auspicious rations like chestnuts, dried *awabi* (a type of shellfish) and *kombu* (seaweed) were regularly included.

The rapid preparation of rations was always a difficult task for any samurai army and while most armies were expected to prepare their own rations, Shimazu clan records show that for the Sekigahara campaign, provisions for approximately 1,500 men and a number of guns were offered and supplied by Toyotomi Hideyori. This is a very rare case in samurai military history. Alternatively, for Tokugawa Ieyasu, preparing for the battle was made easier by a number of allies, particularly those along the Tokaido route such as Yamauchi Katsutoyo and Fukushima Masanori et al, offering various supplies of food, weapons etc, along the way to the battlefield. Fukushima Masanori had some 300,000 180kg bushels of rice in storage at his castle in Kiyosu that had been stockpiled there by the Toyotomi for safekeeping and this too was offered to the Tokugawa.

On both sides, cooks, kitchen staff and fire makers were recruited, as were labourers, grooms, baggage carriers, sandal bearers and the like from the local peasantry. For war, arrangements included the fitting of arms and armour for the foot soldiers who would play a major part in the action, as well as basic training for these men. The polishing of bladed weapons and the maintenance and manufacture of arrows was an important task, along with the melting of lead, poured into scissor-like moulds to form matchlock balls and the weighing of gunpowder into small charges to facilitate the quick reloading of firearms.

Tokugawa Ieyasu had arrived back at his castle in Edo only a few days before and seemed to be in no great hurry. As the Tokugawa forces prepared to attack the Uesugi, the not-unexpected news came of Ishida Mitsunari's uprising in Osaka. Mitsunari had counted on the Uesugi in keeping Ieyasu busy, but Ieyasu's adherents Date Masamune and Mogami Yoshiakira had in fact kept the Uesugi at bay. Surprisingly, instead of increasing the pressure on his enemies, Ieyasu requested that Date Masamune pull out of the conflict with the Uesugi. For his support and loyalty, Masamune would receive 50,000 *koku*.

Detained too long by the Uesugi and stuck in Sendai, it was now too late and too far for Masamune to participate in the battle. In support, the 'One-Eyed Dragon' provided Ieyasu with some 1,200 arquebuses, 850 spears, 200 bows and 330 non-military staff.

Meanwhile, Fukushima Masanori was growing concerned at Ieyasu's perceived reluctance at taking the lead. Nonetheless, Fukushima remained loyal and proved that loyalty on 22 August by launching a joint attack on Gifu Castle with another Tokugawa ally, Ikeda Terumasa. Despite Masanori's concerns, Ieyasu was not afraid of leading the assault and it was his deliberate intention to leave his own men fresh for the real battle by allowing his allies to fight these initial skirmishes.

On the Western side, Oda Hidenobu was well aware that the Eastern troops would not be long in coming but did not know where they would attempt to cross the wide Kiso River and so he ordered fortifications be established along the riverside provincial borders and around Gifu Castle. This dispatch of warriors to the borders served to weaken the main defences of the castle and only managed to temporarily delay the Eastern troops' advance.

The Fukushima forces, including those of Todo Takatora and Hosokawa Tadaoki totalling some 16,000 men, had attempted to cross the Kiso River near the Nakashima district (modern-day Ichinomiya) as it was closer to his fief at Kiyosu, but were prevented from doing so by the large enemy contingent firmly entrenched on the opposite side. Leaving a small contingent to counter these enemy, the bulk of this army went further south, crossing at Higashi-Kaganoi before attacking and defeating a small garrison of Western army troops stationed at the now understaffed Takehana Castle (near present-day Hashima City).

The troops of Ikeda Terumasa had also moved out of Kiyosu Castle that morning and, heading towards Gifu, crossed the river at Koda in the Haguri district. Terumasa's troops met resistance in the form of Hidenobu's crack gunners, but even they failed to stop the advance. This skirmish, known as the Battle of Koda Kisogawa Toko, soon ended with the Ikeda forces overrunning the musketeers. They bulldozed on and in a matter of minutes further clashed with a force of 3,000 samurai under the command of Dodo Tsunaie[8] at Komeno (modern-day Kasamatsu). This battle, known as the Battle of Komeno, saw another defeat for Hidenobu, who had been at nearby Injiki (now called Ginan) and he ordered a hasty retreat to Gifu, rather than risk facing the Ikeda army.

Despite the heavy losses, Oda Hidenobu remained confident in Gifu Castle's invulnerability. He and his younger brother Hidenori waited within the castle, while the remainder of Dodo Tsunaie's men and the troops of Oda vassals Tsuda Tosaburo, Inuma Tadasuke and Kozukuri Tomoyasu, were dispatched to the various passes surrounding the castle for protection.

The very next day, on 23 August, the Fukushima and Ikeda combined their armies and assaulted Gifu Castle. Hidenobu had already sent for reinforcements from Ogaki Castle in the west and Inuyama Castle in the

---

8.   Dodo Tsunaie (c.1548–1609), also known as Yasunobu and Yasuyuki, was a vassal of Oda Nobunaga, Toyotomi Hideyoshi and Oda Hidenobu. He served as the Governor of Echizen Province and as an advisor to Oda Hidenobu. Highly skilled both in field warfare and castle construction, Dodo had implored Hidenobu to join the Eastern coalition prior to hostilities breaking out, but Hidenobu had refused his advice. Following the Battle of Sekigahara he was placed under arrest and detained in Kyoto. He later accepted a position with Yamauchi Katsutoyo and assisted in the construction of the still-extant Kochi Castle. Kochi City's Echizen-cho area was named after Tsunaie, the former Governor of Echizen Province.

east, thinking that these fresh samurai could trap the Eastern forces between them. Aware of the danger, the Eastern commanders arranged to have Yamauchi Katsutoyo, Horio Tadauji, Arima Toyoji and Togawa Tatsuyasu take up positions in the villages to the south-east of Gifu, while the troops of Kuroda Nagamasa, Todo Takatora and Tanaka Yoshimasa prepared for battle to the south-west. However, no samurai were forthcoming from Inuyama Castle. Although not having officially declared his abandonment of the Western forces, Ishikawa Sadakiyo, the lord of Inuyama, had secretly made a deal with the Tokugawa general Ii Naomasa not to participate, thus protecting the rear of the Eastern advance. The samurai that eventually sallied forth from Ogaki arrived too late to be of service. The highly-regarded Gifu Castle fell in one day. From this revelation it appears as though the Eastern forces' attack ran as smoothly as a well-oiled machine, but that was not always the case. For example, throughout the history of samurai warfare, being the first into battle was considered a great honour and many a fight was lost through impatience at being the first to engage the enemy. In this instance Fukushima Masanori had preceded Ikeda Terumasa in the charge to Gifu and was accused of attempting to take the lead.

Further exacerbating this situation was that days before at Kiyosu Castle, the Fukushima and Ikeda had decided to attack Gifu jointly. However, they could not agree on the best way to take the fortress and in their desperation to be first into battle almost came to blows themselves. Eventually they decided that the Fukushima would attack the front of the castle while the Ikeda stormed the rear. A ratio of three attackers to one defender was involved, generally considered the ideal minimum proportion to bring down a Japanese castle. In the severe fighting that ensued, most of Gifu Castle and the elegant palace around the base of Mount Kinkazan was destroyed.[9]

---

9.   After the Battle of Sekigahara, Gifu Castle was abandoned and on the orders of Tokugawa Ieyasu himself, the ruins were put off limits on the penalty of death. Some of remaining structures and stones from the walls of the lower sections were removed and reused to build nearby Kano Castle, which served as the regions main castle until the end of the Edo period. Only the stone walls around the *hon-maru* central bailey and the now filled-in moats remain. The keep-like structure at the top of the mountain was rebuilt over 300 years later, becoming Japan's first castle to be rebuilt as a tourist attraction in 1910, but this was destroyed in a fire in 1943 during the Second World War. The current mountaintop keep was recreated

On the outbreak of hostilities between Tokugawa Ieyasu and Ishida Mitsunari, the samurai of Gifu had advised Hidenobu against siding with the latter. With the fall of Gifu, Oda Hidenobu surrendered to Fukushima, who took him to Imoarai in Yamashiro, Kii Province, where he was confined to a Buddhist monastery. After Sekigahara, Ieyasu ordered him to shave his head and retire to life in the monastery, where he died two years later at the age of 21.

The Eastern allies had captured Gifu Castle and the troops stationed in nearby Inuyama Castle now found themselves cut off and already having agreed not to attack the Eastern forces, subsequently surrendered, giving the Eastern army control of most of the Nakasendo. Interestingly, Inuyama Castle was spared the fighting and is now listed as a National Treasure. It is Japan's oldest surviving castle keep and until recently it was the only privately-owned castle. Inuyama remained in the hands of the Naruse family, handed down since feudal times, until it was given to Inuyama City and a preservation management consortium in 2004.

Ishida Mitsunari was aware of the Eastern units' incursion into Mino and of the fall of Gifu Castle. In response, he ordered troops be deployed to the Godo area on the western banks of the Nagara River that flowed around the base of Gifu Castle. As an extra precaution he ordered Shimazu Yoshihiro further downstream to Sunomata, famous as the site where, in 1567, Toyotomi Hideyoshi in an attempt to take the former Saito clan's Gifu (then Inabayama) Castle for his master, Oda Nobunaga, had constructed a castle 'overnight' to the great surprise of the enemy and his allies alike.[10]

---

in concrete in 1956 and, although slightly larger than the original, today it serves as a fine museum and scenic tower looking out over the wide Nobi Plain.

10   Although it is claimed Sunomata Castle was completed overnight, it is believed the moats were dug, the earth from them was then piled on the inside of the moats to form protective earthen walls, rudimentary fencing was erected around the top and basic gates were constructed. So as to appear to have been constructed overnight, it is believed that Hideyoshi had either erected bamboo frames covered in cloth or woven sheets of straw to give the impression of more sturdy structures having been built and then later over the following weeks completed the buildings properly, or had prefabricated various structures elsewhere and floated the parts down the river to the site where they were hastily put together within around three days. Either way it is believed by most researchers that it took around three weeks to complete the entire castle, even then a most impressive feat to achieve,

By this stage, the Eastern-allied Kuroda Nagamasa and Todo Takatora had advanced towards Ogaki in an attempt to block reinforcements from Ogaki Castle reaching Gifu. The wide Nagara River was enveloped in a thick mist when they arrived on the eastern banks, masking their advance. The Western units there were caught off guard by the sudden appearance of the Kuroda and Todo troops and shocked into making a hasty retreat back into the safety of Ogaki Castle. This retreat would have serious repercussions in the days to come.

The retreat was ordered so quickly that the Western commanders neglected to inform Shimazu Yoshihiro and his troops further along the river at Sunomata, leaving them isolated, vulnerable and feeling very much insulted. The joint Kuroda-Todo army then continued on to the mountains of Akasaka, just west of Ogaki, swelling the numbers of Eastern troops waiting there to around 40,000 men.

October 1600

Word of the fall of Gifu reached Tokugawa Ieyasu in Edo four days later and he soon commenced preparations to leave his extensive castle. On 7 October 1600, Ieyasu headed down the Tokaido with 30,000 troops. At that time, Ieyasu's son, Hidetada and his army had converged in Karuizawa (modern-day Nagano Prefecture) to make an assault on nearby Ueda Castle. Meanwhile deep in central Mino Province, Eastern ally Endo Yoshitaka[11] attacked – and two days later captured – Gujo Hachiman Castle, the property of the absent Inaba Sadamichi,[12] who was at Inuyama Castle at the time.

---

especially right under the noses of the enemy. The modern-day reconstruction of Sunomata Castle, although impressive, is a complete fabrication. No such keep ever existed at the small fortress.

11   Endo Yoshitaka (1550– 10 May 1632). Born in Kigoshi Castle, Gujo, Mino. Served the Saito clan of Mino, later Oda Nobunaga.

12   Inaba Sadamichi (1546–17 October 1603). Born in Mino, originally served the Saito clan, joining Oda Nobunaga's army in 1567. Upon the death of his father he became the master of Mino Sone Castle. A veteran of many campaigns, he was in Kyoto when Nobunaga was killed and fled back to his homeland. He fought at Shizugatake under Hideyoshi, for which he was later awarded Gujo Hachiman Castle. He saw action at the Siege of Odawara in 1590 and in Korea. Although Western allied, he held Eastern sympathies. After Sekigahara he was awarded Usuki Castle in Oita, Kyushu, where he died aged 57.

On 9 October, the leper lord, Otani Yoshitsugu, his face covered by a white cloth to hide his disfigurement and wearing a white *jinbaori* (a sleeveless surcoat covering his heavy armour) arrived at Sekigahara with his 1,500 soldiers. Unable to walk due to his crippling disease, Yoshitsugu was carried in an open palanquin to his command post.

Otani Yoshitsugu was born in Omi Province (Shiga Prefecture) in 1559. At the age of 15, he was accepted into the service of Toyotomi Hideyoshi while in the castle of Himeji. He was awarded the castle of Tsuruga (modern-day Fukui Prefecture) and a stipend of 50,000 *koku*.

By the age of 42, the effects of Hansen's disease had well and truly set in and he was both crippled and partially blind. Yoshitsugu was originally allied with the Tokugawa and was on his way north to assist Ieyasu in the fight against the Uesugi, when he met with Ishida Mitsunari in Sawayama, about 2km east of the currently remaining National Treasure listed site of Hikone Castle. Through his long association with the leader of the loyalist armies, he was persuaded to join the Western forces. He is today chiefly remembered for his leprosy and his staunch friendship. Yoshitsugu had worked closely with Mitsunari as one of the Three Commissioners, along with Mashita Nagamori who had been sent by Hideyoshi to oversee the Korean Campaign, but their connections ran even deeper.

One of the better-known stories regarding Otani Yoshitsugu and Ishida Mitsunari's friendship happened in 1587. During a tea ceremony at Osaka Castle, as Yoshitsugu was drinking from the shared cup, some pus dropped from his disease ravaged nose into the tea. As per tradition, the cup was passed on to the following participating samurai, who having seen the accident looked on horrified as the teacup came their way, further embarrassing the ill Yoshitsugu. However, when the tea was passed to Mitsunari, he drank it, pus and all and then commented on the fineness of its flavour. Whether, as it has been suggested, Mitsunari was an unwitting stooge of the more aware samurai who merely pretended to drink, or whether this was a genuine act of sincere kindness, Yoshitsugu was touched by the gesture and is said to have remarked, 'Mitsunari is an extraordinary man'.

Otani Yoshitsugu had met with Ishida Mitsunari at Sawayama Castle some months before hostilities commenced and listened earnestly to his friend's problematic scheme. Knowing that Mitsunari's lack of charisma and allies would be the first of many hurdles to clear in gathering adequate numbers to pose a threat to Ieyasu, Yoshitsugu did his best to dissuade him from attempting the brazen agenda. The ever-stubborn Mitsunari refused to accept this and so in exasperation, Otani reluctantly agreed to support him.

Along with Kinoshta Yoritsugu, Hiratsuka Tamehiro and Toda Shigemasa, Otani Yoshitsugu had amassed a force of 4,000 Western troops and began to take up positions around the village of Yamanaka-mura near Sekigahara. On the same day, 9 October, another 2,000 Western-allied troops under the joint command of Wakisaka Yasuharu, Ogawa Suketada and Akaza Naoyasu gathered at nearby Fujikawa Village to prepare for the coming conflict.

Four days later they were followed by Kikkawa Hiroie and his 3,000 troops leading the Mori army that included Mori Hidemoto with 15,000, Ankokuji Ekei commanding 1,800, Natsuka Masaie with 1,500 and a further 6,600 under Chosokabe Morichika. This group set up camp just east of Sekigahara and south of the village of Tarui on Mount Nangu.[13]

As with many of the command posts of the major players at Sekigahara, the actual sites can still be visited and are often marked out with stone monuments and the battle flags of the leader. Mori Hidemoto's encampment on Mount Nangu was designed and constructed like a small castle. The main bailey was only around 100m in size, not large enough to fit his entire army in, only the elite samurai. A second smaller bailey was located to the north-east and to the south-east, facing Ogaki, the remains of a dry moat can be seen. Nearby, the Chosokabe camp too was constructed in a similar fashion, with a 10m by 20m rectangular area shaved from the mountain top, surrounded by a walled embankment and dry moat around the south and eastern edges. Mount Nangu is now covered in forest, but in 1600 was bare of any trees and vegetation that may have provided cover for the enemy.

Occupying Mount Nangu, Ankokuji Ekei was not of samurai stock, but a Buddhist monk. Ekei had entered the Tofuku-ji Temple in Kyoto at the age

---

13. At the base of Mount Nangu, facing Tarui is the famed Nangu Taisha Shrine, which at the time also housed the Asakurayama Shinzen-in Temple. East of the temple's bell tower is a cast bronze mausoleum said to have been erected by Hojo Masako in memory of her husband, the first Kamakura Shogun Minamoto Yoritomo (1147–99). The mausoleum's missing upper section is said to have been commandeered and used as a stove by Chosokabe Morichika's men to cook their meals in during the Battle of Sekigahara. The Asakurayama Shinzen-in Temple was relocated away from the Nangu Taisha Shrine site after the Government ordered separation of Shinto and Buddhism during the Meiji Period (1868–1912).

of 11, where he had shown great promise. Mori Terumoto had met the young monk and, much taken by his intelligence, brought him to Aki where he was later made a councillor of the Mori administration. He continued to rise in rank, soon becoming the Chief *Bonze* of Ankoku-ji temple in Aki, where he continued to receive many favours and great rewards.

Ankokuji Ekei held a 60,000-*koku* fief in Iyo thanks to his close connections with Hideyoshi, who very much enjoyed the monk's discourses on military and religious affairs. This close association with Hideyoshi was one that he used to his own advantage, accepting bribes from *daimyo* for arranging an audience with the *Taiko*.

Ankokuji Ekei had been called in to negotiate peace between the Mori and Hideyoshi in 1582, the success of which elevated him to the role of states-man. He had then set his sights on a political career and strongly voiced his support for the infant Hideyori on the death of the boy's father, and had also played a major role in the active gathering of *daimyo* in support of Hideyori under Ishida Mitsunari. His actual role in the coming battle, however, would open a few eyes and not just those of the loyalist armies.

Mori Terumoto had been made *Soutaisho* or commander-in-chief of the Western forces. It was Otani Yoshitsugu who had advised Mitsunari that as Terumoto was the nation's second most powerful *daimyo* after Ieyasu, he should be in command. Mitsunari agreed, but by awarding Terumoto the title of supreme commander, Mitsunari essentially shunted him aside with a position in Osaka Castle, the seat of Toyotomi power, while Mitsunari himself continued to command the forces and make the decisions from the battlefield.

This move naturally angered Mori Terumoto and his subordinates, who were well aware that Terumoto was by far a better strategist than Ishida Mitsunari, a man Kato Kiyomasa had once called 'A commoner interfering in military affairs'. This led Kikkawa Hiroie to advise his cousin, the pow-erful Terumoto, on the best course of action, a strategy that affected the outcome of the battle at Sekigahara tremendously.

On 16 October, just five days before the battle at Sekigahara took place, Mitsunari wrote letters to Mashita Nagamori that were meant to spur on the forces residing in Osaka and to gain further sympathy. In it he wrote:

> Ieyasu seems to be afraid of confronting us, as he has yet to leave
> Edo. We should take comfort from that. I am however concerned
> with Natsuka Masaie and Ankokuji Ekei having to fight in the

mountains. Also, Mori Terumoto still has not confirmed his alliance with us. That too gives me some concern; however, I believe he is with us. I feel that our army is not together spiritually as one. If we do not come together soon, I fear we shall break up from within before the real battle even begins.

Citing other grievances, he closed with the positive news that; 'I take comfort in the fact that Ukita, Shimazu and Konishi are dedicated to our cause and can be counted on as most trusted allies.'

The letter, which is now kept in the National Archives in Tokyo, was intercepted in Omiji, Omi Province and hastily redirected to Ieyasu, who took great delight in discovering that Mitsunari was unaware he had in fact left Edo a week before the letter was penned. In fact, on the day before the letter was written, Ieyasu had arrived at his birthplace and ancestral home of Okazaki Castle. Continuing to follow the route of the Tokaido Highway, the next day he stopped at the nation's second most important shrine after the Great Shrine of Ise, the Great Atsuta Jingu, in the south of Nagoya City, where, like Oda Nobunaga on the morning of the 1560 Battle of Okehazama when he defeated an enemy ten times stronger, Ieyasu too prayed for victory.

When news of Ieyasu's advance was received, the allies of the Tokugawa – Fukushima Masanori, Kuroda Nagamasa, Ikeda Terumasa and Hosokawa Tadaoki – combined their contingents to form an army of nearly 21,000 at Fukushima's castle at Kiyosu. There they awaited the advent of Ieyasu, who arrived on 17 October along with Ieyasu's most trusted friend and advisor, Todo Taketora, ready to advance on Mitsunari who lay in wait at Ogaki. Ieyasu took this opportunity to address his men and reconfirm their loyalty in a special pre-battle ceremony called the *shutsujin-shiki*.

The Pre-Battle Ceremony

Because samurai armies were often made up of higher-ranked *daimyo* with clan members, lesser-ranked lords, or retainers joining their ranks, the *shutsujin-shiki* ceremony was held to reinforce loyalty and ensure the combatants' good fortune. For example, Ieyasu's total force consisted of his own troops amalgamated with those of his generals, such as Ii, Hosokawa, Matsudaira and Honda, amongst others, to create one large army. Furthermore, some lords took command over their more junior counterparts, making it extremely important to implement and develop unity and cohesion before going into battle. In many cases, personal reputation and honour conflicted with the plans and orders that were issued by superiors. Just as Ikeda Terumasa and Fukushima Masanori fought over battle tactics in the attack on Gifu Castle, at times conflicting loyalties could hinder success in battle by thwarting the authority of command.

To combat any problems regarding a breach of orders, rules including threats of punishments such as confiscation of property, loss of titles or even death were not uncommon. This ceremony was for the most part slow and deliberate and carried out with great decorum. It was a chance to show that despite the very real possibility that they would not be returning from battle, they were in control of their emotions and a last chance to show unity and respect to one another.

The ceremony involved all the lords gathering to pay their respects to the leading lord, in this case Ieyasu, and submitting themselves and their men to the disposal of that lord. One by one they would approach and kneel, flicking open their prepared documents, in a loud voice they would state their name, title, the number of soldiers and units they had supplied and then would present such information in writing to the leader. The leader would then acknowledge their loyalty and accepting their documents, sign and return it to them. With this complete, five pieces of *awabi*, a type of shellfish, seven *kuri* chestnuts and five pieces of dried *kombu* seaweed were presented along with three cups of sake of varying size.

The lord would take a piece of *awabi* in his left hand and bite the widest part of it, then turn it around and bite into the narrower part to make a shape not unlike that of Mount Fuji. It represented the Japanese figure eight (八) to mean *sue hiro gari* or 'spreading fortune in battle'. The smaller of the cups would be filled with sake and drunk in three sips by the lord. A single peeled chestnut or *kachi-guri*, representing a win (*kachi*) in battle, would then be consumed, followed by the second largest cup of sake in a similar fashion. After that, a strip of *kombu* seaweed would be taken and broken into three pieces, of which the lord would eat the middle piece and then drink the third and largest cup of sake in three gulps. The *kombu* stood for post-battle peace and happiness, or *yoro-kombu*. The lord would then stand, offer words of inspiration or providence and then thrusting his drawn sword into the air, would lead the *kachidoki*, a chorus of several cheers of '*Ei! Ei! Oh* !' followed in unison by all in attendance.

The lord's bow would be ceremoniously handed to him and an arrow notched and fired for luck. Next, the lord's horse was brought forward. If the horse neighed while being fetched, this was considered auspicious, though if the horse neighed while the lord was mounting it, it was seen as unlucky. If the lord then fell off his horse it was considered unlucky if he fell to the left, yet oddly fortuitous if he fell to the right.

A well-known incident at this particular *shutsujin-shiki* ceremony involves Yamauchi Katsutoyo (1546–1605), master of the small castle at Kakegawa on the Tokaido with a 50,000 *koku* stipend. Early in his career he was viewed as a samurai of little value or note and it was his wife, Chio, who was better known for her ability to provide good advice on military affairs. Katsutoyo's wife had once secretly saved a sum of money without his knowledge and used the money to buy the finest of horses for her husband and it was the splendour of this horse that greatly elevated the reputation of the owner in the eyes of his contemporaries. Prior to gathering before Ieyasu, Yamauchi Katsutoyo had asked his friend Horio Tadauji what he thought the best course of action would be. Tadauji answered easily, with passion and veneration, 'I pledge my lands, my castle, my family, my food, my life, all I can give, without hesitation for the Tokugawa cause!' Katsutoyo was so touched, he agreed to follow his friend's advice and so joined the Eastern forces.

On the day of the great gathering, Ieyasu received many pledges of loyalty, but it was the answer Yamauchi Katsutoyo gave which drew the most response. Stuck for an answer of his own, he repeated verbatim the passionate response of his friend Horio Tadauji. 'I pledge my lands, my castle, my family, my food, my life, all I can give, without hesitation for the Tokugawa cause!' Tadauji's eyes must have bulged, his mouth gaping dumbstruck, hearing his own pledge come from the mouth of his dullard friend. More so when a much pleased Ieyasu praised the man for his sincerity and for going so far in his offer. The other leaders too admired the answer and received it with a rousing cheer.

As was expected, although Yamauchi Katsutoyo took action, he failed to particularly distinguish himself in the battle at Sekigahara, maintaining a position along the Nakasendo route protecting Ieyasu's rear from a potential attack fromenemy forces on Mount Nangu to the east of the battlefield, seeing a little action towards the end of the day as he entered the main arena of Sekigahara. However, Ieyasu remembered his words at Kiyosu and after the battle rewarded him with a new fief, the whole of Tosa Province (Shikoku), a residence at Kochi and a stipend of 242,000 *koku*, while Horio Tadauji received but a minor reward and increase in stipend.

The Siege of Otsu

Just days before the Eastern army set up their war banners at Akasaka, on 13 October another force of Western allies under the command of Tachibana Muneshige, a *daimyo* from Kyushu, along with Tsukushi Hirokado[14] and Mori Motoyasu, had stormed Otsu Castle on the southern shores of Lake Biwa on their way to join Ishida Mitsunari. Otsu was a strategically important base, directly along the route between Kyoto and Sekigahara. This would be the route the Western forces' nominated commander-in-chief, Mori Terumoto, or possibly Toyotomi Hideyori himself would take to reach Mino if – and when – they departed Osaka Castle.

The master of Otsu Castle, Kyogoku Takatsugu (1560–4 June 1609), had been ordered by Ishida Mitsunari to support Western operations in the Hokuriku region and had gone to the trouble of marching his troops out of the castle on a northward path, before suddenly about-facing, returning to Otsu and with around 3,000 samurai, shut himself inside the castle. Kyogoku Tadatsugu's younger brother, Takatomo had already allied himself with the East and Tadatsugu himself had secretly been sending information regarding Ishida Mitsunari's movements to Tokugawa Ieyasu. It appears he had considered supporting the Tokugawa-led faction from the start and now had decided to follow his instincts.

Although Mori Terumoto's uncle Mori Motoyasu was in command of the overall attack, it was the popular General Tachibana Muneshige who was actually leading the troops. He was a fine warrior and such was his reputation as a fighter that of all the men within the Western forces, he was one of the very few that genuinely concerned Tokugawa Ieyasu, especially as he was known to have had a number of cannon in his arsenal. Tachibana Muneshige's armour was made from thicker-than-average steel, in order for it to withstand close-range matchlock fire. The size of his remaining armour shows Tachibana to have stood 1.77m tall. He had long been associated with the Toyotomi clan and had played an important role in Hideyoshi's Korean

---

14. Tsukushi Hirokado (1548–22 May 1623). Former *daimyo* of Chikuzen Province (modern-day Fukui Prefecture) and master of Katsuno Castle. Loyal to Toyotomi Hideyoshi, he saw action and distinguished himself in the Korean campaigns. For his role in the attack on Otsu Castle, Tsukushi was deprived of his lands and title, but later accepted a position as a retainer of Kuroda Nagamasa, then Kato Kiyomasa and finally the Hosokawa clan.

campaign. Together with the young Kobayakawa Hideaki he had defeated the Chinese army and in another battle, it was Tachibana who had rescued Kato Kiyomasa and his troops from the siege of Ulsan. Now, assisted by a number of ships belonging to Mashita Nagamori, the 15,000-strong force surrounded Otsu Castle, which had been given to Kyogoku Takatsugu in 1590 by Hideyoshi, along with a stipend of 60,000 *koku*.

The castle had been exceptionally well designed. Its outer moat had been dug from a south-west shoreline of Lake Biwa, forming three small islands connected by a series of bridges, with the lake feeding the outer, central and inner moats. These islands consisted of a crescent-shaped outer bailey, the *san-no-maru*, and two central precincts, the *ni-no-maru* and the main *honmaru*.

The attackers set up camp around the outer moat, effectively blocking and barricading the four bridges that connected the castle to the mainland and in an effort to cause further psychological distress to the defenders, the villages north, south and west of the castle were set alight and burned to the ground. The lakeside was patrolled by a flotilla of ships, making any attempt at escape futile for those inside the castle. Despite these efforts and the continued cannon bombardment from the Mori side which caused great destruction and started many fires, the men in the castle refused to capitulate.

Six days into the siege, on 19 October, an interesting occurrence took place. At night, the castle's commander, Kyogoku Takatsugu, sent one of his ninja into the surrounding enemy camp. The stealthy spy stole a number of Mori banners and the next morning, as a taunt, there were Mori battle flags being flown from the castle walls. Instead of demoralising the attackers as had been planned, it only enraged them.

Mori Motoyasu, insulted by this, intensified his efforts to take the castle, as did Tachibana Muneshige, who, having seen the banners fluttering from the keep, thought that the Mori had already taken the castle overnight and, embarrassed at his own lack of action, redoubled his efforts to enter the citadel. For a total of eight days Kyogoku Takatsugu and his 3,000 troops held the attackers at bay until Otsu Castle lay in ruins.[15] On 21 October, the very

---

15. Nothing remains of Otsu Castle as it was demolished in 1601 and the stone and surviving timbers were used in other construction projects begun by Ieyasu. Otsu Castle's keep was dismantled in 1603 and the top three of its five floors were used as the new keep for Ii Naomasa's elegant castle of Hikone, currently one of just five

day of the battle at Sekigahara, Takatsugu made peace and then fled with his family to the temples of Koya-san on the Kii Peninsula, long considered a place of exile for persons of rank.

Through his efforts, Kyogoku Takatsugu had managed to keep 15,000 Western samurai away from the main battle at Sekigahara, as well as providing a spectacle for the citizens of Kyoto who arrived in droves with lunchboxes and picnics to watch the samurai fight from the Miidera Temple on Mount Hiei. In all, when combined with the sieges at the castles of Fushimi and Tanabe, the Western army was short of over 40,000 men for the battle at Sekigahara. Despite having abandoned his post and fled, Kyogoku Takatsugu was awarded with a new fief in Obama, Wakasa (modern-day Fukui Prefecture), with a 92,000-*koku* stipend not long after Ieyasu had claimed victory.

According to the *Ritsusai Kyubunki,* Tachibana Muneshige's diary, he was unaware until 22 October that the battle between East and West had been fought and lost the previous day at Sekigahara and that Sawayama Castle was already under attack. Knowing that Otsu was only one day's march from Sekigahara, the following day he gathered his men and quickly began to retreat, leading his battle-weary troops out of Otsu and towards Osaka.

The Road to Akasaka

During this time, the Western army had firmly entrenched themselves in Ogaki Castle. Here, they thought, they held the upper hand. However, before Ieyasu had left Edo on 7 October, he had been busy writing some 169 letters. Many of these were intended for those loyal to Mitsunari's cause and were dispatched en route to Akasaka, just outside of Ogaki.

These letters, whose recipients included, amongst others, Takenaka Shigekado, Inaba Sadamichi and also Kato Sadayasu (whose participation at the Battle of Sekigahara cannot be confirmed), outlined the intentions of the Mori and Kobayakawa forces. Half of the letters written were to warlords with ties to the Toyotomi, with the letters to Fukushima Masanori and Hosokawa Tadaoki promising rewards of land upon victory. To prevent the letters from being found by the Loyalist forces, they were written on strong

---

National Treasure-listed castles across Japan. As for Kyogoku Takatsugu, following his mother and brother Takatomo, he became a Christian and was baptised in 1602, dying a few years later in 1609 aged 49.

Japanese *washi* paper before being twisted into strings and used as straps on the messengers' hats. All the messengers were also carrying other hidden letters with false information as decoys in case of capture.

Slowly, the two armies began to assemble on the plain closest to where the Tokaido and the Nakasendo met, the plain that bottlenecked at the gateway between the mountains, at the pass called Sekigahara. Making camp in Mino Akasaka on a small hill known as Okayama, overlooking Ogaki Castle from the Sekigahara side and in the small villages surrounding the strategically important pass, Tokugawa Ieyasu's allies sent word of their progress and awaited his coming. Ieyasu arrived about midday on 20 October with 30,000 men.

By all accounts, despite the rain that had begun to fall during the last leg of his journey, Ieyasu was in a jovial mood. This rain had forced him to travel not by horse, but inside a closed palanquin. He was dressed in a short-sleeved kimono and baggy *yoroi bakama* trousers together with just the body armour, or *do*, of a *gussoku*-style armour. Over this was a wide-sleeved coat and in place of a helmet, a triangular *nurigasa* rain hat.

What had put him in such a fine mood was not just the speed at which they neared the camp, but also the very large persimmon that had been presented to him by the head priest of a temple just outside of Gifu's Godo-Cho area, near the famed Shiroyama Shrine. It was not that Ieyasu had a particular liking for the fruit, but the pronunciation of 'big persimmon' or '*O-Gaki*' that gave rise to Ieyasu joking that he 'now held *O-Gaki* (Ogaki) in his hands', and this was seen as an auspicious sign.[16]

Soon after arriving in Akasaka, he was approached by the Loyalist Kikkawa Hiroie who submitted a plan and made his contract with Ieyasu not to fight against the East in an effort to protect the Mori clan, while saving face on his own behalf. Hiroie had already made a vow 'Not to make the mistake of joining losing dogs'. This plan would keep another 27,900 Western samurai from participating in the battle.

---

16.   Another version of this story tells of how the head priest, in presenting the large persimmon to Ieyasu, accidentally let it roll off the tray and watched embarrassed as it fell to the ground. Without missing a beat, the old priest smiled and said, 'Ogaki has fallen before you, my lord'.

Ogaki Under Siege

Ishida Mitsunari was of course unaware of the stand-off at Ueda Castle and he had not counted on such losses in the smaller skirmishes at Tanabe and Otsu. He was particularly surprised at the speed with which the Eastern forces, especially those of Ieyasu, had moved into position. At first he refused to accept that Ieyasu had arrived at Akasaka and suspected incorrectly that it was a ruse by the Eastern forces to cause confusion within Ogaki. After all, he figured, Ieyasu was supposed to be in the northern districts fighting the Uesugi.

Reports of Ieyasu's followers gathering at Akasaka had been confirmed one by one by the banners seen flying from the hilltop. Some had been at the site for a couple of weeks and that number was increasing noticeably. Finally, clearly visible to all in Ogaki Castle, fluttering in the breeze above Akasaka's skyline, along with the hollyhock crest of the Tokugawa, were a number of tall, plain white banners. These were the white flags representing the once powerful Minamoto clan, a clan from which Ieyasu's family claimed to have descended. Final proof was confirmed when the great golden war fan was spotted high above the camp. This fan was made of ten black lacquered bamboo ribs, each 2.31m long, with a gold-foil covered *washi* paper fan blade that was fitted atop a 5.73m-tall pole. It was a battle standard, used to command troop movements from the strategic campsites. This was a symbol of the future shogun, a symbol that would only be used when Ieyasu himself was present.

Confidence in Ishida Mitsunari's leadership abilities fell yet again and a number of lesser samurai considered abandoning him. Behind the scenes talk focused on ways of possibly deserting the castle. Mitsunari recognised a lessening of certainty within his own ranks. His intelligence network had lost a great deal of credibility in not reporting Ieyasu's advent sooner and, furthermore, Ieyasu had positioned himself well. His men had chosen the mountain known as Akasaka and right at the bottom, the hill called Okayama as both overlooked Ogaki Castle from the north-west, the vital Nakasendo from the north and was in sight of the equally important route linking the Tokaido highway. This left Mitsunari restless and feeling trapped. At a council of war, Mitsunari and his generals contemplated the situation.

At the suggestion of a few of his generals Mitsunari decided to test the Eastern armies. He ordered a contingent of his forces to dress as farmers and attack a small garrison of Eastern troops near Kuisegawa under the command of Nakamura Kazuuji. Western forces strategist Shima Sakon set out from Ogaki Castle with 500 soldiers, followed by Akashi Masataka (also known as Teruzumi) commanding 800 troops. The troops split up around the bridge near the villages of Kido and Isshiki. Half went across the river while the Akashi samurai waited in ambush.

When the opportunity presented itself, the Shima troops made their attack, then turned and fled back towards the castle. The trick was a success and Nakamura Kazuuji was drawn out and sent his men after the attackers. Despite assistance from Arima Toyouji, the Nakamura samurai were routed when they crossed the narrow bridge over the river and were ambushed by the waiting Akashi forces. Ieyasu had witnessed this skirmish from the watchtower on Okayama and at first was pleased with the Nakamuras' reactions and counter-attack, but as they crossed the river, Ieyasu immediately realised they had been tricked. The head of Nakamura Kazuuji and those of over thirty of his leading warriors were taken and displayed near the gates of Ogaki Castle, boosting the morale of the Western troops stationed there.

Western morale did not remain high for long, however. The Eastern forces had been watching them like hawks from high on Akasaka and Okayama for two weeks now. The veteran general Shimazu Yoshihiro noted from within the walls of Ogaki that 'The Eastern forces have been conducting manoeuvres almost incessantly, their men have been in armour all this time and are no doubt near exhaustion. Now would be the ideal opportunity for a surprise night attack.'

Shimazu Yoshihiro's plan was seconded by Ukita Hideie, but Mitsunari's chief strategist, Shima Sakon, was against it. Despite having just taken part in the previous ambush on Nakamura Kazuuji, Sakon called the plan an outright cowardly idea, greatly insulting Shimazu Yoshihiro. Sakon was counting on the Westerners' numerically-superior force achieving victory in an open battle, pointing out quite hypocritically that ambushes and night attacks were for weaker armies against stronger opponents. Having been left to his own devices and forgotten about in the retreat from the Sunomata area and now being accused in front of the Western alliance members of cowardice by someone who had just taken part in ambushing a small contingent of enemy left the elder Shimazu in an even fouler mood and Shima Sakon would pay for this insult before long.

While the Western generals bickered over strategy in Ogaki, Ieyasu was making plans to flush the Toyotomi loyalists out of the castle. In a letter addressed to Date Masamune, Ieyasu had written that he was considering damming and redirecting the nearby Ibi and Kuze rivers, causing them to flood Ogaki Castle, a strategy Toyotomi Hideyoshi had used successfully against Shimizu Muneharu in the protracted siege of Takamatsu Castle in 1582.

This was probably a ruse, as a faster and less costly plan was devised whereby information was planted among spies of both camps that the Eastern army would simply about turn and head west and having passed through the mountain barrier at Sekigahara, first attack Ishida Mistunari's own castle, Sawayama, before advancing to capture Osaka Castle and Toyotomi Hideyori. Mitsunari was alarmed at this news and despite advice from other members of the Western forces, left Ogaki Castle in the hands of his senior retainer, Fukuhara Nagataka, with 7,500 men and set off with the remaining troops back towards Sawayama and Osaka. He likened the move to 'risking his head to save an arm'. It was 7 p.m. on the night of 20 October when the first of the Western troops pulled out of Ogaki Castle in cold, driving rain.

Mitsunari had decided to gather his forces in the narrow valley called Sekigahara, where Kobayakawa Hideaki, Otani Yoshitsugu and a few other allies were already waiting. Mitsunari figured that if he could get to the valley via the southern slopes of Mount Nangu, where Kikkawa and the Mori clan's troops were also waiting, he could block and trap Ieyasu's army as it followed him in the push towards Osaka. Tokugawa Ieyasu was well aware of the situation and, as field battles were his forte, gained confidence knowing he now held the upper hand.

That, and the fact he secretly held a trump card or two up his sleeve.

Chapter 2

The Flight from Ogaki

21 October 1600: 1:30 a.m.

Ishida Mitsunari finally left Ogaki Castle about 1:30 a.m., backed by his 6,000 samurai, arriving at Sekigahara in the rain-drenched early hours of 21 October 1600. Under cover of darkness Mistunari's men busied themselves setting up camp on Mount Sasao to the north of Sekigahara, overlooking the narrow plain. The site had been previously chosen and recommended by the Mori strategists as an ideal location from which Mitsunari could command. It had been a 14km march from Ogaki for his men along a narrow and winding road, made muddy by the driving rain and churned up by the feet of the horses and samurai ahead.

Mitsunari's *ashigaru* and labourers were scrambling in the dark and wet, felling trees and constructing rudimentary log and bamboo fences and barricades. With simple wooden shovels they dug moat-like trenches in the wet soil at various levels around the hill. Other units of labourers set up the tall banners and war flags used to stake out territory and for the soldiers in the field to identify rallying points. Towards the top of Mount Sasao, the hill that served Mitsunari as his *jin*, or war camp, his samurai set up the large white curtains featuring the Ishida crest as an enclosure and beside that, a small, simply-built wooden hut.

Using the lights of the brazier fires of Chosokabe Morichika's camp high on Mount Nangu as a guide, Mitsunari rode to meet Nagatsuka Masaie, Ankokuji Ekei and then Chosokabe Morichika, giving each last-minute instructions and encouragement. From there he went to the fortress on Mount Matsuo where Kobayakawa Hideie had been among the first to be stationed. He told the young Hideie and his lieutenant Hiraoka Yorikatsu to wait for a signal flare to be sent up. 'That's when we'll have Ieyasu trapped and begging for his life'.

Finally, on his way to his headquarters, he made a final stop in Sekigahara's Yamanaka Mura area, where his friend Otani Yoshitsugu had set up his command post high on Fujikawadai Hill. It was to be their final meeting.

Armed with his much-favoured longbow, Shimazu Yoshihiro and his nephew, Toyohisa, had left Ogaki not long after Mitsunari and, cold and wet, stationed themselves together with 3,000 men to the south of Mitsunari's camp. Situated between the Shimazu and Ishida was a joint army of 2,000, led by Ito Morimasa and Kishida Tadauji.[1] This company was all that remained of Oda Hidenobu's troops following the fall of Gifu. Both were former loyal retainers of Toyotomi Hideyoshi, serving as elite bodyguards, and had now gathered to assist Mitsunari under the direction of Konishi Yukinaga. These valiant warriors would play a major role in supporting the forces of Shima Sakon and Gamo Bitchu at the foot of Mount Sasao and in protecting Mitsunari from the fierce assault of the Eastern forces. For now, they and the Shimazu were positioned near the Hokoku-kaido, an important route to stop the possible westward advance of the Eastern forces.

Arriving at about 4:30 in the morning were another 6,000 Western troops under the command of Konishi Yukinaga, who had been among the third group to leave Ogaki. The disciplined Konishi ranks made camp at the base of Mount Kita-Tenma, while to their left, on the lower slopes of Mount Minami-Tenma, Ukita Hideie arrived with some 17,000 samurai.

The Ukita samurai were among the last of the larger Western armies to arrive at Sekigahara. They too had taken the same circuitous route, south of Mount Nangu to the valley, while the Eastern troops, who pulled out of Akasaka about 2 a.m. with Fukushima Masanori taking the lead, had taken a more direct course north of Mount Nangu. Both armies arrived at approximately the same time and in the mist and heavy rain, Ukita's rearguard had accidentally been run into by the forward troops of the Eastern-allied Fukushima forces. A small fight had ensued in the darkness, but it finished just as quickly as it had started, doing minimal damage to either side.

Ieyasu soon received reports of the skirmish and was pleased to hear that the eager Fukushima had wisely refrained from causing a larger fight. Around 5 a.m., while working his way from Akasaka towards Sekigahara and with the majority of armies on both sides mostly in place, Ieyasu dispatched his spies and scouts forward in an effort to determine the positions and numbers of the Western forces.

1.　Kishida Tadauji (?–20 January 1616) was lord of Yamato Province, south of Kyoto.

The Ukita samurai wore tall blue *sashimono* flags on the backs of their armour with the character for *ko* (兄) emblazoned twice upon it. This was in reference to the Ukitas' famed ancestor, Kojima Takanori (1331–29 December 1382), a hero of the early Muromachi period (1336–1573). The Ukita forces were divided into five divisions and were lined up one behind the other. It is popularly believed that among the Ukita men was a 17-year-old foot soldier who had run away from home seeking glory and fame in battle. However, it wasn't at Sekigahara that he made a name for himself: he was to achieve fame in the years to come as the master swordsman, strategist, artist and writer Miyamoto Musashi.[2]

A further 13,000 Western-allied troops had been waiting in Matsuo Castle, a fortress high on Mount Matsuo across the valley from Mount Sasao. This strong force was under the command of Kobayakawa Hideie, while a contingent of troops under Ogawa Suketada, Wakisaka Yasuharo, Kuchiki Mototsuna and Akaza Naoyasu held strategic places in the south, below Kobayakawa Hideie's command post on Mount Matsuo. To the northeast was a smaller force of 4,000 soldiers led by Kinoshita Yorichika, Otani Yoshitsugu and his son, Yoshikatsu, as well as Toda Shigemasa and Hiratsuka Tamehiro, camped below at nearby Fujikawadai. Initially Ishida Mitsunari had planned to have the Mori troops stationed at the top of Mount Matsuo, but the Kobayakawa had occupied the fortress site instead. Had Mitsunari's plan taken effect, the outcome of the battle may have been different, as the Kobayakawa were to play a major role in reversing the fortunes of the Western forces later that day. The Mori were based east of Sekigahara high on Mount Nangu with a 30,000-strong force ready to attack the Tokugawa forces from the rear,

---

2.   Musashi is said to have fought in the front ranks of the Western-allied Ukita forces at Sekigahara, but the extant *Kuroda Han Bugencho*, the Kuroda Clan Registry, has an entry which suggests it is possible both Shinmen Munisai and his teenage son, the future Miyamoto Musashi, were serving under the Kuroda clan in Kyushu, subduing the Tokugawa enemy and fighting against the Otomo clan at the Battle of Ishigakibaru in Beppu, northern Kyushu, just two days prior to Sekigahara. Other sources, including researcher Kenji Tokitsu in his 2004 book, *Miyamoto Musashi, his Life and Writings*, suggests Musashi was in fact involved in three battles during 1600; the attack on Fushimi Castle, then the defence of Gifu Castle and finally on the battlefield of Sekigahara in support of the West.

By early morning the Western army, although cold, wet and tired, had itself in position for the Battle of Sekigahara, with over 83,000 soldiers strung out across the valley.

The Eastern Army's Positions

Tokugawa Ieyasu had barely slept when he was awakened at around 2 a.m. with the news that the Western forces were vacating Ogaki Castle. This is one of the very few times that the usually alert Eastern forces' intelligence system appears to have been lax, for it had been almost seven hours since the first of the Western troops commenced their rain-drenched march towards Sekigahara, right under the Eastern forces' noses. Ieyasu hurriedly gave the orders to decamp and pursue the Western troops.

As field battles were his forte, Ieyasu's plan from the beginning had been to fight Mitsunari on the plain between the mountains east of Sekigahara and Ogaki. Fukushima Masanori and Kuroda Nagamasa's troops were the first to leave the Akasaka base, followed closely by Kato Yoshiaki, Todo Takatora, then the joint Ii Naomasa–Matsudaira Tadayoshi units. Leaving 1,300 samurai under the command of Horio Yoshiharu at Akasaka, Ieyasu ate a quick, simple meal and then having given his final orders, moved out to assume a position with 30,000 soldiers setting his headquarters above Tarui-Hara on the small hill known as Mount Momokubari just east of the Sekigahara battlefield.

Ieyasu's highly trusted and charismatic carpenter, a rare breed of common man permitted wear the two swords of the samurai and to enter the great lord's presence and with whom Ieyasu would often share a drink, Nakai Masakiyo,[3] had been among the first of Ieyasu's men to leave the Akasaka site and arrived around 2 a.m. at Mount Momokubari to begin constructing

---

3. Aged around 37 at the time of Sekigahara, Nakai Masakiyo would go on to build keeps, watchtowers and other structures at Nijo, Edo, Sumpu, Akashi and Osaka Castles amongst many others. In 1610, employing a team of 541 hand-picked carpenters arranged into four groups, he completed the largest castle tower in samurai history, the Tokugawa's magnificent 57m-high keep at Nagoya Castle within just seven months – a month earlier than expected. He had promised Ieyasu he would cut himself open if he failed in his task. One of his final jobs in the service of Ieyasu was in 1616, constructing what is considered to be the final resting place of Ieyasu's remains, the gloriously carved and decorated Kunozan Toshogu in

a shelter for his lord. When he arrived only a few hours later, Ieyasu was so impressed by the speed with which the cabin had been built and by its quality of the cabin, that he presented Nakai Masakiyo with a *jinbaori* after the battle and appointed him the official Tokugawa clan castle carpenter.

The site of Ieyasu's first command post, Mount Momokubari itself, was a historic place well before the Battle of Sekigahara. It was here that the 40th emperor, Temmu, had handed out peaches (hence the name *momo kubari*, or 'peach-distributing mountain') to his soldiers during the Jinshin No Ran civil war of 672.

The headquarters had been hastily relocated from the previous base at Okayama overlooking Ogaki Castle and, besides the cabin crafted with great speed earlier that morning, consisted of a tall white curtain strung up in a large square between stakes. This curtain, or *jinmaku*, sported the Tokugawa clan crest of three inward-pointing, circularly enclosed hollyhock leaves, the Aoi-no-Go-mon crest, which had been adopted by Ieyasu's father, Hirotada. Their vassals, the Honda family, used a similar crest, only with smaller leaves and longer stalks. Hirotada was once served cakes on hollyhock leaves by members of the Honda clan following victory in battle, a recognised show of subservience to the Tokugawa. The hollyhock had long been regarded as a symbol of a loyal retainer, bowing his head and following his master, as the leaf does to the sun. Anecdotally Hirotada is said to have admired this crest and asked Honda for its use, to which Honda replied '*O ha-bakari*', or 'Only the leaves'. Here Honda was making a clever play on words as '*O Habakari*' also meant 'By your command'.

The Tokugawa (left) and Honda crests.

Shizuoka, a feat he and his men completed within six months. Nakai Masakiyo followed his master in death three years later in 1619.

Surrounding this *jinmaku* were seven banners sporting the Tokugawa crest and another twenty plain white banners. Smaller banners featuring a rising sun motif were also placed at intervals around the camp. Set high on a pole above the site was Ieyasu's large golden fan standard, used to command troop movements and act as a rallying point. The secondary standard was a silver *kurihangetsu*, or crescent moon device. The site also featured some very large rocks which are said to have been covered with tiger and leopard skins and used as seats for Ieyasu, his generals and his audience. A modest outdoor kitchen had been set up a short walk behind the camp.

A special standard presented to Ieyasu by the head priest of the Jushoku Temple and flown at the Battle of Okehazama in 1560 had been set up along with a flag of the Jodo sect of Buddhism, to which Ieyasu belonged. On it was written '*Onri Edo Gongu Jodo*', or 'Renounce the living world and embrace death. The afterlife is greater!'

This slogan was flown above Ieyasu's camp to show his soldiers that death was nothing to be feared in the expectation they would fight with greater vigour. Interestingly, this was the complete opposite to the positive philosophy prescribed in Ishida Mitsunari's crest, which featured the characters representing '*Dai Ichi, Dai Man, Dai Kichi*', ('Great One, Great Abundance, Great Destiny'), or understood to mean 'As One, As Many, Great Fortune Awaits'. With everything in place by 7 a.m. on 21 October, the Eastern army was also ready to fight. In position in the north on a hill above the plains was Takenaka Shigekado under Kuroda Nagamasa, with 5,400 troops. They were around 600m from Mitsunari's location, within easy striking range. Directly below Kuroda's elevated encampment to the south, waited Furuta Shigekatsu[4] leading 1,000 samurai. Alongside them were the 500 men of Oda

---

4. Furuta Shigekatsu is better remembered today as the tea master, artist and potter Furuta Oribe. Oribe was originally a *tsukaiban* (messenger) reporting directly to Oda Nobunaga. Later he was apprenticed to the great tea master Sen no Rikyu and it had been Oribe who had influenced Rikyu in recognising *wabisabi*, the seeing of beauty in flaws, pointing out the marks, scars and impurities in pottery that until then had been viewed as inferior, simply added to its appeal. Oribe created the *Oribe-Ryu* style of tea ceremony and *Oribe-Yaki*, a type of pottery famed for its use of dark green and brown glaze painted in geometric patterns. He was also the tea instructor to Tokugawa Hidetada when he became shogun. Oribe was ordered

Nagamasu, then Kanamori Nagachika's 1,100 warriors and then the 1,800 men of Ikoma Kazumasa.

A short distance ahead of this line-up, from north to south and camped either side of the River Ai, were the 5,000 troops under Hosokawa Tadaoki. Beside them a little further south was the campsite of Kato Yoshiaki and his 3,000 samurai. To Kato's left was Tsutsui Sadatsugu commanding 2,850 and next to them, Tanaka Yoshimune headed another front-line force with 3,000 men. Although the distance from these Eastern positions to their visible target of Mount Sasao was a little over 550m, the fields in between formed a rising gradient that would no doubt prove to be a disadvantage and slow their progress.

To Tanaka Yoshimune's left, across the Teradani River, sat Fukushima Masanori. His 6,000 men were the southern vanguard of the Eastern forces and had been ordered to fight just south of the Nakasendo. They had taken a position beside the Kasuga Shrine, where an 800-year-old cedar tree depicted in the remaining battle screens still stands.

Ieyasu had ordered his 21-year-old son Matsudaira Tadayoshi and his trusted general Ii Naomasa to set up camp in the centre of the plain directly behind the armies of Kato, Tsutsui and Tanaka where the Sekigahara railway station now stands. The Ii camp was easily seen, being marked out with a wall of fluttering red banners, the taller ones featuring prayers to the god of war, Hachiman, written on small strips of silk, dangling from the top.

The Ii army were resplendent in their bright red lacquered armour and *sashimono* battle flags. Ii Naomasa was among Ieyasu's four most trusted senior generals and was always on the front lines of any engagement the Tokugawa entered. The Ii's distinctive red armour, a trademark of sorts, was an idea Naomasa borrowed from Yamagata Masakage, a general in Takeda Shingen's army, who realised the importance of uniformity when facing an enemy and so would select any warrior happening to be wearing red to serve in the front rank.

Originally hailing from modern-day Gunma Prefecture, Ii Naomasa had a 120,000-*koku* revenue and commanded 3,600 soldiers. Ieyasu's son led another 3,000, while yet another body of 1,830 positioned themselves directly behind the Ii and Matsudaira. These were the samurai of Ikoma Kazumasa of Owari, whose family had also long served the Tokugawa. Both Kazumasa's father, Chikamasa and his son, Masatoshi, were also on

---

by Ieyasu to commit *seppuku* in 1615 accused of having communicated with the enemy during the Siege of Osaka.

the battlefield that day, but were on the opposing side in support of Ishida Mitsunari. This strategy was chosen as a means of preserving the Ikoma name regardless of which side prevailed.

This was not as uncommon a tactic as may be thought. Sanada Nobuyuki, son of Sanada Masayuki of Ueda Castle, was fighting for the Tokugawa side, while his father and brother faced off against the Eastern forces at Ueda. Similarly, while Kuki Yoshitaka, the famed naval commander under both Oda Nobunaga and Toyotomi Hideyoshi, supported Mitsunari at Sekigahara, his son, Kuki Moritaka, would be on the other side of the battle-field in support of Ieyasu. Following the battle, Moritaka petitioned Ieyasu to spare his father's life. Ieyasu granted the man's request and a messenger was dispatched immediately with the good news. However, Yoshitaka committed ritual suicide on 17 November, shortly before news of his pardon arrived.[5]

Terazawa Hirotaka's 2,400 battle-ready samurai waited directly south of the old village of Sekigahara, between the Nakasendo and the Teradani River. Just ahead of them, 2,490 of Todo Takatora's warriors composed themselves beside the 3,000 men under Kyogoku Takatomo for the approaching engagement.

Honda Tadakatsu, Ieyasu's most trusted senior advisor, was strategically positioned together with only 500 of his troops, just south of where the Isekaido bound for the Tokaido intersected Sekigahara and the Nakasendo. His position allowed him to monitor the Western forces on Mount Nangu behind him to the east, as well as act as a line of defence between Tokugawa Ieyasu's main troops and those of recent Tokugawa allies, such as Fukushima Masanori and others. This was to be the 57th battle of Tadakatsu's life.

Also on the Isekaido and the most southern site held by the Eastern troops, in what is now a residential area, was Togawa Michiyasu's small retinue of 400, who were situated less than 100m to the left of Honda's 500 men. Togawa Michiyasu was from what is now Okayama City and had until recently been a high-ranking retainer under the command of Ukita Hideie. Since his first battle at the age of 13, he had always been on the front lines of the Ukita forces, demonstrating great courage, wisdom and skill in battle. A veteran of many battles, including the siege of Bichu Takamatsu Castle

---

5.   Kuki Yoshitaka (1542–17 November 1600) was buried on an island in the calm clear coastal waters of the Shima District in modern-day Toba City, Mie Prefecture. His body is interred at the bottom of a hill and his head buried separately at the top facing towards the Kuki clan's Toba Castle.

with Toyotomi Hideyoshi, Komaki Nagakute in 1584 and Odawara in 1590, he had been one of the Ukita's most trusted vassals, but found himself being shunted out of his role as an advisor due to his religion. Togawa Michiyasu was of the Nichiren Buddhist sect, while Ukita Hideie had embraced the religion of the foreigners and was therefore partial to other samurai of the Christian faith. As such, Michiyasu had defected to the Eastern camp at the invitation of Tokugawa Ieyasu just before the battle. His small but powerful unit completed the Eastern forces' line-up, snaking its way along a north-south line like a sleeping dragon across the Sekigahara plains.

Far behind the front lines and stretching back towards Tarui were the 900 troops of Arima Toyouji positioned between the River Ai and the Nakasendo, just north-east of Ieyasu's position on Mount Momokubari. East of Ieyasu's position and sitting directly on an intersection of the Nakasendo were Yamauchi Katsutoyo's 2,058 samurai. Further east along the Nakasendo waited Asano Yoshinaga and an army of 6,510, while Ikeda Terumasa sat just south of Tarui Village, his 4,560 warriors positioned to watch the forces under the Mori banners on Mount Nangu, as Ieyasu still distrusted the Mori clan.

Samurai Armour and Provisions

The word 'samurai' means 'to serve' and there were various types of samurai, those who served as warriors and those that served as administrators and clerks. Since Hideyoshi had unified the nation bringing hitherto-unknown peace, the gap between the warrior faction and the administrative faction had widened. Warriors such as Kato Kiyomasa, Fukushima Masanori, Kuroda Nagamasa, Hosokawa Tadaoki and Ikeda Terumasa watched as their significance as fighting men decreased and their positions of power were eclipsed by pen-pushers such as Ishida Mitsunari, involved in mere administrative affairs rather than the true calling of the military man, fuelling a growing animosity.

At the forefront of every army were the well-organised *ashigaru* foot soldiers. Highly trained in the use of their weapons, either long spear or matchlock, and drilled in battlefield tactics, they were uniformly fitted with lightweight (about 5–8kg), mass-produced munition armour, or *okashi gusoku* ('borrowed armour') that was supplied by their respective lord.

One such common type of armour was the *okegawa do*, featuring a two-piece body shell hinged on the left and tied shut on the right like most armour of the time. How the *okegawa do* differed was by its thinner steel and lacquer covering, and also the use of simple *kusazuri*, or 'grass scrapers', these being multiple plates of steel or raw leather, lacquered and laced together and dangling below the main body armour. Unlike samurai of a higher rank, the *ashigaru* had less *kusazuri* plates attached and the sword or swords were put on first, with the armour worn over the top. Even simpler was a *hara-ate* (lit. 'stomach plate'), an open-backed armour, rather like a modern-day kendo breastplate with three or four rows of leather or steel-plated *kusazuri* hanging below to protect the hips and upper thighs.

Another type of armour frequently used for the lower-ranking troops was the *tatami gusoku*, consisting of steel plates linked together with chain mail and sewn onto a cloth backing. This armour was easily folded for carrying in a backpack-like bag. Both the *okegawa do* and *tatami gusoku* types would usually be fitted with simple *kote*, plate-covered sleeves, and occasionally with *suneate* or lower leg armour. Some were lucky enough to receive a simple but effective *zunari*-type helmet, made of a thick steel crown plate with rounded sides.

Zunari kabuto became very popular, as they were easier, cheaper and faster to produce than the older, often seen *suji kabuto*. *Suji kabuto* are identified by their having been made of multiple triangular lames, hammered into a concave shape before being riveted together to form the crown. Around the base of this crown was a *koshi-ito*, a base plate to which the *shikoro*, or neck guard, was attached. The *shikoro* was formed from rows of steel plates, held in place concertina-like with dyed braids of silk or cotton hemp. It was structurally very strong, but could prove to be heavy. *Zunari kabuto* were also structurally strong, made from concave plates of steel covering the sides and a wide strip of steel covering the crown to create a bowl shape. Like the *suji kabuto*, a *koshi-ita* held the *shikoro*. The design of the *Star Wars* villain Darth Vader's helmet was partly based on the *zunari kabuto*. *Zunari kabuto* were usually only issued to higher-ranked *ashigaru*, the rest usually receiving a *jingasa*, a flat conical hat of lacquered steel or raw leather with cloth flaps back and sidex. The *jingasa* were not just protective headgear: in some cases, they were also used as cooking pots for boiling water and rice, as well as to water and feed the horses.

For the swordsman as well as the spearman, the main points of attack against an armoured samurai included the face, the throat, the neck, the armpits, the inner wrists, the inner elbow, the lower stomach area below the *do* and *gessan*, the backs of the knees and the groin area between the *haidate* plates. These are target areas with major veins and arteries running through them, the cutting of which could dispatch a man in as little as 8 to 12 seconds.

The *ashigaru* knew how to care for themselves and were used to hardship. Many were of agricultural stock and so an *ashigaru* culture of sorts was created, using both military training and rural know-how to survive the rigours of war and life on the march during military campaigns.

Following the Battle of Sekigahara, a popular book called the *Zohyo Monogatari* ('Handbook for Foot Soldiers') was published. It was basically a survival guide written especially for *ashigaru* that gave them hints and tips for getting through a battle. This book was written using first-hand accounts of over thirty veteran *ashigaru* and provided information handed down from campaigns of old. For example, the resourceful *ashigaru* was taught to use the straw wrappings from rice bails as blankets in the cold, to chew peppers to stay warm when on duty and to make stomach medicines from apricot and plum stones. Most were also adept at making medicines from wild herbs too. Fire making was a common skill and horse manure was often used for fires when wood was scarce, the smoke of which kept the mosquitoes away in summer. The *ashigaru* knew to use *zuiki*, the platted vines of a potato plant, dried and then soaked in *aka-miso* (a nutrient-rich paste made from fermented soybeans and salt), as a tie for packhorses and the like. The miso-impregnated cords could be chopped up finely and boiled to make soup once supplies ran low and the used vine ropes were no longer required.

Ieyasu was well aware of the importance of maintaining one's health during military campaigns. He showed particular concern for the common foot soldiers and had often warned his troops not to chew raw rice as it would upset their stomachs and that whenever possible, rice should be soaked for two hours before being cooked and eaten. For health reasons, Ieyasu himself would only take rich foods once or twice a month and preferred to dine on simple fare, sometimes contenting himself during battles with the rations eaten by the samurai in the field.

Some *ashigaru* would carry their rice rations with them, rolled in a long white cloth and tied at intervals for daily use. Three to four days' worth was usually prepared. The pre-soaked rice would only have to be popped into hot water to be ready to eat at a moment's notice. Known as *juzu*, these ration packs were carried slung around the shoulder and resembled the large, white Buddhist prayer beads from where they derived their name. Only a few days' rice rations were doled out at a time to discourage the lower ranks from making their own sake from the excess rice.

Another popular and handy food was *hyo-ro-gan* (warrior food rations), which were dried dough-like balls roughly 4cm across, made of buckwheat flour, soybeans, sesame seeds, pickled plums and sometimes wild potato or even pounded rice mixed with sake to make a dough. The *ashigaru* would eat two or three of these a day, especially during campaigns when the wearing of heavy armour combined with the rigours of battle necessitated a quick meal providing proper nutrition. A type of traditional instant soup called *imokaranawa* using the aforementioned bundled stalks of potato plants was also prepared with miso stock and dried so all the warrior had to do was add water and boil.

Despite their rather lowly status, these foot soldiers were well trained and for the most part, quite loyal. The *ashigaru* knew that it was their job to fight and, if need be, die for their lord. Particularly with the advent of the gun, the professional *ashigaru* knew that part of his job was to act as cannon fodder. If an *ashigaru* could take a bullet, he knew that by doing so he could possibly save a higher-ranked samurai. Further, as the role of the *ashigaru* increased, there was a need for greater numbers and so many were recruited from the farming community. Many joined up simply for money and thus often attached themselves not just to their local lord, but also to any rich and powerful *daimyo* in the hopes of getting a good wage in a large army and increasing their chances of coming through a battle alive. For some, the chance to participate in a battle provided a little extra income through the frowned-upon though often overlooked practice of looting the dead. Not only could they supplement their own meagre armour and add to their weapons collection, but by reselling various pieces, could gain financially too.

It has been estimated that a third, or about 150,000, *ashigaru* nationwide found themselves made redundant following Sekigahara due to the deaths or deposition of their lords who had sided against Ieyasu. Most returned to the fields, or took up jobs as labourers building castles. When war broke out again in 1614 and 1615 with the winter and summer battles of Osaka, many took the opportunity to bear arms once again.

Higher-ranked samurai were expected to provide their own armour and each was made to suit the tastes and finances of the wearer rather than to provide any uniformity or show any allegiance. By the mid-sixteenth century, *kachushi* (armour craftsmen) faced an overwhelming demand for armour and so simpler, more practical armour came into being. The new styles, known as *tousei gusoku* or 'modern armour', featured major improvements over the older, more cumbersome *domaru*, or 'stomach wrap', styles of the past.

Among the most common *tousei gusoku* styles were the *nuinobe do* and *mogami do* types. *Mogami do* consisted of an average of five individually-hinged or laced strips of horizontal steel with a further three strips covering the upper chest. These were shaped to fit the body better than the much earlier types of samurai armour known as *yoroi*, which were often squarish in shape and quite cumbersome when it came to the energetic business of war. The waist of the *tousei gusoku* was tapered so that the bulk of the armour's weight rested on the hips once the outer *uwa-obi* sash was tied tight, rather than being borne on the shoulders. This body armour was comprised of a shell of two pieces hinged on the left and tied with cords on the right. Below this was attached the *gessan*, also known as *kusazuri*, being six or seven sets of four or five plates of lacquered steel or *nerikawa*, raw leather. For the armourer, the most difficult part of the armour set to make was not the helmet as might be expected, as helmet sizes were relatively uniform, but the *do*, as it had to be tailor-made to fit the samurai perfectly to remain comfortable during long marches, sieges and battles when it would be worn over extended periods of time.

The samurai's helmet provided the best opportunity to display the wearer's individuality, with flamboyant designs sported by creative or attention-seeking samurai. Fanciful names were imagined for often-produced helmet styles and were created not only to describe the helmet, but to attract purchases. The Japanese preference for simple things rose from the Tokugawa Shogunate's enforced practice of austerity. Prior to the peaceful Edo period, samurai enjoyed eye-catching costumes and armour.

Aside from the lords, soldiers of all rank wore a tall identification flag, a *sashimono*, bearing the crest or symbol of the samurai's commander, on their backs. These banners were held in a brace on the back of the body armour. As most samurai chose their armour based on personal taste rather than having a uniform look, further identification was required and provided by small coloured flags called *ai jirushi* that were attached to the back of the helmet, the left *sode* (shoulder armour) and to the front right waist area. Occasionally, during heavy fighting, these identification tags came off and so verbal passwords were also used, though in the heat of battle, some samurai forgot their side's password and were cut down by their allies. These passwords also helped ensure spies could not infiltrate the camps. At Sekigahara, for example, the Shimazu clan's password was *Zai*! The word had no meaning and was written in the simple *hiragana* form. These *ai jirushi* often carried the personal information of the samurai himself. Should he be killed in battle and his head be taken, his body would be identifiable and his opponent would know whose head he had taken back to camp for registration.

Ii Naomasa's bright-red lacquered armour, specially crafted to fit his large figure, was of a simple design, but was heavier than the average samurai's, apparently weighing in at around 30kg. This was almost twice the average weight of the armour of the time. This armour is still in existence at the Hikone Castle Museum and while it looks like it has been beaten out of a single sheet of steel, it was in fact made in the standard fashion. Five lower and three upper horizontal strips of steel were joined together and when all of the parts were assembled, it was thickly lacquered, effectively hiding the ridges and joints. This style is known as *hotoke do*, which refers to the smooth, unblemished figure of the Buddha Hotoke. This sleek surface would allow arrows or spears thrust at the lord to glance off and not catch in the lacing and therefore featured rolled edges. Likewise, musket balls could be stopped or at least deflected by the thickness of both steel and lacquer.

While Ii Naomasa's armour was among the heavier of those worn at Sekigahara, another of Ieyasu's great generals, Honda Tadakatsu, had one of the lightest suits. Honda's set was made mostly from *nerikawa*, raw leather, dried, cut and held in position with steel rods before being lacquered over. The armour was lightweight, yet protective.

Ieyasu was wearing a suit of armour known as the *kuro ito shida-gusoku* at the Battle of Sekigahara. Built to specifications dictated by Ieyasu after having seen it in a dream, this very dark brown lacquered armour with black silk lacing features a *nuinobe*-style body armour of multiple horizontal plates laced together to form two pieces hinged on the left. Seven sets of five-plate *kusazuri* hang from the base of the body armour. The sleeves are a simple *tsutsu-gote* type, in which the crafted plates covering the forearm are hinged together to form a protective tube, while the upper arms were encased in a thick mesh of chain mail. This particular armour lacked *sode*, the rows of plates covering the upper arm and shoulder. Small rectangular card-like plates of raw leather, lacquered and laced like the rest of the set, covered Ieyasu's thighs, while *tsutsu suneate,* lower leg protectors in a manner similar to the forearm protectors, and a lacquered steel mask featuring a moustache of white horse hair completed the outfit.

A noble of Ieyasu's rank would probably have had as many as five other suits of armour on hand at such battles. There have been a number of suits of armour owned by Ieyasu attributed to this battle and it is possible that a few *kagemusha* or doppelganger Ieyasus, used as decoys to mislead the enemy, could well have been used. The armour he wore at Sekigahara is now kept at the Kunouzan Toshogu Shrine, burial place of the great lord, in Shizuoka Prefecture. Although unconfirmed, it is believed that he also wore this same armour during the attack on Osaka almost 15 years later.

Weapons and Tactics

Among the most common weapons of the day were, in order of importance, the matchlock, the long spear, bow and arrow, various polearms including short spears and *naginata*, and the sword. Although many believe the bow and arrow had been effectively made redundant by the gun by late 1600, it is interesting to note that Shimazu Yoshihiro and his army were observed carrying longbows into action at Sekigahara, something seen by many as being charmingly old-fashioned. However, the bow and arrow were still considered a major battle weapon. We can see in the extant battle screens that archery was still prevalent, as guns were vulnerable to weather conditions and because they took time to reload, were not ideal in close combat situations.

Japanese bows, called *yumi*, are said to have been amongst histories' longest and most powerful bows. Perfected in the sixteenth century and made from laminated bamboo and hardwood, the *yumi* averaged around 2m in length. Japanese Sengoku (Warring States) Period (1467–1615) and even Edo period bows are said to be far superior to even modern-day martial arts kyudo bows. The asymmetrical bow was held not in the centre as with European longbows, but at a point around the lower third of the bow. European arrows averaged around 75cm, while Japanese arrows, called *ya*, were made from *yadake* bamboo a metre or longer and with fletching of large birds of prey or geese. Owl feathers were said to bring misfortune and so they were never used. Strings were made of a hemp twine. An arrow shot from a Japanese bow had an effective range of over 100m and could penetrate steel plate at distances of 20–30m. The various types of arrowhead were forged from *tamahagane* steel, produced from iron sand in the same labour-intensive way as *katana* and *tachi* swords were made. Arrows could be notched and fired in three to five seconds, making them ideal support weapons on the battlefield.

Despite swords being placed last in importance on the battlefield, all samurai carried a set of blades but these were still considered weapons of last resort. Various kinds of swords could be seen on the battlefield. Worn with armour and with the edge downwards, *tachi* swords were on average over 60cm in length from hilt to tip, with a pronounced arc to their shape. Some samurai even tied cords around or through the hand guard (*tsuba*) and then looped the cords around their wrists to avoid dropping the sword during battle. *Tachi* were more a stabbing sword, being slighter than the *utsugatana* (*katana*) or cutting sword. The *katana* was usually worn with normal clothing tucked into an *obi* sash, with the cutting edge upwards. Shorter companion swords, known as *wakizashi*, 30 to 60cm in length, and *tanto* daggers, with blades under 30cm, were often carried. Oversized swords worn slung across the back and known as *nodachi*, field swords, or *odachi*, great swords, were sometimes carried by stronger warriors. These were usually carried to intimidate the enemy and had longer hilts than standard *tachi*, often being used with the lower part of the blade wrapped in thick *washi* paper to act as an extended handgrip to increase effectiveness and control of the oversized weapon. A great deal of skill and strength – and a different form of fighting skill compared to use of the *tachi* or *naginata* – was required when using the *nodachi* or *odachi*, which never enjoyed the popularity of similar weapons such as the *nagamaki*, a polearm somewhere between a *naginata* and a *nodachi*.

Cavalry charges were not unheard of and were used most effectively in many samurai battles, in particular those involving the Takeda clan. For mounted samurai, apart from the *tachi*, a spear 2 to 3m in length was the norm. These spears were not thrown, but used as thrusting or cutting weapons. A mounted samurai was usually surrounded by numerous foot soldiers to protect him and his horse from attack. This was most important, as anyone on a horse was obviously of rank and significance and therefore made a ready target for any samurai or *ashigaru* looking to take the head of a general and advance their position and standing. Scouts and messengers were often on horseback and being part of the enemy's intelligence operations would also make them valuable targets.

Rows of spearmen were often used front and foremost as a line of defence and the long spear was ideal for front-line foot soldiers. The *ashigaru* spearmen would be equipped with spears of around 3 to 6m in length. During the Sengoku Period, the lengths of *nagae-yari* (long spears) varied between clans and according to the preferences of the generals. For example, the armies of Takeda Shingen and Uesugi Kenshin had spears averaging 4m, while Uesugi Kagekatsu's samurai carried 4.8m spears around the time of Sekigahara. The armies of Toyotomi Hideyoshi, Tokugawa Ieyasu and the Hojo clan also carried 4.8m-long spears, while the longest of all, at 5.6m, were those of Oda Nobunaga's troops.

These longer spears, although occasionally made of a lacquered laminate of wood and bamboo, were usually a long, strong single pole of wood topped with a 15 to 90cm steel head, often of a flattened diamond shape or triangular in cross section. Some shorter, 2–3m, spears featured cross-shaped or right-angled L-shaped blades.

When approaching the enemy in battle, these long spears were often not pointed at the enemy as would be expected, but carried raised vertically, with the left hand high and the right hand holding the lower end. As the opponents came within range, by manoeuvring the pole slightly at the end, a larger movement could be affected at the sharp end and the spears were brought down heavily onto the enemy. The force of a long-spear strike from above was enough to cause concussions, break wrists, arms, collar bones and shoulders and the highly sharpened spear blades could then be used to stab and cut into the face or vulnerable neck, shoulder, armpit, wrist or groin areas where major arteries are located.

In a horizontal position, the spears continued to be used with the left hand held slightly forward. The rearward right hand could suddenly thrust the pole forward in a stabbing motion, increasing reach, or be held still in the forward left hand, while the right hand could be used to control a manoeuvre even slightly, causing a wider action at the sharp end to block opposition stabs or cause the spear head's blade to slice into the opponent's unprotected points. Some schools of spear fighting adopted a twisting motion on the forward thrust, causing the head to spiral, tearing a larger hole in the opposition. Cross and L-shaped spear heads could be used to catch and deflect enemy spear attacks and also to stab past an opponent, only to catch the razor-sharp protruding element against their neck, or the back of their legs on a reverse pull.

While primarily used against oncoming rows of lower-ranked samurai and *ashigaru* in the opening moments of a battle, the long spear was also used against mounted samurai. Crouching along the defence line, the very first row of *ashigaru* held their spears straight out in front of them, with the spear tips resting on the ground. As the horsemen approached, the *ashigaru* would remain still, keeping their eyes on the advancing steeds. The horses, seeing the row of crouching men holding long slender poles, would become frightened and shy away, arresting the advance. Should they continue, the spears could be lifted to skewer oncoming man and beast.

Another tactic was for the *ashigaru* to cross the upper ends of their spears and hold them pointed at the ground, again while crouching, in an effort to trip advancing men and horses. The dagger-like tipped spears, while held low, could also be used to flick at the legs of both animals and enemy warriors alike. This most effective formation was called *yaribusuma* and was a frequently-used tactic during a battle. In these cases, it was often the horse that became the primary target of attack. Once the horses were down, the foot soldiers would concentrate on the high-ranking samurai who were now forced to fight on foot and often some distance from their main forces.

Guns

The use of guns had become widespread by the time of Sekigahara, changing samurai battles considerably as strategy and tactics developed. The first guns arrived with the Portuguese in 1543 and their potential was quickly recognised. While archers were previously used first and foremost, the simplicity of the gun allowed the *ashigaru*, with their limited training, to become a formidable fighting force. Guns were now front-line weapons, often backed by archers, who were themselves backed by spearmen, ready to rush forward. Just 32 years after guns had arrived, Oda Nobunaga had more than proven their value in defeating Takeda Katsuyori 25 years before Sekigahara at the Battle of Nagashino in 1575, when, according to legend, his 3,000 men in ranks of three provided near-continuous volleys of fire at the approaching enemy, with devastating results.

The matchlock guns, known as *hinawaju* or *teppo*, were of relatively simple construction, having a steel barrel around 1m in length with a bore averaging 18.7mm was fitted to a wooden stock. A priming pan on the right of the bore sat below a serpentine lever holding a length of saltpetre-impregnated cord. When the trigger was pulled, the spring-loaded serpentine dropped the slow-burning match into the priming powder in the open pan. Bang!

The average matchlock at Sekigahara fired a lead ball weighing six *mon*, or around 22.5g. While these smaller-bore guns were used primarily against enemy personnel, there were a number of larger-bore guns known as *O-zutsu* usually used against structures such as castles and fortresses, but also against troop formations. These *O-zutsu* were smaller than actual cannon and either hand-held or frame-mounted, weapons firing 200 *mon* (750g), 300 *mon* (1.125kg) and even 1,000 *mon* (3.75kg) shots.

Tokugawa Ieyasu had ordered ten 800-*mon* (3kg) shot *O-zutsu* from the gunsmiths of Kunitomo five months before the Battle of Sekigahara. Both Ieyasu and the Western leader Ishida Mitsunari had approached the gunsmiths of Sakae, near Osaka and Kunitomo in Omi Province (Shiga Prefecture) in the hopes of securing large numbers of firearms. Ieyasu had been wise enough to move first and, employing the warrior Wakisaka Sukedayu as a secret mediator, placed a large order for weapons, particularly with the smiths of Omi. When Ishida Mitsunari went to place his own order with the smiths of his own domain, the Kunitomo smiths were forced to turn him down, as they already had too many orders to fill. Two months before the battle, an infuriated Mitsunari ordered the skilled metalworkers to cease filling orders from anyone not loyal to the Toyotomi cause. By this stage, the Kunitomi gunsmiths had come to the decision that Ishida Mitsunari had already lost to Ieyasu and considering the generous orders received as well as their own futures, decided to continue to produce guns for the Tokugawa. Evidence of Kunitomo-forged *O-zutsu* having been used at Sekigahara was discovered in the early 1900s when the Sekigahara train station was being constructed and two 3.75kg shot were unearthed.

The *ashigaru* matchlockmen were given either a small flask of gunpowder and a smaller container of priming powder, or pre-measured charges in paper tubes kept in a small box tied around their waist. This made reloading quicker and so, using the wooden ramrod housed in the gun's stock to pack in the powder and ram home the lead ball, meant that all could be performed ideally in as little as 45 seconds. However, during the pressure of battle, or on damp or windy days, reloading a matchlock weapon would take significantly longer.

Because it was lightweight, easy to use and most importantly, an effective weapon, the matchlock was ideal for *ashigaru*. The weapon had an effective range against armoured warriors of about 50 to 75m, but at Sekigahara, with so many enemy soldiers at such close proximity, there was no real need to aim as one could quite easily hit an opponent by pointing in their general direction and firing without paying too much attention.

It has been estimated that 25,000 matchlock guns, or 30 per cent of all the guns in existence worldwide at the time were used at Sekigahara. In all of Europe, only 30,000 guns were believed to be in use. Japan had a total of approximately 55,000 of these projectile weapons and in fact had more guns than any other country at that time. Had the weather conditions not been so poor and the supplies of gunpowder and match not become so damp the night before, the death toll in the Battle of Sekigahara may well have been significantly higher.

Research conducted on Sengoku-Period battle casualties has produced some interesting results. Most people, even the modern Japanese, tend to think that swords would have produced the most combat-related deaths in samurai battles,

Leader of the Eastern forces and future shogun, Tokugawa Ieyasu. This statue stands in the grounds of his birthplace, Okazaki Castle, Aichi Prefecture.

Ishida Mitsunari, leader of the Western forces at Sekigahara. This statue stands in Ishida Village, Shiga Prefecture.

Honda Tadakatsu in his distinctive antler-fitted armour and carrying his famed spear, the 'Dragonfly Cutter'.

Statue of a mounted Ii Naomasa in full armour of the type worn at Sekigahara.

Fukushima Masanori waves a *saihai* baton to command his troops.

Fushimi Castle, Fushimi Ward, Kyoto.

Kiyosu Castle, Aichi Prefecture.

Ogaki Castle, Gifu Prefecture.

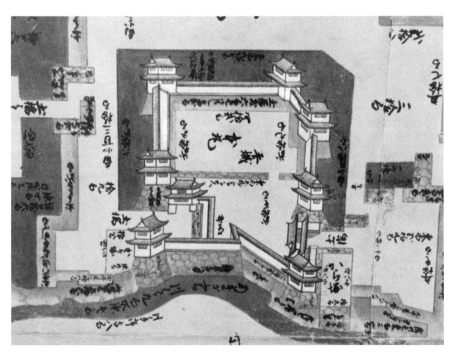

Plan of Ueda Castle.

Tokugawa Ieyasu's armour, worn at the Battle of Sekigahara. (Photo courtesy of Kunouzan Toshogu Shrine, Shizuoka Prefecture)

Set of typical samurai armour of the early 1600s.

Edo period *ashigaru* armour

Battlefield memorial marker and battle flags pinpointing the site where the Konishi forces launched the flare signalling the beginning of the battle having just witnessed a small contingent of around thirty mounted Ii and Matsudaira samurai emerge from the mist and attack the Ukita forces front lines.

Mount Sasao, Ishida Mitsunari and the Western force's command post seen across the killing fields of Sekigahara, with the battlefield memorial on the site of the most violent of the day's fighting.

View from Ishida Mitsunari's command post on Mount Sasao looking south easterly across the battlefield and Sekigahara central. To the far left is Mount. Nangu, and Ieyasu's original command post can be seen below the red and white power pylon bottom left of Mount. Nangu. Ieyasu's second command post was positioned within the clump of pine trees, at the very centre of the photograph. The Eastern forces' front lines were where the houses border the rice fields.

The battlefield of Sekigahara, seen from the Kobayakawa positions on Mount Matsuo.

Troops prepare for the attack during a re-enactment.

Kobayakawa and Ukita spearmen clash. (Sekigahara Town photograph)

Samurai battle action at Sekigahara.

関ケ原合戦絵巻2000

Over 850 re-enactors in full samurai armour take to the field for the 400th
anniversary in 2000. (Sekigahara Town photo)

Site of Tokugawa Ieyasu's second and centrally-located command post, around 800m south of the Western forces' headquarters on Mount Sasao.

The site of Ieyasu's first command post, Mount Momokubari.

Site of the Shimazu force's encampment at Sekigahara, marked out with the clan's war banners.

The site of Fukushima Masanori's command post. The large tree on the right is featured in the Sekigahara battle screens.

Otani Yoshitsugu's grave, not far from his main command post. Behind it is the grave of his loyal vassal, Yuasa Gosuke.

The Eastern *Kubizuka*, or Head Mound, where hundreds of both Western and Eastern heads taken in battle are buried together below this huge old tree. Many visitors to the battlefields pay their respects to the fallen from both sides here to this day.

Palisades surrounding Mount Sasao and Ishida Mitsunari and the Western forces' headquarters.

The site of Konishi Yukinaga's command post, with the Shimazu encampment in the background.

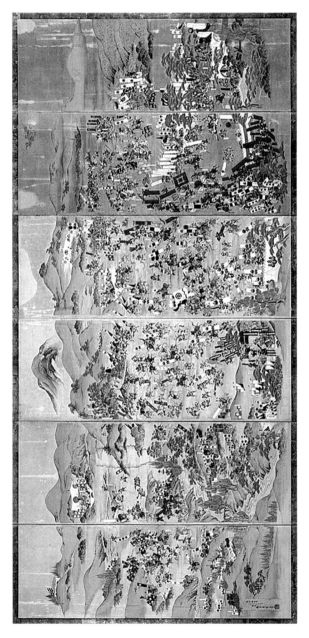

The Sekigahara Battle Screen. This large six-panel screen depicts the battle
at its peak. (Courtesy of the Gifu Sekigahara Battlefield Memorial Museum)

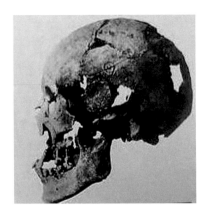
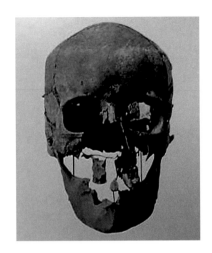

2Ishida Mitsunari's skull was rediscovered in Kyoro's Sangen-in Temple in 1907. Using the skull as a base, Mitsunari's facial features were recreated by Dr Nagayasu Shuichi, former Chief of Engineering, Tokyo National Research Institute of Police Sciences at the request of photographer and descendant of Mitsunari, Mr. Ishida Takayuki. It appears that Mitsunari had a pronounced defect in his teeth that caused them to bow outwards. The rest of his skeleton was later studied by Dr. Ishida Tetsuro (no relation) of the Kansai Idai Medical University.

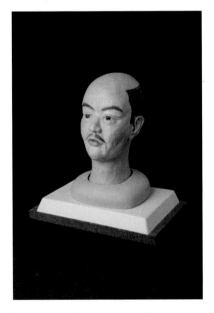

The forensically-recreated face of Ishida Mitsunari. (Ishida family collection)

but researchers have shown that deaths attributed to archery came to an average of 41 per cent. Matchlock fire was responsible for an average of only 19 per cent of kills. Spears accounted for 18 per cent of all casualties. Rocks were the cause of 10 per cent of deaths in samurai battle. Indeed, many battles began with both sides facing each other and then throwing rocks at one another, a most un-samurai like beginning to a battle. Rocks to be used as weapons are known to have been piled at strategic locations around medieval and early-modern castles and fortresses and these piles of stones are regularly unearthed during excavations particularly in inaccessible, rarely visited sites that have not been contaminated by tourists or unknowing site caretakers. At the siege of Hara Castle, part of the Shimabara Rebellion (December 1637–April 1638) the renown warrior Miyamoto Musashi was struck in the leg by a rock thrown by a defender and injured to the degree that he was unable to participate further in the battle. Although swords are considered the 'soul of the samurai' and the preferred weapon, it appears they caused the least number of combat related deaths at just 4 per cent.

This information tends to dispel the myth of the samurai being close-quarters combatants, armed simply with swords. We see from the figures that the longest-ranged weapons were responsible for the most deaths, becoming progressively shorter-ranged further down the list. The figures show that like modern-day warfare, battles were usually fought at a distance, with warriors generally preferring to be as far away from the enemy as possible.

Battle Formations
Although many elaborate battle formations with fanciful titles existed, many were not properly formalised until the peaceful Edo period that was forged by the Battle of Sekigahara. Loyal vassals and clan members would occupy strategically important points within the formation, while the *daimyo* or leader would be stationed to the rear in his war camp. From there he could control the battle through the use of visual standards, flags, fireworks and smoke flares, also conch shell, war drum, bell and gong signals and through the dispatch of messengers with specific orders for the captains of the many formations of an army. The commander in this case was seen as the main rallying point and indeed his presence would have quite an effect on the outcome of a battle, rousing his men into fighting harder, as well as psychologically upsetting an enemy. If the leader was taken or killed, it usually signified the end of a battle, as his men would flee or simply capitulate and would often be absorbed into the victor's forces if not executed.

The *hoshi no jin* arrangement was one of the older battle formations. Highly mobile, it was shaped like an arrowhead with lightly-protected flanks. It was used primarily to drive deep into an enemy's ranks. Archers, and later matchlockmen, would first open a hole in the enemy's lines, allowing the warriors to enter.

When faced with either the *hoshi* or *kakuyoku* (crane's wing) formations, the *koyaku no jin* (cattle yoke) formation, named due to its resemblance to the yokes fitted to cattle, was often employed. The twin ranks of front-line troops could receive the initial attack and reveal the enemy's intentions, allowing the following lines of fighters to then counteract the attack by changing positions to either envelop the enemy, or even change formations for a different strategy.

The *saku no jin*, a circular formation likened to a keyhole, was considered one of the best formations when facing the *hoshi* formation and easily formed from the *koyaku no jin*. The multiple angled ranks of matchlockmen and archers in the front line were designed to meet the initial *hoshi* formation with a crossfire of bullets and arrows. Pressing forward, the circular ranks could surround those of the enemy while protecting the *daimyo*.

Based on the patterns of birds in flight, the *ganko no jin* was another formation that was easy to take up and highly flexible, featuring solid ranks of matchlockmen supported by archers, with ranks of samurai surrounding the general and a rearguard complete with archers and matchlockmen. This was a basic, yet formidable, order.

When up against a numerically superior enemy, the *gyorin no jin* was adopted. Resembling fish scales, hence its name, the *gyorin* formation was used to bulldoze a small section of the enemy in order to break their ranks, rather like a snub-nosed *hoshi* formation. While the Western forces adopted the *kakuyoku* formation to block the western end of the Sekigahara pass, in response Ieyasu's troops had set themselves out in the *gyorin* formation.

The *kuruma gakari no jin* was a formation favoured by the Uesugi at the earlier Battle of Kawanakajima and consisted of well-trained troops in a spoke-like order radiating from a central marker point. The 'wheel', as the name *kuruma* suggests, would advance while rotating, so that fresh troops could continually take the place of those in front, which would then be rotated out.

There are many variations of the above-mentioned formations with equally fanciful names and imagery, affording the samurai the adaptability to face various situations such as terrain, weather, enemy numbers and so on. Due to the penchant of the samurai for being first into battle, these formations

were often broken as personal glory was sought and as confusion in the heat
of the battle reigned.

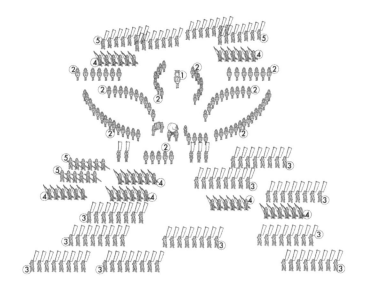

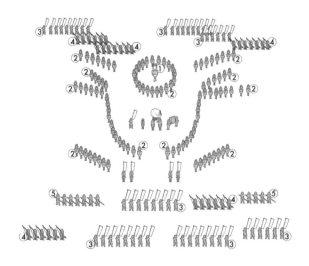

The *Kakoyoku* formation (top) adopted by the Western army, and the *Gyorin* formation (bottom) of the Eastern army.
Key
1. Commander
2. Cavalry
3. Marksmen
4. Archers
5. Spearmen

Chapter 3

The Battle

The Villages of Sekigahara

In 1600, the Sekigahara basin was mostly rice paddies and fields and consisted of around ten villages. Rice and barley were the main crops, grown in rotation, making for two sowing and two reaping seasons annually. The main central village was that of Sekigahara, consisting of 120 houses built up along the Nakasendo route with a population of 552 residents, mostly famers. The majority of the *minka* folk dwellings and *machiya* townhouse-style wooden homes were of *irimoya* construction, being hipped and gabled roofed, with a mostly reed or straw thatch, suggesting an architectural influence from the Kyoto or western Kansai region. Because properties were taxed according to the width their street frontage, the homes along the roadways were narrow fronted and two to three times as deep.

East to west along the Nakasendo, close to Tokugawa Ieyasu's first command post on Mount Momokubari, was Nogami Mura. The village had 54 houses for 221 residents. Around 2km west was Sekigahara, then the rice paddy surrounded Oseki, with 66 villagers and 14 houses. During the battle, the Ukita and Fukushima troops fought with such intensity here, most of the homes and fields were destroyed.

Across the Fujikawa River was Fujishita Mura with a population of 104 in 25 houses. During the battle, the small village was surrounded by the troops of Hiratsuka Tamehiro, Toda Shigemasa, Akaza Naoyasu, Ogawa Suketada, Kutsuki Mototsuna and Wakisaka Yasuharu. Records show the villagers, possibly under duress, assisted in setting up the command posts and camps and prepared food while the village headman was commandeered to explain the lay of the land.

Yamanaka Mura, west of Fujishita Mura and also established along the south side of the Nakasendo, featured over 40 dwellings and was home to 166 people. With the help of the villagers, Otani Yoshitsugu made his camp directly above the village's Wakamiya Hachimangu Shrine. Yamanaka Mura was prone to flooding in heavy rains as it was situated in a narrow valley. A little further along was Imasu, one of Mino's larger post towns on the Nakasendo with 62 houses and 250 residents.

On the road leading north from Sekigahara village was Koike, Koseki and then Tamamura below Mount Sasao. When the samurai began entering the region en-masse, the villagers of Tama Mura quickly reaped their fields so as not to lose their crops, then fled to the nearby hills. Along the road directly south of Sekigahara village was Makita Mura.

Over 1,360 people lived and worked in the vicinity of what was about to become the greatest of samurai battlefields.

Saturday, 21 October 1600: 6 a.m

Heavy rain the night before to the battle had left the ground thoroughly saturated. The samurai of both armies, East and West, who had travelled through this pouring rain to the battlefield were as damp as the surrounding long grass and ripened rice crops they waded through.

On the morning of 21 October 1600, the rain subsided just after 6 a.m., but a heavy mist, conjured up by the sun-warmed earth from the previous few days' fine conditions being suddenly drenched by the cold autumnal rains, cloaked the valley and plain. Fires lit by the samurai to warm themselves, to dry their sodden armour and weapons and to clear the mist, soon spread out of control and caused more residents of the area's few villages to flee to the safety of the surrounding mountains. The majority of the locals had already escaped to the hills during the night when they saw the large numbers of armoured warriors pouring into the valley.

Tokugawa Ieyasu was aware of the smoke rising from the campfires on the western side of Sekigahara and he cautioned his generals on the dangers of overestimating the numbers of enemy troops based on the number of fires, advising them that 'Numbers appear to swell in a confined area'. In the meantime, both sides waited in relative quiet for the fog to disperse.

Initially it appeared that the Loyalist army held the upper hand. They had a greater number of men on the field and importantly held the higher ground. Although difficult to confirm as estimates vary, the Western samurai are believed to have numbered well over 83,000 men. Another 13,000 waited at Ogaki and over 30,000 more were engaged in other sieges around the country. The Eastern side meanwhile came to little more than 80,000, some 38,000 men less, as Ieyasu's son and heir had failed to arrive at the battlefield in time. Approximately 163,000 troops were on the central Sekigahara fields that morning.

Most modern studies on the battle are based on the research of one of the earliest works on the subject, the *Japanese Military History, Sekigahara Campaign*, part of a series written and published by the Imperial Japanese Armed Forces General Headquarters in 1893. At the time, where historical records could not confirm numbers of troops in each army, figures were deduced, based on a letter from Tokugawa Ieyasu to Shimazu Yoshihiro, who was initially set to join the Eastern forces before suddenly allying himself with the West. In the extant letter, Ieyasu orders the Shimazu to 'Send three men for every 100 *koku* produced by the domain'. The Shimazu were ranked at around 900,000 *koku* at their peak, with Yoshihiro having an income of 560,000 *koku* and so should have furnished at the very least 5,600 men, yet Yoshihiro and his nephew Toyohisa combined to supply just 1,500 men. This same ratio was apparently used by the authors of the 1893 book when details regarding other *daimyo* warlords could not be confirmed.

For that reason, the exact numbers of each unit and army are disputed to this day, although most scholars basically agree on the following breakdown of the main armies at Sekigahara, listed here:

WESTERN ARMY App. 83,000
(in alphabetical order)

Akaza Naoyasu 600
Ankokuji Ekei 1,800
Chosokabe Morichika 6,600
Hiratsuka Tamehiro 360
Ishida Mitsunari 6,000
Kikkawa Hiroie 4,200
Kinoshita Yoritsugu 750*
Kobayakawa Hideaki 15,600
Konishi Yukinaga 6,000
Kutsuki Mototsuna 600
Mori Hidemoto 15,000
Natsuka Masaie 1,500
Ogawa Suketada 2,100
Otani Yoshitsugu 848

Shima Sakon 1,000
Shimazu Yoshihiro 1,500
Toda Shigemasa 1,500
Ukita Hidie 17,000
Wakisaka Yasuharu 1,100

EASTERN ARMY App. 80,000

Arima Toyouji 900
Asano Yoshinaga 6,510
Fukushima Masanori 6,000
Furuta Shigekatsu 1,020
Honda Tadakatsu 500
Horio Tadauji*
Hosokawa Tadaoki 5,100
Ii Naomasa 3,600
Ikeda Terumasa 4,560
Ikoma Kazumasa 1,830
Kato Yoshiaki 3,000
Kanamori Nagachika 1,140
Kuroda Nagamasa 5,400
Kyougoku Takatomo 3,000
Matsudaira Tadayoshi 3,000
Oda Nagumasa 500
Takenaka Shigekado 200
Tanaka Yoshimasa 3,000
Terasawa Hirotaka 2,400
Todo Takatora 2,490
Tokugawa Ieyasu 30,000 men
Tsutsui Sadatsugu 2,850
Yamauchi Katsutoyo 2,058

*Figures are either unavailable or unconfirmed

Samurai of all levels studied military manuals such as the *Toryu Gunpo Kousha Sho* ('Winning Ways of Strategy'). A list in that particular manuscript outlines the 'fourteen best moments in which to take an enemy':

Attack in the following instances:

1. Before the enemy amass completely.
2. Just before the warriors and horses feed.
3. When the enemy is geographically lost.
4. Before the enemy have decided upon their campsite.
5. Before the enemy have had time to plan their defence.
6. Before the enemy have fully planned their offense.
7. When the enemy are tired.
8. When the leading commander is away from the main encampment.
9. When the enemy are en-route to their desired destination.
10. When the enemy are crossing a river.
11. When the enemy are traversing difficult terrain.
12. When the enemy are content, feel confident or relaxed.
13. When the enemy are confused or unsure of their next move.
14. When the enemy is scared.

On the morning of the battle, both Eastern and Western forces were facing most of the above-mentioned conditions, which meant that, according to this list, the situation was ideal for an attack.

The Mist Lifts

In the early hours the two great armies waited in the dark and gloom of Sekigahara. An air of tension, fear and uncertainty filled the plain. The sounds of clattering armour, weapons and horses and the barked shouts and final orders of captains steadying their men could be heard across the small area that was about to become the battlefield. Contemporary reports mention that visibility had been reduced to as little as 30m in places and so the opposing armies had little idea of who they were facing or just how close to each other they really were.

Like a curtain on stage, the thick mist began to lift just after 7:30 a.m., prompting Ii Naomasa to begin giving orders to ready for the attack. Messengers from both sides were dispatched to the various front-line battalions enquiring after their preparedness.

The Eastern forces' Ii Naomasa and Matsudaira Tadayoshi began their advance with a division of around thirty mounted samurai. They got as far as their ally Fukushima Masanori's strategically positioned camp, when they were stopped by Kani Saizo, a 47-year-old samurai under Masanori, who challenged them and questioned their movements. Kani Saizo had served under Oda Nobunaga and the man responsible for his death, Akechi Mitsuhide, as well as Nobunaga's father-in-law Saito Dosan and even at one stage, the only man who could have prevented Tokugawa Ieyasu from splitting the nation in two, Maeda Toshiie.

Kani Saizo (also known as Yoshinaga) was a native of Kani in modern-day Gifu Prefecture, not far from where Akechi Mitsuhide had also been born. Saizo had quite a reputation as a brave, strong fighter and although a loyal samurai, was somewhat of a maverick. Instead of a standard *sashimono*, the tall identification flag worn on the back of the armour, he wore a stalk of freshly-cut bamboo grass, which he claimed brought him luck. Strips of strong *washi* paper were twisted into strings and tied between the lower ring of his helmet's neck guard, the *shikoro*, and the shoulder braces of his body armour. This was a practice that would have hindered his mobility, but was done to prevent other samurai from getting a sword or *naginata* to his vulnerable neck area.

Kani Saizo brashly reminded Ii Naomasa and the young Matsudaira Tadayoshi that the honour of being first into battle had been awarded personally by Lord Ieyasu to Fukushima's army and that he, as captain, was to lead that first attack.

Ieyasu had indeed granted this honour to Fukushima Masanori some months earlier, during a council of war held in Oyama. The reason was that Masanori, upon hearing Ieyasu's plan to destroy Mitsunari, was among the first to agree and it was his enthusiasm for launching an attack that had pleased Ieyasu. Masanori had at that time muttered something about wanting to eat Mitsunari's flesh, '*Mitsunari no niku o tabetai*'; the phrase was used with such regularity that it became a slogan Fukushima Masanori would often use to express his desire to bring about Mitsunari's demise.

Ieyasu's decision to award Fukushima Masanori the honour of being first into battle raised not only more than a few eyebrows, it also raised the voices of a number of Ieyasu's loyal generals, concerned that if Masanori was successful in battle, his position, reputation and confidence would also rise, making him unbearably arrogant, leading to future potential problems. Ieyasu for his part attempted to placate his generals by offering them front-line positions in his formation, promising them all an equal chance of first drawing enemy blood. Ii Naomasa too had thought it unacceptable that Masanori should be first into battle as he had only recently become a vassal of the Tokugawa. The honour of being first should belong to a long-term, close and loyal follower of Ieyasu, a distinguished retainer of rank, such as Naomasa himself.

Naomasa looked down on Kani Saizo from his horse and, pointing out that he was with Lord Ieyasu's fourth son, Tadayoshi and that as this was Tadayoshi's first experience of war, gave his assurances that they were merely going on a short reconnaissance mission to gain intelligence on the enemy's positions. Saizo recognised they were but a small group and begrudgingly allowed them to pass, but in doing so, he and the Fukushima were thus denied their chance to be the first to enter the fray.

When going in to battle Naomasa would often wear a monkey mask to protect his face under his helmet and although unconfirmed, he was believed to have been wearing it when his mounted samurai suddenly emerged from the remaining mist and attacked the opposition's front ranks. This small group, fronted by the Ii clan's future *Hitto karo*, head of the chief retainers, Kimata Morikatsu, unleashed the first volley of gunfire before driving deep into the front lines of the largest force at Sekigahara, the Ukita troops. Certainly, they could not have hoped to achieve much but glory from this David versus Goliath situation of 30 cavalry taking on the 17,000-strong Ukita, but glory was theirs. Quickly realising they were out of their depth just as the startled Ukita realised they were being attacked by only a small force, they hastily beat a short retreat. Watching in surprise, the Konishi troops situated less than 100m north of the Ukita urgently sent up a signal flare in report of the battle having commenced. As the small unit of Ii and Matsudaira samurai quickly extracted themselves, they were quickly replaced by Fukushima's front-line soldiers who rushed forward and opened fire on the Ukita troops at around 8 a.m. hoping to make up for having missed their chance of first blood. Wanting to join their master in the thick of the action and in their bright red armour, Naomasa's 'Red Devils' too flowed like boiling hot lava onto the battlefield. They were backed by Matsudaira Tadayoshi's forces for a combined 6,600 men. The greatest and bloodiest of samurai battles had begun. East and West then commenced the barbarous work of butchering one another.

Kimata Morikatsu (1555–29 August 1610), who spearheaded the initial charge, was a well-respected and strong fighter hailing from Okazaki in Mikawa Province (eastern Aichi Prefecture), where he served the Tokugawa clan as a senior retainer, achieving the status of *hatamoto*, or bannerman, to Ieyasu. A descendant of the great general Kusunoki Masashige (1294–4 July 1336), one of histories' finest samurai warriors, Morikatsu was leading some 800 of his followers in the fight under the Ii clan's banners. However, of that 800, only about 300 took to the field, as just 36 per cent were warriors, while the others were bearers, assistants, cooks and so on. This can be considered the case for most contigents at Sekigahara.

For example, Kimata's approximately 800-strong group was recorded by an Ii-clan scribe as consisting of:

10 generals or captains
80 inner guard samurai
30 mounted samurai with seven grooms each
50 foot samurai
30 matchlockmen
20 archers
30 assorted samurai
10 samurai with cross-headed spears
40 long spear-armed *ashigaru*
20 light-armed *ashigaru*
20 matchlock accessory bearers
20 arrow carriers
10 *sashimono* bearers
20 standard bearers
40 baggage porters
20 baggage handlers
10 medicine bearers
40 rain hat and cape bearers
80 armour stand and box bearers
20 *jinmaku* war camp labourers
40 lantern bearers
20 cooks
10 sandal bearers

As another source of reference, that of the Western forces' Otani Yoshitsugu, a mid-ranking *daimyo* with an income of 50,000 *koku* and with an army of just over 800, consisted of:

70 mounted samurai
30 foot archers
15 backup archers
150 matchlock-armed *ashigaru*
50 reserve gunners (secondary)
80 *ashigaru* spear men
10 banner bearers
40 non-mounted samurai
2 bow carriers
2 marchlock carriers
2 *naginata* carriers
6 armour bearers
8 standard bearers
4 accessory porters
2 rain hat and cape carriers
2 lunch box carriers
1 Buddhist priest (for the dead)
1 sandal bearer
6 horse handlers
3 horseshoe fitters
8 *ashigaru* inspectors/leaders
4 arrow box bearers
4 matchlock accessory attendants
56 horse grooms
46 attendants
56 horse-mounted samurai attendants
56 pack horse armour bearers
8 accessory box bearers
1 Chief of Staff
14 attendants for the Chief of Staff
2 banner handlers
3 *yari* (spear) caretakers
6 armed troop inspectors
40 sub inspectors
30 pack horses
30 pack horse handlers

This list suggests approximately 505 warriors, or around 63 per cent of Otani's 848 listed army, were active fighting men, more than double the recorded figures for Kimata's retinue, despite their similar size.

Confusion on the Field: 7:30 a.m.

Overlooking the battle site from Mount Sasao, the Western leader Ishida Mitsunari is popularly believed to have been dressed in a dark blue laced suit of armour under a blue and black *jinbaori* and topped with a most resplendent helmet featuring a prominent gold visor under a long shaggy black mane of yak hair. Conspicuous were the large, flat gold-leaf covered wooden horn-like flanges attached to either side of the helmet and standing tall above this ensemble.[1]

The cool, damp weather and the wearing of wet and heavy armour no doubt added to Mitsunari's nasal problems, which apparently caused him to habitually huff through his nose in an effort to clear it. This is said to have made people uncomfortable when reporting to him, as it seemed as though he was displaying continual dissatisfaction. Despite his undeniable abilities as a statesman and his administrative skills, his short temper and brashness when dealing with others were obviously major factors leading to his eventual downfall.

Now that the mist had cleared somewhat, Mitsunari commanded a fine view of both the East and West armies on the plain below and was expecting an easy victory. He had positioned his armies well, blocking the roads leading westwards to Osaka and with the Mori and other allies in the east on Mount Nangu and the Kobayakawa on Mount Matsuo to the south, his units were completely surrounding the Tokugawa troops in the valley.

This formation was seen as superior even in more modern times. During the early to mid-Meiji Period (1868–1912) a number of foreign experts were invited to become advisors to the Meiji Government in its efforts to rapidly modernise Japan that had been in isolation for 260 years of Tokugawa rule. These included industrialists, engineers, agricultural consultants and military strategists. According to the 1893 *Japanese Military History, Sekigahara Campaign* by the Japanese Armed Forces General Headquarters, when

---

1.   Despite this most popular image, there remains no evidence of such an armour ever existing and it is possible that this image was created based on similarly-designed extant armours also belonging to Ishida Mitsunari.

shown a map of the battle at Sekigahara, the military experts[2] noted that the Western army had created a very strong battle formation and went on to note that the *kakuyoku* or 'crane wing' formation was most intimidating. The forward troops constituted the body of the crane, while back-up samurai units would then fan out and sweep down, surrounding and enveloping the enemy like the downward beat of a crane's wing in flight. Viewing these maps of the battlefield and positions, the majority of these military experts stated that the Eastern army, being surrounded and with numerically inferior troops, must have lost the battle. They were no doubt surprised to discover that they were wrong and even more so when they heard the reasons why.

If Ishida Mitsunari did not see Ii Naomasa's initial advance, he certainly would have heard the great roar of gunfire and of men as the first wave of samurai swept across the sodden southern plains in three ranks. Having seen the flare fired by the Konishi units signifying the commencement of fighting, Mitsunari ordered a similar flare be launched from the Western forces' headquarters on Mount Sasao, officially starting the battle. Almost simultaneously, a smoke flare was shot into the hazy morning sky from the Eastern side's Kuroda camp, instructing the Eastern troops to commence action.

By this time, Fukushima Masanori's force had already begun to draw Western blood, taking the lead from the westernmost position of the Eastern forces they entered the killing zone closely followed by the troops of the Ii clan, then Todo Takatora and Kyogoku Takatomo who had been positioned at nearby Shibai and from their shadow, the then 37-year-old Terasawa Hirotaka who would distinguish himself in battle by dealing an early blow to the enemy Otani contingent. A grand strategy had not been properly formulated and even though each army was well trained, the battle quickly became something of an orderly free-for-all.

Immediately following the first rounds of gunfire between the Fukushima and Ukita forces came a great white cloud of gusmoke, as thick as the mist that had just cleared, and moving quickly through the smoke came ranks of Fukushima's *ashigaru* wielding long spears averaging around 4m in length

---

2.   The story often identifies the Prussian general, military strategist and Meiji government advisor Klemens Wilhelm Jacob Meckel (1842–1905) as being the military expret who viewed the formations and made the assumptions regarding the outcome, but this cannot be verified.

and held upright as they advanced. The *ashigaru* were followed by mounted samurai, supported by archers keeping up a volley of arrows. The narrow gap between the enemies' front lines quickly closed and having brought the long spears crashing down on the opposition, both sides then commenced ferocious hand-to-hand combat on the muddy rice fields across the central plains. The Fukushima matchlocks smashed away at the opposing Ukita soldiers, leading to heavy losses, although the Ukita soon regained control and fought back with devilish ferocity.

The violent fighting was close. Within the first 15 minutes, the battle seemed to bode well for the West with Fukushima Masanori and Ii Naomasa being driven back some 600m by the mass of counter-attacking Ukita troops. From there it seemed an even match as the Eastern forces again rallied and soon regained their lost ground, only to be forced back again shortly after.

Mounted samurai darted into the action armed with spears of various lengths, *naginata* and the frequently preferred razor-sharp *tachi* swords. The horses they rode were mostly the sturdy *Kisouma*, native horses that resembled stocky ponies rather than modern-day thoroughbreds. They were stub-faced, long-haired, short-legged, shaggy-looking creatures, their backs averaging about 1.20 to 1.40m in height. Despite this, they were quick and agile creatures.[3]

Some of the mounted samurai also sported large cloth capes on their backs. These *horo* were popular in the Kamakura period (1192–1333) and were originally a type of cape worn tied to the top and waist of the armour and opened at the sides allowing it to balloon out like a parachute when charging. Although the real reason for this device is lost to history, it is believed the *horo* served a number of functions, including catching arrows fired by the enemy, also, to intimidate an enemy, rather like a puffer-fish bloating itself for protection, as well as a form of identification on the battlefield. The *horo* could also have been an attempt to imitate the Gods of Wind and Thunder, who were often depicted with air-filled capes billowing out behind them. In later years, during the Sengoku period, use of the *horo* was revived and a frame of bamboo or whale baleen was used to hold it in shape.

---

3.   In tests performed by NHK in 2015, a *Kisouma* carrying a 62kg samurai equipped with around 30kg of armour and weapons was able to cover 100m in 12.03 seconds at full gallop. The smaller *Kisouma* also proved to be more agile and could perform tighter turns than a larger modern horse.

An important point to remember is that while Europeans would fight from horseback and Heian (794–1185) and early Kamakura (1185–1333) period samurai warfare also involved shooting arrows at the enemy from the saddle, warfare had changed dramatically over the years. Luis Frois (1532–97), a Portuguese Jesuit missionary to Japan, had noted that 'The Japanese ride into battle, dismount, then fight on foot'. Frois was to a degree correct, but then again, he had only witnessed samurai of the Chubu (central Japan) and Kansai (eastern Japan) regions and was not aware of the samurai of the Kanto (far eastern and northern Japan) regions, particularly those of the feared Takeda clan who had developed effective cavalry tactics. In some cases, mounted samurai fought by charging their horses at their opponent, often causing a collision that would unbalance or even injure the other's steed. In some instances, the horses were the first attacked in a charge rather than their riders, particularly when it came to a charge against ranks of spear, bow or matchlock-armed troops. They would first shoot at or spear the horse, which would in turn bring down the warrior too. However, the value of horses also meant that whenever possible, they would be taken alive to add to the stables of the victor.

Various techniques were developed for fighting against other mounted samurai. There were a number of ways of attacking, using polearms, swords, clubs and even hand-to-hand methods. For swordfighting, such approaches included positioning oneself on the left side of one's opponent. This was an obvious advantage when fighting on horseback, as it meant the average right-handed swordsman would be an easier kill, finding it more difficult to avoid and parry blows. Other techniques against horsemen would include spear practices not unlike the European knights, or grappling techniques almost akin to judo on horseback in an effort to pull the other from his horse.

Among the 6,000 men under the command of Fukushima Masanori was Kyoto-born Ono Harunaga (1569–4 June 1615). He too had long served Hideyoshi loyally as *Shuri Tayu*, or Minister for Structural Repairs, and had for some time been regarded with suspicion by Ieyasu due to his Toyotomi loyalties. In 1599, Ieyasu had Harunaga exiled to Yuki in Shimosa (Ibaraki Prefecture) for his role in a plan to assassinate him. Despite this, Ono Harunaga shared Fukushima Masanori's conviction that taking Ieyasu's side was essential for the survival of the Toyotomi family and this view shaped his decision to take up arms against the Western forces. Forgiven by Ieyasu for his actions and offered a position in the Eastern forces, Harunaga gratefully accepted.

In an effort to prove his loyalty to Ieyasu, Ono Harunaga fought brilliantly from the outset and led his men in numerous counter-attacks against the Ukita. Surprisingly, 15 years after Sekigahara, he would return to serve the Western loyalists during the Summer Siege of Osaka Castle where he acted as an advisor to Hideyoshi's widow. He was to perish at his own hand, defeated in battle in 1615 when Osaka finally fell to the Tokugawa.

Another of Fukushima Masanori's captains, the previously-mentioned Kani Saizo (1554–10 August 1613), was naturally among the first of his men to enter the fray, quickly dispatching a number of enemy warriors. He was an expert in the *Hozoin-Ryu* spear-fighting techniques, yet is depicted holding a *naginata* in four of the known surviving folding screens illustrating the Battle of Sekigahara (kept at the Gifu Sekigahara Battlefield Memorial Museum, the Gifu City Museum of History, Hikone Castle Museum and Fukuoka City Museum) and is easily identifiable by his stalk of green bamboo grass in place of *sashimono* carried on his back. The *naginata*, such as the one wielded by Saizo, is said to be amongst the most difficult of weapons to master. Similar to the European glaive, it consists of a pole with a curved, single-edged blade at the end. The advantages of the weapon include the fact that both the cutting end, the shaft and the shaft end could be used to block and strike, like a halberd. At an average 2.5m in length, the Naginata had greater reach than a sword and offered more striking power. It also allowed for cuts to be made to the lower legs, targets normally considered too low for swords.

Among the first with whom Kani Saizo clashed with in bloody hand-to-hand combat was a samurai under his direct opponent, the captain Akashi Takenori (also known as Teruzumi) who fought under the Ukita banner. He was an expert in matchlock tactics, hence being in the Ukita front line. The veteran Saizo charged into battle alongside the Fukushima forces' leading spearmen and challenged this first enemy while the gunner was reloading, swinging his *naginata* in well-controlled arcs. The closeness of this battle and the numbers of men fighting in such limited space, would have hindered usual mobility greatly. The opposing samurai would have attempted to keep his distance, using a spear, sword or *naginata* to block and parry while the *naginata* wielder would seek an opportunity to get within the striking distance of the slender weapon. The fight continued in this manner for some moments before Saizo's blade found its mark. Akashi Takenori fell wounded and Saizo quickly moved in for the kill. Having dispatched the man and cut off his head, the blood-spattered Kani Saizo moved on to his next victim.

The taking of heads in battle was a custom by which a samurai could distinguish himself. Once an enemy was defeated he was decapitated. Mounted samurai hung trophy heads from the left side of the saddle before bringing them back to camp where the head was then cleaned, perfumed and mounted for inspection and registration. Powdered rice was used to mop up and stop any blood or other fluids leaking from the head. For lower-ranked samurai, thick *washi* paper or even dried leaves and dirt would suffice. Women specially trained in the art of arranging the heads were employed for this gruesome task. Unafraid of freshly decapitated heads and used to the sight and smell of blood, these women would also blacken the teeth of any head upon order. Only the nobility could afford to have their teeth blackened with betel nut in life and so to increase the perceived value of a head, those with white teeth were sometimes inked to make them appear of higher rank.

Registration of a head taken in battle involved writing the details on a folded piece of strong *sugiharagami* paper. On it was recorded the day, date and time of taking, as well as the name of the battle. Beside that in thick letters but in a light ink was the name and rank of the deceased, along with any known family history. The name of the victor was then recorded in dark ink, but with narrowly-written characters. Following that, details such as the type of weapon used and even the brand or blacksmith's name were written down.

Fukushima's captain Kani Saizo left many of his victim's heads on the battlefield, not wanting to miss even a moment of the action and excitement of the fight. Other lesser samurai sometimes took advantage of finding a head on the ground and a number were taken back to camp with the finder claiming it as his own kill. These unscrupulous soldiers were later to be disgraced, however, as the clever Saizo had not just left the heads on the ground, but had hidden his 'calling card', a rolled-up bamboo leaf taken from his unorthodox *sashimono* , in the ear, nose or throat cavity. When it came time to inspect the heads, Saizo claimed to have taken over twenty heads, but a few appear to have been misplaced. All the same, he was found to have taken a record seventeen enemy heads at Sekigahara alone.

During a battle, if a samurai found himself too 'busy' to take the head, or if his assistants had already left the field with other heads, cutting off the upper lip and nose together was also acceptable. Then, after the battle had ended and after reuniting the pieces like a macabre jigsaw puzzle, the head could be properly cut off or reclaimed. For reasons unknown, although possibly because it was bereft of a moustache, any heads missing the lip and nose were known as *onnakubi*, or 'women's heads'.

Bloodbath Below Mount Sasao: 8:15 a.m.

Kuroda Nagamasa and Takenaka Shigekado had positioned themselves less than a kilometre directly east of the spiked wooden palisades that had been hastily set up around Mount Sasao by Mitsunari's troops the night before. With a burning desire to present Mitsunari's head on a spike to Ieyasu, Nagamasa and his allies had planned their moves from their northernmost position on the front line, a camp marked out by the tall dark blue banners bearing Kuroda's swirling wisteria-like crest at the top.

Kuroda Nagamasa had long been associated with the Toyotomi. Like many others formerly loyal to Hideyoshi's cause, it was not so much that they had turned traitor, but rather it was their intense dislike of Mitsunari that put them on the side of the Tokugawa. As Inspector General in the Korean campaign, Mitsunari had at one time come to oversee Nagamasa's army. Nagamasa was, at the time, midway through concentrating on a game of *Go* (a type of Japanese checkers) and had kept Mitsunari waiting for a moment. Mitsunari in turn relayed this perceived disrespect directly to Hideyoshi, complaining that Nagamasa was more interested in playing board games than achieving success on the field. For that, Nagamasa was severely reprimanded by Hideyoshi.

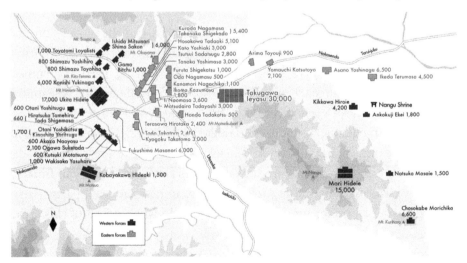

The Battle of Sekigahara, 8 a.m. 21 October 1600.

The 32-year-old veteran Nagamasa[4] never forgot the reprimand, nor forgave the man who had been the cause of it. Now Nagamasa looked out over his assembled force, over the war flags marking out his territory and over the hundreds of front-line *ashigaru*, all armed with 5m-long spears and smouldering matchlocks. His gaze then drifted across the hazy hillside to Mitsunari's place of command, Mount Sasao.

At about 8:30 a.m., the long, mournful wail from a *horagai* conch-shell horn and the tinny clanging of war gongs signalled the start of the joint attack by the 5,400 samurai under Kuroda Nagamasa, including those of 27-year-old Takenaka Shigekado. Until the night before the battle, Shigekado had been a member of the Western loyalists and was holding out in Inuyama Castle. Relying on his gut feeling that the West would lose at Sekigahara, Shigekado defected to the East with his remaining 100 samurai. Being very familiar with the Sekigahara region, he offered his services to Kuroda Nagamasa.

Takenaka Shigekado was much indebted to the Western cause. His father had died while he was still an infant and it was Toyotomi Hideyoshi who had brought the boy up. At the age of 16, Hideyoshi had given Shigekado the fief of Tango with a stipend of 6,000 *koku*. Later he was awarded lands in Mino, where his father had hailed from, and so at the time of Sekigahara the battlefield was part of his domain. His sudden defection came as a surprise to the other *daimyo* under Ishida Mitsunari. It was Takenaka Shigekado who suggested that Nagamasa set his camp and defence line along the steep sloped hills above the River Ai.

On the other side of the Ai, to the south and just to the left of Kuroda Nagamasa's forces, ready to charge at a moment's notice, was the contingent of 5,100 belonging to Hosokawa Tadaoki. Having fired the smoke flares announcing the start of the battle some 25 minutes ago, Nagamasa had wanted to move even earlier, but harboured initial concerns over the Hosokawas' intentions, as the senior-ranked Hosokawa Tadaoki had made no signs of commencing the attack. Tadaoki was looking towards the Kuroda camp above him, watching Kuroda Nagamasa's confused hesitation. In fact, Hosokawa Tadaoki was waiting for Nagamasa to take the lead, particularly as Nagamasa had under him Takenaka Shigekado who, as lord of this area,

---

4.   Kuroda Nagamasa wore a notable helmet known as an *Ichinodani kabuto*, the shape of which was supposed to represent the cliffs of Ichinodani where a major battle was fought between the Minamoto and Taira clans in 1184.

should have been afforded the honour of being the first into battle. When that misunderstanding was finally cleared up, Nagamasa's voice could be heard repeatedly screaming '*Kakare!*' 'Attack'!, the barrage finally commenced and with Kuroda Nagamasa and Takenaka Shigekado in the lead, Hosokawa Tadaoki soon followed and the bloodbath below Mount Sasao began.

Close on the heels of Hosokawa Tadaoki, Kato Yoshiaki's 3,000 troops sent up their war cry. Known as one of the 'Seven Spears of Shizugatake', Yoshiaki[5] was one of the bravest of fighters. Leading his men on a bee-line for the Western headquarters, the Kato army pounded away at the forces of Gamo Bitchu guarding the lower slopes.

As per the standard formation of troops, the front-line *ashigaru* spearmen were sent in right behind Yoshiaki's famed crack matchlockmen under the command of Ban Danemon, supported by a unit of archers to maintain the volley of covering fire while the gunners reloaded. However, the matchlock corps' efficiency was fast quelled by the fact that they were soon left leaderless: it was not that Ban Danemon had been killed, but that in all the excitement and in an effort to gain personal glory, he had grabbed a spear and run off alone into the thick of the battle, leaving his *teppotai*, marksmen unit, without a captain.

His abandonment of the marksmen rendered them temporarily virtually impotent and caused great confusion amongst the Kato ranks, leaving them vulnerable, a situation which greatly angered Yoshiaki. After the Battle of Sekigahara, Danemon was called before his lord and severely reprimanded. Not liking his terms of punishment, he ran away from Kato Yoshiaki's castle, but not before writing a letter and posting it to the castle gates. It read: 'I, Ban Danemon, a hero of the Sekigahara campaign, hereby resign myself from the employ of the fool Lord Kato, who failed to distinguish himself in the great battle because he lacked leadership qualities.'

Ban Danemon was a heavy drinker, often getting into fights and being fired. Under Kato Yoshiaki, he was awarded the post of captain of the arquebusiers. After Sekigahara, he joined the army of Kobayakawa Hideaki and then, upon the unexpected death of that young lord, the forces of Matsudaira Tadayoshi. When Tadayoshi passed away in 1607, Danemon secured a

---

5. Kato Yoshiaki's helmet at Sekigahara was conical with thin triangular fins protruding from either side. The effect was supposed to represent a silhouette of Mount Fuji, but more closely a squid's head.

position among the followers of Fukushima Masanori. When Kato Yoshiaki discovered Danemon was working for Masanori, he asked for the decapitated head of his former captain. Danemon somehow escaped the death penalty and at the Winter Siege of Osaka in 1614, he achieved renown on the night of 2 February. The story goes that at 2 a.m. he took his small band of twenty men and made a surprise attack on the camp of Hachisuka Yoshishige, taking the head of a high-ranking general while he slept. Danemon was richly rewarded for his efforts and had souvenir wooden plaques on which his name was inscribed distributed to remind people of his heroic deeds.

The following year, 1615, during the Summer Campaign at Osaka Castle, he had been promoted and was in command of a force of 3,000 men. Stationed beside the troops of one Okabe Noritsuna, Danemon was horrified to see the Okabe troops pull out one morning and begin an advance before he was able to rouse his men. In an effort to be the first into battle, Danemon ran ahead alone, caught up with Okabe, challenged his ally to a fight, physically beat the man and then ran ahead to be the first to engage the enemy. Having left his 3,000 troops behind, the maverick Ban Danemon then faced the countless enemy alone and was soon overwhelmed and killed instantly.

Also making efforts against the north-western flank of Mount Sasao were the Kuroda troops. One among Kuroda Nagamasa's captains was a mounted samurai named Goto (Mototsugu) Matabei (5 May 1565–2 June 1615). It was said that Matabei was born ready to fight. He was a much-respected professional warrior who often proudly boasted of the fifty-three scars on various parts of his body, trophies of the many wars in which he had participated.

Ohashi Kamon was Goto Matabei's counterpart under the Western leader Ishida Mitsunari. Kamon competently wielded a long spear, topped with a large, vicious-looking cross-shaped head. Having found each other among the masses on the field below Sasao, the two horse-mounted captains clashed vigorously. Charging like jousting European knights, the two galloped at each other in their first melee, Kamon swinging his polearm in a sweeping arc, only to have it countered by Matabei's blade. Turning, Ohashi Kamon swung once more, though yet again the blow was parried. Surrounded by a sea of yelling, screaming, fighting, dying men, the two continued to manoeuvre their mounts until Matabei could get close enough to render the polearm ineffective. Repeatedly striking Kamon, he knocked him from his horse and with the wounded Kamon down, quickly dismounted and pouncing on the injured man, dispatched him with a slash across the throat with a short sword and then cleanly severed his head. With blood surging from the gaping throat, Goto Matabei handed the bloodied head to one of his followers to register, clean and prepare for later inspection, remounted his horse and continued to lead the remainder of his command through the rest of the battle.[6]

Meanwhile, Ii Naomasa and Matsudaira Tadayoshi had left Fukushima to continue to fight the Ukita and noticed that while the Western forces headquarters was now under a fierce attack from the Kuroda, Hosokawa, Kato and Kanemori forces and the Western allies to the south were being assaulted by the Eastern forces, there was no one facing the Shimazu army in the very middle. Working their way west, north-west from their initial encampment, they halted mid-field, stopping right in front of the Shimazu, and watched and waited.

While the Ii moved to a north-westerly position to face the Kyushu samurai of the Shimazu, Tsutsui Sadatsugu, the Lord of Ueno Castle in Iga (present-day Mie Prefecture) was working his way south. Tsutsui Sadatsugu had accompanied Ieyasu in his campaign against Uesugi Kagekatsu in Aizu and had arrived back from the northern districts just in time to join his lord at Sekigahara. On this day, he was to again distinguish himself, leading his contingent of 2,850 across the battlefield, directly through the masses engaged in fierce fighting below Mount Sasao, to a position where he could assist Fukushima Masanori's troops in their push against the Ukita. After achieving this objective he returned to Mount Sasao with his troops, reinforcing the front lines and coming to the aid of Kuroda Nagamasa, Hosokawa Tadaoki and the others who were being forced back. However, before they could get to Mitsunari, Tsutsui and his men had to first overcome the superior fighting forces of Shima Sakon and Gamo Bitchu.[7]

6.　Goto Matabei was another of the samurai fighting under Tokugawa colours that day who would later side with Toyotomi Hideyori in Osaka. He was shot while fighting against Date Masamune's troops in the Summer Battle of Osaka in 1615 and, unable to stand let alone continue to fight, committed *seppuku*. Matabei's armour survives and is on display in the keep of the National Treasure-designated Matsue Castle.

7.　Despite his fine efforts on this day and his closeness to Ieyasu, Tsutsui Sadatsugu would be dispossessed eight years later on the grounds of poor governance and was finally ordered to commit *seppuku* in 1615.

The Fury of War

Fluttering in the wind below Mount Sasao were the tall black and white flags bearing the inscription '*Oni kodomo haha, zenshin jura*', an ancient invocation to the god of war Hachiman and amongst various geometric designs, at the lower extreme, a three-leaf crest. This was the crest and slogan used by Shima Sakon, regarded as a key ally and chief strategist to Mitsunari's force. It was Sakon who had orchestrated the successful sneak attack on the Eastern forces at Ogaki just days before. His army was based at the foot of Mount Sasao below Mitsunari's main position and, from Mitsunari's point of view, to the left of another trusted ally, Gamo Bitchu.

Shima Sakon was dressed in a simple *okegawa do*, a barrel-shaped torso armour made of horizontal steel plates, cross-laced together and worn under a sleeveless dark green *jinbaori*. His *kabuto* featured a red-lacquered, wooden elongated horseshoe-shaped, horn-like device known as a 'Focus of Heaven' crest, standing some 3 *shaku*, or about 99cm, high from the brow. Sakon's wife was from a medical family and she and their sons are said to have set up a rudimentary field hospital to the rear the western base on Mount Sasao.

Sakon's troops waiting behind the hastily-built log palisades numbered just 1,000 and in confronting Mitsunari's army bore the brunt of the Eastern matchlock fire backed by some 3,000 soldiers. Unlike some commanders who led from a safer position behind their troops, the gallant Sakon personally led his men into the monstrous fight against the overwhelming numbers of samurai under Kuroda Nagamasa and Hosokawa Tadaoki.

Despite the great efforts of both the Kato, Kuroda and the Hosokawa forces, one amongst their numbers appears to have been uninterested in combat and was more a spectator to the bloody fighting around the base of Mount Sasao: Tanaka Yoshimasa. Yoshimasa was a veteran samurai and had long been a friend of Ishida Mitsunari. He was indebted to Mitsunari for a number of reasons and as such, was hesitant to make an attack on his mentor. On this occasion he decided that rather than dying, it would be better to simply watch the younger, less experienced generals, Kuroda and Hosokawa, battle Shima Sakon, a man he knew to be a better strategist and a fierce fighter.

Tanaka Yoshimasa had quickly realised that the huge army on Mount Nangu loyal to the Toyotomi were not moving and that although the Western forces were superior in number, fewer than expected were actually participating in the battle. This, he deduced, lessened his obligation to enter the fray and it was this rationale that temporarily kept a formidable force from fighting, allowing Shima Sakon's samurai some respite.

Meanwhile, Kuroda Nagamasa and Hosokawa Tadaoki struck time and again only to be repelled by the powerful samurai guarding the Western headquarters. During one such melee Nagamasa met with Tadaoki and is said to have expressed his fears of losing to Sakon.

'We are both doing our best, but to no avail', Nagamasa explained. 'Shima Sakon is too strong an enemy. After the battle, I will tell Lord Ieyasu that the Hosokawa did their best if you can promise to tell our lord that the Kuroda fought well too'.

Hosokawa Tadaoki answered angrily 'We haven't lost yet, what a foolish thing to think! Try harder!' And with that he let loose a terrifying war cry of 'Ei! Ei! Ei!', to which his surrounding subordinates responded with a deep rousing 'Ooooh!' and returned to the thick of the battle. Kuroda Nagamasa followed suit, but both armies were soon forced to retreat once again back to near their original starting lines. This fierce fighting continued for around four more hours and at the end of the day, Hosokawa Tadaoki would be able to present to his master with over 130 enemy heads taken by his men.

Various war cries were used at battles such as Sekigahara. The often heard 'Ei! Ei! Ei!', three times from a commander, was an order for everyone to move out immediately. 'Ei' was a general call asking for readiness to fight, with the responding 'Oooh' an affirmative answer. Other rallying calls of 'Ei Tou Ei!', 'Ei Oh! Ei Oh!', and 'Eiya! Eiya!' would have been heard across the battlefield from the various warlords.

In the case of Shima Sakon, each repeated yell of 'Ei!' commanded his foot soldiers to take a single step forward in unison. After the battle Kuroda Nagamasa and his comrades talked about the psychological effect it had on both sides and remembered the intimidating ferociousness in Sakon's voice, how it boomed across the field as his troops advanced, slowly, robotically and menacingly.

Displaying a banner that proclaimed him a follower of the Nichiren sect of Buddhism, Shima Sakon entered the fray with gusto time and again in the course of the early morning's skirmishes. During such action, Sakon was caught in the sights of at least three of the 100 matchlockmen under the command of the masked Suga Rokunosuke. Suga wore a white kerchief around his face at all times to cover a missing lip, the result of having been shot in the face and disfigured by a poisoned arrow during the Korean campaign.

The Suga matchlockmen took aim and on the command of '*Utte!*' blasted at the advancing figures.

Being in the forefront meant the mounted Sakon was an easy target. While galloping into action, Sakon and his horse suddenly tumbled forward and ploughed into the muddied field, the rider rolling to a stop not far from his terror-stricken steed. The Shima samurai were horrified to see their lord felled by the gunfire. Two bullets had caught Sakon – one smashed into his left elbow and another entered his chest on the far left, while a third lead ball sank into his horse's front leg, dropping man and beast alike. One of the shots was attributed to Kan Rokunosuke, a samurai in the employ of Kuroda Nagamasa. Sakon's leading captains quickly seized control of the situation, rallying his men to advance with even greater fury. Badly wounded, Shima Sakon was forced to temporarily retire from the battlefield and was carried back to his main camp by two of his closest followers, one of whom seems to have been his son, according to the scene as depicted in a surviving screen painting of the event.

News of Sakon having been shot just 90 minutes after hostilities broke out quickly spread throughout the Western armies. Sakon was a popular and trusted general and his temporary departure from the field had a damaging effect on Western morale. A popular saying at the time was that both 'Shima Sakon and Sawayama Castle [Mitsunari's fief] were wasted on Ishida Mitsunari!' Mitsunari had noted Sakon's past influence on his allies and recognised the tactician's importance: in fact, Mitsunari had lured Sakon out of retirement by offering the man half of his own personal income to retain his services and so Mitsunari must have felt the great general's wounding as if it were his own.

Hour of the Dragon: 9 a.m.

By all accounts Hosokawa Tadaoki was like his father, Yusai, a man of letters and poems, an able practitioner of the tea ceremony having studied under the great tea master Sen no Rikyu, as well as a renowned warrior and administrator. For someone so well versed in gentle affairs, Tadaoki was also known to have had a fierce temper. This temper was no doubt further fuelled by a desire to avenge the premature death of his wife, Gracia, due to Mitsunari's vile actions in Osaka and the fact that his father remained besieged in Tanabe Castle by Western allies. The Hosokawa units would continue to strike hard at the Western base over the first few hours, slowly but surely eroding its defences' effectiveness.

Meanwhile, Oda Yuraku and his son Nagataka, together with Terazawa Hirotaka, Togawa Michiyasu and his followers had commenced their clash with the armies of Konishi Yukinaga's Eastern forces, repeatedly inflicting great damage as they went. Oda Yuraku, younger brother of the warlord Oda Nobunaga, was regarded as a weak samurai, more attuned to the world of the teacup than the world of weapons, yet his performance at Sekigahara would greatly elevate his standing in military circles.

At about this time, approximately 9 a.m., Mitsunari is thought to have put into use the five cannon he had specially ordered from a blacksmith from Kunitomo-Mura in Omi, not far from his hometown in Nagahama. Cannon in this age were primarily used against castles and ships at sea and not in pitched battles. Years earlier, Oda Nobunaga had been interested in cannon for use in the field, while Toyotomi Hideyoshi, citing the difficulty in transporting the heavy guns, had little interest. Mitsunari himself had seen first-hand the devastating force a cannon could inflict when the Koreans had used them most effectively against the invading Japanese just two years earlier.

The 1m-long cannon used at Sekigahara weighed in at around 80kg apiece and were mounted not on wheeled carriages but on wooden stands and were situated high on Mount Sasao, just in front of the small hut that marked Mitsunari's HQ. About two *shaku*, or approximately 400g, of gunpowder was poured into the mouth of each one. An *ashigaru* would then load a large 4kg shot into it, ram it home and then insert fifty to sixty small stones and assorted small shot wrapped in thin paper. When used on the enemy it caused great damage and confusion, particularly as the cannon had a range of about 2km.

Within range of those guns, 2km south-east of Mount Sasao, was where Honda Tadakatsu had set up his command post. Among the most easily identifiable characters centre-stage at Sekigahara, Tadakatsu was a veteran of the Tokugawa forces and a more than able samurai. He had assisted Ieyasu in all his campaigns, including the defeat at Mikatagahara by the feared Takeda near Hamamatsu and at Nagakute on the outskirts of modern-day Nagoya City, more than proving his merit time and again. Tadakatsu wore a standard *nuinobe-do* style suit of dark blue laced, black-lacquered armour with a string of large wooden Buddhist prayer beads slung across his chest. His armour is said to have been made partially from dried raw leather in place of the usual steel scales, lessening the weight, but lacquered to make it both as strong as and indistinguishable from the steel armour of his companions. Armed with the traditional pair of swords, he also carried his favourite spear, known as the 'Dragonfly Cutter'.[8] However, what made him stand out most of all was his distinctive *kabuto*, with large, thick antlers resembling those of a stag rising from the top of the crown rather like a stereotypical Viking. His *maedate*, the crest-like motif fronting a samurai's helmet, was that of a big-eared, horned and grinning devil face. The large antlers he sported on his helmet were something he is said to have adopted following the defeat of the once-powerful Imagawa clan at the Battle of Okehazama in 1560, when he led his lord, the young Ieyasu, back to his ancestral home in Okazaki. Their desperate escape was thwarted by a rain-swollen river they had to cross. While searching for a way across, Tadakatsu witnessed a stag ford the shallower section of the river. Seeing this as an auspicious sign and recognising that as the deer had led them to safety, just as it was his destiny to lead his liege, he adopted the stags' antlers as part of his armour.

Initially, Honda Tadakatsu had positioned himself to be able to watch the actions of the and other former Toyotomi retainers ahead of him, as well as the forces atop Mount Nangu behind him to the east. About two hours after the conflict had begun and assured that the Fukushima were indeed fighting to the best of their abilities against the Western units and that those on Nangu were staying still, Tadakatsu could be seen steering his men across the battlefield in a northerly direction in an attempt to attack Mitsunari on Mount Sasao, nipping in between a number of advancing allies and enemies alike, all the while participating in their skirmishes in the process. Surprisingly for a lord of such rank and importance, Honda Tadakatsu commanded just 500 men on the battlefield at Sekigahara.

Tokugawa Ieyasu had expected the battle to end within two hours of the first action, but the Western forces were fighting back harder than expected and this was irritating the normally patient Ieyasu. By about 10:30, he felt his current command post on Mount Momokubari was too far behind the lines and so was determined to advance as a means of spurring on his own allies further, while psychologically upsetting Mitsunari's side. Ieyasu was confident enough to order the bulk of his samurai to advance to just outside

---

8.   Honda Tadakatsu's treasured spear was so named as it was said to be so sharp that a dragonfly that landed on the tip supposedly cut itself in two.

of the village of Sekigahara. This area, now preserved as a small grassed reserve beside the Sekigahara Museum, is even now referred to as *Jinbano* or 'War Campsite Field' in memory of Ieyasu having moved his HQ there.

Battle Behind the Lines: 10 a.m.

From early that morning, the Western forces of the Mori on Mount Nangu were being watched by the Eastern-allied Yamauchi Katsutoyo and Arima Toyouchi, both situated far behind the lines along the Nakasendo route between the villages of Sekigahara and Tarui. These two armies were now called upon to join the front-line forces, leaving Asano Yukinaga with his 6,510 samurai and Ikeda Terumasa's 4,560 on either side of Tarui Village to monitor the Western battalions posing a threat to the rear of the Eastern forces.

Asano Yukinaga then rallied his Eastern troops and led them in a direct assault on the 1,500-strong army of Natsuka Masaie. The Natsuka spearmen formed the front rank but were nearly decimated by volley after volley of matchlock fire and supporting archery from the approaching Asano. The Asano samurai continued to push forward, carving deep into the Natsuka lines. Matsuda Hidenobu was a warrior under Natsuka Masaie whose preferred weapon was the *Oo-kumade*, a large, pole-mounted steel rake, rather like the large amulet bamboo rakes sold at Shinto shrines on New Year's Day. At Sekigahara, Hidenobu used this rake to reap in the enemy and pull Asano-clan samurai off their horses, allowing his retainers to behead them. Together they took eleven heads during the battle.

Meanwhile, Mori Hidemoto remained high atop Mount Nangu, Ankokuji Ekei was on the lower slopes and on the south-eastern side was Chosokabe Morichika. These Western commanders looked on idly as the samurai of Natsuka Masaie were being battered by the Asano troops. Natsuka Masaie must have then wondered why the others weren't coming to his aid; why wasn't Kikkawa Hiroie leading a counter-attack against the Asano forces?

Without Kikkawa Hiroie taking the lead, the others would never find the courage to confront Asano's men. Hiroie, in his effort to protect his clan, would not break his promise to Ieyasu and risk the destruction of the Mori. Earlier, when the sound of the main battle had risen to such a level it could be heard even on the eastern slopes of Mount Nangu, the statesman priest Ankokuji Ekei, who had done much to bring many of the Western leaders together, had gone across to Mori Hidemoto and with uncharacteristic bravery asked 'Are we not going to enter the fight?' He was told to wait for Kikkawa's command.

Later, a messenger arrived from Mount Sasao asking the same question of the Kikkawa and Mori forces, 'Are you going to fight?'

'Not right now', Kikkawa Hiroie answered brusquely, 'The men are having their lunch'. The same messenger returned sometime later with the same question and received the same reply from Hiroie. 'When my men have finished their lunch!' Later again the same situation occurred, with the same answer supplied and so Mitsunari, like the others, waited for Kikkawa Hiroie to lead the defence, but he remained inactive. It appears that his men, and indeed the large numbers of other warriors atop Mount Nangu, enjoyed a long lunch that day.

Back at centre stage, on the Western side of the valley, the Ukita were continuing to face a strong contingent of samurai under the banners of Fukushima Masanori with quantifiable success. A large company of Fukushima samurai had first formed into ranks, with the matchlockmen in front. Running some 300m towards the Otani camp, they stopped within effective range and opened fire. Otani Yoshitsugu had sent large numbers of his men to assist those further down the slopes from their base on Mount Tenman. As they entered the battle zone, they too were again assailed by the massed forces of Todo Takatora and Kyogoku Takatomo, who had moved into position from behind Fukushima. These units then formed a wedge between the Otani and Ukita, reaching as deep as the base of mountains. The hand-picked front-line samurai had been well trained. Stepping over the bodies of their fallen comrades, they launched a vigorous counter-attack. The Ukita response was to send forward ranks of spearmen who formed lines of the intimidating *yaribusuma* formation and, slowly shunting forward, were able to temporarily repel the 5,500 eager Fukushima samurai. As the Ukita advanced around 200m, Terasawa Hirotaka saw an opening and came at them from their flank. The violent attack was a devastating blow and the disruption to the Ukitas' advance allowed Fukushima's samurai to recover and regain lost ground.

According to a Battle of Sekigahara manuscript researched, penned and presented to Ieyasu in 1601 by Ota Gyuichi, better known as a close vassal of Oda Nobunaga and the author of the *Shincho Koki*, the 'Chronicles of Lord Nobunaga', 'Such was the amount of continual gunfire that the noise was louder than thunder. Arrows filled the sky and by around 10am, the smoke from the guns had blotted out the sunlight, making the area dark.'

The Kobayakawa Dilemma: approx. 10:30 a.m.

The Western army had just over 80,000 troops on the field, but only around 35,000 were actually fighting. Ishida Mitsunari had noted how well Ukita Hideie's troops were holding up despite the aggression of Fukushima Masanori's forces. Otani Yoshitsugu too appeared to be gaining ground and so now, especially with Ieyasu advancing to the middle of the valley, he thought, would be a good time to bring in a little extra help. He ordered flares to be fired, a signal that was to bring the 8,000 Kobayakawa troops streaming down from high on Mount Matsuo onto the Eastern army. The flares were fired, but not one of the Kobayakawa men moved.

Having seen the signal flares and noting the reluctance of the Kobayakawa to enter the battle, both Otani Yoshitsugu and Konishi Yukinaga sent messengers ordering Kobayakawa Hideaki to advance his troops into the fray, but each messenger returned with a non-committal reply. This intrigued Yoshitsugu, who then sent word to his forward flanks to prepare for the possible turning of the young lord Kobayakawa stationed high on the mountain to his right.

Kobayakawa Hideaki was not the only one failing to enter the battle. Shimazu Yoshihiro had remained idle in his central position as well, refusing all orders to advance – not even the attacking enemy could get him to move. Mitsunari had sent numerous messages ordering the Shimazu men into action but to no avail. His retainer Yasojima Sukezaemon was dispatched to the Shimazu camp to see what the problem was. Sukezaemon knelt before Toyohisa first, who dismissed him with a wave of his hand, informing him that all was understood, yet still no action was taken.

Mitsunari sent Yasojima Sukezaemon back a second time and then a third, each time requesting Shimazu Yoshihiro order his men into action. Finally he was told by the elder Shimazu that he refused to fight on behalf of Mitsunari. Mitsunari was both shocked and angered when he heard this and so he sent the messenger back a fourth time demanding that the Shimazu fight.

Pulling up to the Shimazu camp this time, the messenger in his haste failed to dismount before delivering his missive. Shimazu Yoshihiro, seated in his curtained-off camp and further insulted by the lack of protocol, quickly rose to his feet and, knocking over his stool, drew his sword and brandished it at the now frightened Yasojima Sukezaemon. 'Get off your horse before you dare address me!' roared Shimazu. Fearing for his life, Sukezaemon turned his steed and fled back to Mitsunari.

Such a breach of etiquette was considered quite rare, although two similar occurrences have been chronicled from the day of fighting at Sekigahara. In one instance, according to the *Keichoki*[9] diaries' *Keicho Gunsho* volume, Ieyasu drew his sword and threatened to cut at the legs of one of his own men, one Nonomura Shiroemon, who in the excitement had mounted his horse before his lord. While Shiroemon escaped injury, the same diary also mentions that Ieyasu had become so frustrated at that stage, that he instead turned and swung his *tachi*, the blade cutting cleanly through the wooden pole of a nearby battle flag held by his vassal, Monna Chosaburo. Another similar incident occurred when Ieyasu sent a messenger, Yamagami Goemon, to Kuroda Nagamasa's site to enquire as to whether the Kobayakawa would come to the East's defence or not. Nagamasa had been instrumental in organising the young lord's promised betrayal of the West, but as their positions were now separated by quite a distance, communication had been lost. Entering the camp, the messenger called Nagamasa not by his personal name, but by that of his fief, Koshu. What's more, Yamagami failed to alight from his horse when he addressed the lord. Outraged by this insolence, Nagamasa replied coldly that he knew as much as anybody and that if Kobayakawa refused to come through as promised, then he, Kuroda Nagamasa, would just have to cut him down too.

It was just before 11 a.m. when Mitsunari's messenger to the Shimazu camp returned for the fourth time, again empty-handed though bearing the

9.   Compiled in late 1615, the *Keichoki*, also known as the *Keicho Gunsho* and the *Keichoshu*, is a 52-volume manuscript and a valuable historical source for the Keicho period (Keicho is a Japanese Imperial era name, being from 27 October 1596 to July 1615) in which the Battle of Sekigahara and the two Sieges of Osaka were fought and the establishment of the Edo Shogunate took place. By traditional reckoning, the Battle of Sekigahara was fought on the 15th day of the 9th month, 5th year of the Keicho period. Many modern Japanese to this day make the mistake of remembering the battle as having taken place on 15 September, as they are usually taught the old lunar calendar and Imperial name-era dates in their history lessons.

additional tale of Shimazu's threats. Mitsunari himself then took the great risk of leaving his hilltop base and, making his way behind the front lines, rode the short distance over to Shimazu's camp to remonstrate with the 65-year-old Kyushu *daimyo*. Shimazu Yoshihiro bluntly responded that, 'In times of war, each commander has to fight his own battle and not be concerned with the actions of others', and that he was merely waiting for his opportunity. 'Besides', he added contemptuously, 'there have been too many unpleasant dealings between us, I won't fight for the likes of you!' Mitsunari returned to Mount Sasao greatly disappointed, though when he told the injured Shima Sakon of the situation, the great tactician showed little surprise. Sakon was well aware of Mitsunari's unpopularity and of the resentment felt by many of his allied *daimyo* in regards to Mitsunari being in control of the Western forces. Indeed, Tokugawa Ieyasu had been correct in allowing Mitsunari to live after his assassination attempt some months earlier.

The Hour of the Serpent: 11 a.m.

At just before 11 a.m., the Ukita army had successfully regrouped and responded to the continual arquebus fire from the Fukushima ranks by launching an even more powerful thrust, forcing the Fukushima troops to retreat almost 600m from their starting point. Enter Tsutsui Sadatsugu and his 2,800 troops, who came to the withdrawing army's assistance. Sadatsugu led his force across the path of Konishi Yukinaga and into the Ukita flank. This allowed some breathing space for Fukushima Masanori who had been fighting non-stop and who had already lost a large number of his original 6,000 men.

One of the noted warriors amongst the many in Fukushima Masanori's army was Kosaka Katsumasa.[10] His golden *kirisaki* crest of three paulownia leaves and *sashimono* banner stood out as being one of the more coourful on the battlefield that day. Armed with his preferred spear of nine *shaku* (approximately 2.7m), the mounted Katsumasa had sustained numerous thigh

---

10. After Sekigahara, Kosaka Katsumasa was awarded 1,000 *koku* by Ieyasu for his valour. However, two years after the battle, at a veterans' reunion held in Kiyosu Castle, it was discovered that the bulk of Katsumasa's exploits were largely due to the initiative and leadership displayed by his friend and saviour Ikoma Hayato. In shame, Katsumasa quit the life of the warrior and retired to live out his days as a humble farmer.

injuries from the spears of enemy foot soldiers. In his weakened state, he was attacked yet again, only this time he toppled from his horse with a crash. His attacker quickly pounced on him and prepared to take Katsumasa's head. Ikoma Hayato, a friend of Kosaka Katsumasa, had seen his comrade fall and came to the rescue, promptly slaying Katsumasa's would-be killer. Kosaka Katsumasa was helped back onto his horse and the two returned to the battle side by side. Katsumasa's younger brother took two heads, while another of his retainers, Maeno Kiyozo, claimed another one over the next half-hour of bloody fighting.

During the third hour of the battle, Honda Tadakatsu and Togawa Michiyasu, in their quest to strike at Mitsunari's flank, were still working their way north between enemy and ally alike when they came across a division of troops under the command of Konishi Yukinaga. Honda Tadakatsu's small army broadsided the Western fighters, by now near exhaustion, engaging them on the bloodied field where Konishi had first set up his standards and banners.

The smaller Honda force was well trained and Tadakatsu's brilliance as a tactician shone through in field battles like this. He was a veteran of over fifty-five battles and even though he had been in the thick of each and every one, had come through completely unscathed. Ieyasu, in recognising his extraordinary abilities, had even called him a reincarnation of the *Hachiman Dai Bosatsu*, the God of War. Such was his reputation that there was a saying that went; 'There are only two things above Tokugawa Ieyasu, – his helmet and Honda Tadakatsu'. Tadakatsu would froth at the mouth with excitement in the heat of battle and today was no different. He was mounted on his favourite horse, a big black animal named Mikuniguro, said to have stood a huge 2.73m tall, much larger than the usual beasts. The horse had been a present from Ieyasu's son and future shogun, Hidetada.

The story goes that as Honda Tadakatsu worked his way towards Mitsunari, his army then engaged that of the Shimazu. The initial engagement at relatively close quarters saw the Shimazu archers let loose with a volley of arrows, one of which struck Tadakatsu's horse, killing it instantly. Tadakatsu crashed to the earth but was unhurt. Pausing only momentarily to offer a brief prayer for his fallen horse, he then took the reins from one of his captain's mounts and continued to fight.

In fact, despite the abundance of bloodshed that surrounded his violent life, Honda Tadakatsu was never once injured by a blade, at least not until well after the brutality of Sekigahara had brought peace to the land. In 1609, the largely retired Tadakatsu had taken up woodcarving as a hobby. The well-known story tells of how one day while carving at Edo the blade slipped and cut his hand. Watching the blood flow from the cut, his first ever from a blade, he decided his life was over and within weeks the veteran warrior had willed himself to die, aged 63.

Time: 11:15 a.m.

The battle had now been raging for just over three hours. The noise had reached a crescendo, with gunfire crackling across the plain and great war cries going up here and there, mixed with the screams of the dying and injured men and horses alike. The deep wailing of conch-shell horns drifted across the plain like the smoke from the guns and fires, while war gongs and drums sounded, directing the troops. The rumbling of horse-mounted divisions charging, sounds of spears, swords and arms clashing and armour clattering, added to the hellish cacophony.

Interestingly, the 30,000 samurai under the direct control of Tokugawa Ieyasu were yet to take action themselves, but remained ready and alert in the very centre of the battlefield. As usual, this was a standard ploy used by Ieyasu time and again: have your allies do all the hard work, keep your own men fresh and intact.

While Hosokawa Tadaoki concentrated on smashing his way through the front lines of what was left of Shima Sakon and Gamo Bitchu's defences, Kuroda Nagamasa took his men around the side of Mount Sasao and made a direct north-easterly assault on Mitsunari's main troops. In response, the Ishida troops descended to confront Nagamasa's samurai, but were repelled and forced back up the small mountain. Meanwhile, around 500m south-west, Fukushima Masanori too was again aggressively counter-attacking after having been repelled by the superior Ukita troops.

The scene remained one of utter chaos, a bloodbath, as unit after unit darted into the thick of the battle, climbing over slain comrades, horses and opponents to either cut down or be cut down. This, the third hour of the battle, saw some of the most savage fighting of the day, leading to heavy loss of life on both sides. Continual streams of arquebusiers and spearmen were sent forward in ranks, backed by archers and blade-armed samurai.

It was through lines of warriors such as these that the Eastern-allied governor of Nagasaki, Terazawa Hirotaka (also known as Masanari), led his men far into the Konishi front lines, cutting their way so deep that the main Konishi force waiting behind the front lines were thrown into confusion and its formation was disrupted.

At about 11:30 a.m., Terazawa Hirotaka's battle flags of three black circles on a white background could be seen weaving their way south, away from Mitsunari's camp. Having first taken his men through the frontline enemy ranks of the Konishi, Hirotaka, waving his *saihai*, the tasselled baton carried by generals to control the movements of their troops, then turned his army 90 degrees to the right, straight into the flank of the Ukita forces. Terazawa Hirotaka's attack on the Ukita greatly assisted the Fukushima counter-attack and helped them gain further ground. Hirotaka again rallied his troops and continued to drive the remainder of his 2,400 men hard at the Otani, who were then being pressed from the front by the samurai of Kyogoku Takatomo and the noted castle designer Todo Takatora.

Within half an hour, at around 12 p.m., the last of Tokugawa Ieyasu's troops had entered the central Sekigahara area, barely 800m from Mitsunari's position. This surprise move and the speed by which it was achieved, prompted Mitsunari to once again order that the signal flares for Kobayakawa be fired. Another firework was shot into the air, but as before, the Kobayakawa army remained motionless.

Ieyasu knew that his current central position was a dangerous one. His army was hemmed in between the massed Western troops ahead of him and the potentially dangerous Kikkawa-led Mori and Chosokabe contingent behind him on Mount Nangu. The Kobayakawa units on Mount Matsuo would be blocking his south-western flank if they failed to defect.

Now he found himself in a most frightening situation. He was biting his nails as he was prone to do in times of stress – particularly the little finger of his left hand – to a point that they began to bleed. He pummelled his fist in frustration on the saddle of his prized horse, Shiraishi (literally, 'White Stone', despite the fact that it was black). Ieyasu now urgently required the Kobayakawa promises of defection to be fulfilled in order to win.

To ensure those defections came through, he decided a new course of action was necessary. Aware of the lack of action on the part of the Kobayakawa army on Mount Matsuo and of their value at this critical moment, Ieyasu ordered Fuse Genbei and his small body of ten *ashigaru* matchlockmen to advance a short distance and fire on the distant stationary Kobayakawa ranks in an effort to coax them into moving.

This often-told episode, known as the *Toi Teppo* incident in Japanese, is among the best known and much loved of the Sekigahara campaign stories, but contemporary reports of the battle fail to mention the occurrence, which first appears in later Edo-period accounts. The author has long thought that the use of matchlocks at such a range would have little to no effect on the Kobayakawa and would barely be noticed amongst the cacophony of the thousands of guns being fired simultaneously across the battlefield. That and the short range of the firearms makes it seem most unlikely that the matchlocks of the time would have disturbed Kobayakawa enough to have roused him into action as had been the intent, had he even been aware that he was being targeted. Instead it is suggested a small cannon such as the ones taken from William Adams' ship may have been used. The Kobayakawa were supposedly fired upon, but the men on Mount Matsuo failed to move. Ieyasu was livid.

Days before the battle, Tokugawa Ieyasu had confirmed with Kobayakawa Hideaki what his role in the battle was to be. Hideaki too had reiterated his pledge to assist Ieyasu in the fight, but the future shogun had remained suspicious and so sent a trusted retainer, Okudaira Sadaharu, to join the Kobayakawa army with the orders that should Hideaki betray the Tokugawa, Sadaharu was to kill him. If this were to occur, the Kobayakawa men would cut him down immediately; Sadaharu was fully prepared for the suicidal consequences.

In fact, Kobayakawa Hideaki is known to have had meetings with Tokugawa Ieyasu as early as four months before the battle at Sekigahara. A surviving letter sent by an intoxicated Hideaki to the monk Konyo, the 12th Head Priest of the Jodo Shinshu sect Hongan-ji Temple in Osaka, thanks the bonze for his hospitality received the day before and states that 'I have to go visit Lord Tokugawa Ieyasu today, so I will visit you again as soon as I have time'. This document dated June 1600, months before the Battle of Sekigahara, proves that such an exchange took place between the young lord and Ieyasu. It is also known that the monk Konyo sympathised with Ieyasu and so he may also have encouraged Kobayakawa Hideaki to lend his support to the Eastern leader.

After Mitsunari's visit to the Mount Matsuo camp earlier that morning, Okudaira Sadaharu had confronted the 19-year-old leader and reproached him for turning his back on the Eastern army and for losing sight of what had been arranged. Surrounded by the hempen war camp curtain and tall battle-flags featuring his family's crest of two crossed sickles, Hideaki angrily kicked the man away, shouting that all was going to plan and for Sadaharu to mind his own business. The battle was about to change direction, but it would still take time. Hideaki remained unsure as to whether his course of action was a wise one. The young lord had found himself in a difficult situation long before the day's hostilities began.

Kobayakawa Hideaki was born to Kinoshita Iesada in 1582 and was adopted by his uncle, the great Toyotomi Hideyoshi, being brought up by Hideyoshi's principal wife, Nene. The Kobayakawa were descendants of Mori Motonari and Hideaki was later adopted again at the age of 15 by the third son of Motonari, Takakage. At the age of 16, Hideyoshi had made his nephew commander-in-chief of the Korean expedition with Kuroda (Kanbei) Yoshitaka, Nagamasa's father, as his counsel. Kobayakawa Hideaki was blamed for the campaign's failure and viciously attacked in reports by Ishida Mitsunari, who had acted as inspector general under Ukita Hideie on the first campaign. It is believed the campaign's perceived failure was a result of the petty squabbling and inability of the other generals to cooperate properly rather than any incompetence on the part of Kobayakawa Hideaki.

Still, Mitsunari's influence in the Toyotomi court was strong and Hideyoshi ordered the youth to give up his position. Greatly insulted, Hideaki refused and the two became estranged. Reconciliation between uncle and nephew only came about through Tokugawa Ieyasu's later intervention.

Hideaki neither forgot the stings of Mitsunari's barbs, nor the kindness shown by Ieyasu. Upon the death of Hideyoshi and as war grew imminent, Mitsunari courted the services of Kobayakawa Hideaki by offering him tutorship of the young ruler, Hideyori. Ieyasu too had made various enticing offers, but due to his extensive blood ties, Kobayakawa Hideaki at first sided with the Western army, only later offering his services to Ieyasu.

Ieyasu had ordered the Kobayakawa attack on the Otani to begin immediately upon the outbreak of war, although no action was taken until around midday when most of the battle had been fought. It was nonetheless an important turning point, as the Kobayakawa forces outnumbered the Otani troops by an estimated six to one. Considering his predicament, Kobayakawa Hideaki had chosen his campsite well. Perched atop the 293m-high Mount Matsuo behind an extensive array of palisades, gates and defensive earthworks in what was known as Matsuo Castle, he commanded a fine view of the battlefield, while remaining far enough away from the actual fighting as to render his troops useless. Ishida Mitsunari had originally planned to have the Mori troops stationed there before the considerable Kobayakawa forces occupied the fort. Unlike today, Mount Matsuo at the time was bereft of vegetation. All the trees had long been cut down, removing any hindrance to visibility on part of the defenders and leaving no cover for potential attackers. Matsuo Castle had been first developed during the Oei era (1394–1428). The mountain ridges had been flattened to create spaces used as baileys, with the summit also levelled to create the *honmaru*, the main central bailey. As such, Matsuo Castle boasts the greatest ground space of all the *yamajiro*, or mountain castles, in Gifu Prefecture.

Kobayakawa Hideaki, like an increasing number of Western 'allies', had never felt completely happy with Mitsunari's plans, leadership or even with Mitsunari himself, but fought as true loyalists. Their allegiance was to the Toyotomi clan, not to Ishida Mitsunari, whom many feared would later attempt to usurp the power of the Toyotomi.

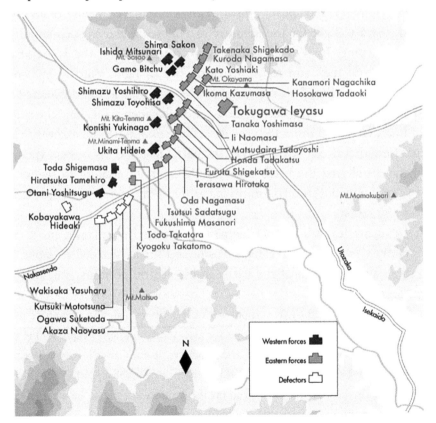

The Battle of Sekigahara, 12 p.m. 21 October 1600.

The Great Defection: 12.30 p.m.

At about 12:30 p.m. and not long after having been fired upon by Ieyasu, or most probably encouraged by his successful advance, Kobayakawa Hideaki made up his mind. 'We fight for the Tokugawa!' he cried and with that order, the young lord's men broke into contingents and charged down the mountainside. With the leaders yelling and screaming '*Kakare*! *Kakare*, 'Attack! Attack!', they entered the fray, viciously assailing the Otani warriors below, – all except for one group, that lead by Matsuno Shigemoto, also known as '*Yari-Oni*' or the 'Spear Devil' due to his prowess with the long slender weapon. He had joined the Kobayakawa force on Mount Matsuo out of his loyalty to Toyotomi Hideyoshi. Matsuno and Hideyoshi had been on such close terms that Hideyoshi had even offered the devoted samurai use of the family name Toyotomi, a great honour. When Kobayakawa Hideaki announced his defection, Matsuno Shigemoto was shocked. In protest he threw down his prized spear[11] and admonished Hideaki, saying that he was at Sekigahara to fight for the memory of Hideyoshi and as such could not consider turning. Instead he stated his intention to quit the Kobayakawa force there and then and refuse to either flee or fight. Putting his words into action, he gathered his retainers, mounted his horse and descended the mountain onto the central battlefield. Leading his men right along the enemy front lines, he placed himself in the direct line of musket and arrow fire and waited for either death or the end of the battle to come. As it was, Matsuno Shigemoto survived the battle and days later, in an attempt to secure his own future, joined Tanaka Yoshimasa's army in the search for Mitsunari as ordered by Ieyasu.

If Tokugawa Ieyasu's advance hadn't spurred the Kobayakawa into action, it certainly was the reason Tanaka Yoshimasa finally decided to move. He had spent the early part of the battle in his central position, watching the

---

11. The samurai treated their weapons with great respect, almost reverence, and it was a serious offence to knock against or even touch another's weapons. One such offence was known as *Saya-ate*, the knocking of one's sword scabbard against another, or bumping someone or thing with one's scabbard, which could lead to a deadly duel. A weapon placed on the ground was not to be stepped over. Even today in many dojos that would be a serious breach of etiquette. A samurai throwing his own weapon to the ground was considered the most extreme form of protest.

action unfold around him. When Ieyasu moved into the centre, right beside his encampment, it prompted Yoshimasa to suddenly enter the fight and he led his men towards Mount Sasao, where he engaged with the troops of Gamo Bitchu guarding the southern face of the small mountain.

Along with the smell of the damp soil, of horses, of spent gunpowder and the increasing smell of blood and death came yet another scent: the scent of fear, as the Western army saw ally after ally defect to the East. The battle was about to take a turn for the worse for those forces loyal to the Toyotomi. Fresh fighting, just as bloody and just as fierce as that of the early morning, was breaking out, only this time the Otani were to fight with even more determination, angered by the traitorous Kobayakawa samurai.

Otani Yoshitsugu of the Western forces continued to be carried into battle and command from a simple open palanquin. Although nearly blind and his body crippled with leprosy, his mind remained sharp. It appeared his suspicions about Kobayakawa Hideaki were correct. In fact, so strong had these suspicions been that Yoshitsugu had ordered a barricade built to protect their southern flank from a possible Kobayakawa attack and slow the attackers. Remains of this 100m-long trench and 1m-high rampart can still be seen today at the top of the steep slope above the former Nakasendo route. Interestingly, the trench appears to have been built in haste, as the usual practice was to dig the trench and pile the displaced earth on the inside of the trench to create a protective rampart. This offers two obstacles to the attackers, first the trench to cross, then the rampart. The obstruction around the Otani camp, however, was built with the rampart on the outer side of the trench.

Otani Yoshitsugu had astutely placed the 660-strong samurai of Toda (Katsushige) Shigemasa and Hiratsuka Tamehiro of nearby Tarui Castle ahead of his own troops, with those of Kinoshita Yorichika and his nephew Otani Yoshikatsu on his right flank, fearing the defection of the Kobayakawa. Those shock troops were already battling a combined force of Eastern samurai under the command of Todo Takatora, Kyogoku Takatomo and Oda Yuraku.

Now came a further problem for Otani Yoshitsugu's troops. Wave after wave of turncoat Kobayakawa forces swept through the combined ranks of Yoshitsugu's men, inflicting heavy casualties on the Western forces. As cries of treachery went up, the Otani were able to quickly about-face and repel the first wave of fresh attackers. However, the mass of Kobayakawa fighters bore down and soon overcame the battle-weary Otani soldiers. Although the crippled lord's men put up a strong fight, they were unable to hold out against such numbers and one by one the Otani captains were cut down and their remaining men slain or scattered.

The warlord Hiratsuka Tamehiro fought directly alongside 62 of his original 900 loyal retainers and was equipped with both a helmet-splitting *tachi* nearly twice the weight of the average battle sword and is reported to have been fighting with a *jumonji yari*, a barbarous-looking cross-shaped spear with forward-facing prongs like a shallow trident, also shown in the Sekigahara battle screens. Incidentally, rather than a spear, Tamehiro's usual weapon of choice was the *naginata*. He and his men had been fighting arduously all morning and Tamehiro was beginning to tire. The Kobayakawa were still fresh and while taking a brief rest, he penned a short death poem that read; 'How regrettable that life is discarded to make a name for one's self in this floating world' which was dispatched to Otani Yoshitsugu. A reply was written by Yoshitsugu, saying; 'Having reached a fork in the six roads, I will wait for you in the afterworld', but it is unknown if the Lord of Tarui Castle ever received the message.

Having spent the morning repelling the repeated savage attacks of Todo Takatora and Kyogoku Takatomo and now the turncoat Kobayakawa, an exhausted Hiratsuka Tamehiro was said to have been sitting on the ground when he was suddenly attacked from behind by an enemy samurai named Kashii Tahei, a retainer of Yamauchi Katsutoyo, who rammed a spear into him. It is said that with the spear still lodged in his body he rose, turned to face his assailant and drew his *tachi*. Although horribly injured, Tamehiro put up a strong fight, soon dispatching his attacker.

He pulled out the spear, and bleeding profusely from the gaping wound, continued to fight as the Kobayakawa troops came nearer. Soon Hiratsuka Tamehiro had samurai bearing the crossed sickle crested flags of the Kobayakawa in sight and despite his injuries, charged at them. The Kobayakawa saw the bloodied Tamehiro running at them and quickly formed a protective circle around their captain. He could not even get close enough to take a swipe at the officer before he was again met by a wall of spearmen and cut down. A monument at the ruins of Tarui Castle lists Hiratsuka Tamehiro's son, Shobei, as also having been killed in action that day at Sekigahara.

Having witnessed the end of the Hiratsuka and Otani, the Eastern ally Todo Takatora then led his men north to the foot of Mount Sasao, where they engaged the remainder of Shima Sakon's Western contingent. Sakon had already fallen once, but had re-entered the battle despite his serious wounds. His 17-year-old son Nobukatsu also remained active, taking his injured father's place on the front line. Shima Nobukatsu was wearing an old *iyo doshi*-style suit of armour made from small scales of lacquered steel intricately bound by silken braids, topped with a helmet fitted with the wide ear-like *fukigaeshi* and distinctive antler-like flanges known as *kuwagata*, common to helmets from years earlier. Both pieces were considered family heirlooms. The mounted Nobukatsu was leading from the front when the first of Todo Takatora's samurai attacked.

Todo Takatora's cousin, 41-year-old Todo (Gemba) Yoshimasu, was among his leading warriors and was widely recognised as being a most able commander. Being in the front lines, he soon found his quarry, Shima Nobukatsu, directly ahead of him. Spurring his horse into action, he led the next charge straight at the evenly matched 42-year-old son of Sakon.

The two horsemen came alongside each other, viciously trading blows, Nobukatsu was armed with his trusted short spear, and by using both ends to their best advantage, he finally succeeded in knocking Todo Gemba from his horse, but in the act unseated himself and the two fell in a sprawling heap beneath their mounts. Being on top, Nobukatsu was quickly able to regain his footing and seeing his opportunity, reached behind him and grabbed the short knife mounted in the rear right-hand side of his armour's *uwaobi*, the tightly tied cloth sash used to close and carry the weapons and armour at the waist and thrust the short blade deep between the openings around the neck of Gemba's armour and helmet. While the mortally wounded Todo Gemba was struggling to stay alive, Nobukatsu again pounced on him, cutting his throat open wide before slicing the newly-dead man's head clean off with a short sword.

With his grisly trophy in hand, Shima Nobukatsu rose and staggered backwards, looking down on the still-twitching headless body and was promptly impaled by a spear wielded by one of his victim's retainers and fell to the ground. Yamamoto Hansaburo had seen his lord felled and had disengaged from his own duel to assist him. Seeing he was too late, Hansaburo rushed his master's killer and took the man's life and then head, in revenge.

Shortly thereafter, Shima Sakon found himself under further attack as the armies of Kyogoku Takatomo and Ikoma Kazumasa moved in. Sakon was still suffering from the bullet wounds received in the early hours of the battle and even more injuries had been inflicted in the subsequent melee. He now resembled the devil incarnate, covered head to toe in sticky red blood, his face a scowl of pain and anger. Despite this, his voice could still be heard booming across the plain for his men to continue to fight.

And fight they did, as wave after wave of Eastern samurai, all vying to take Ishida Mitsunari's head, attempted to break the Shima and Gamo lines. Mounted troops again stormed the base of Mount Sasao, trampling over mounds of bodies in the process. Soon, less than a hundred of Sakon's men remained standing and it was suggested that he retreat from Sekigahara. Instead he replied that as he had no more reason to live. Having just lost his son Nobukatsu on the battlefield that day, it would be best for him too to die a glorious death on the field. So saying, he once again entered the hellish battle for the last time.

After that it remains uncertain as to whether he was killed in action, or died from his injuries, or even escaped to the west and survived. Either way, his head remained unaccounted for at the end of the battle and a squad was sent by Ieyasu to look for it but to no avail. One theory states that Sakon's second son may have taken his father's head from the battlefield that day to prevent it from falling into the hands of the enemy and fled to Nara with it. The head is believed to be buried under Shima Sakon's gravestone at the Mikasayama Temple. The blood-soaked cord from Sakon's helmet is now on display in the Togawa Family Archives, a small museum in Hayajima-Cho, Okayama.

Alternatively, the Osaka Castle Keep Collection contains a picture scroll of the Battle of Sekigahara known as the *Sekigahara Kassen Ezu*. At the end of the scroll is a scene depicting Shima Sakon trying to retreat, bolstering the opinion that he did indeed escape alive. Also, on the wooden box housing a portrait of Shima Sakon by Kano Sanraku, an artist in the employ of the Toyotomi clan, is a note explaining that Sakon fled the battlefield and went into hiding in Kyoto's Kitayama district, only later coming forward and that he died on 26 June 1632 having lived his final days on Mount Ibuki in Omi Province. Kyoto's Ryuhon-ji Temple records confirm the same date of death.

Either way, so fierce was the fighting around the foot of Mount Sasao that many of the heads taken there were unrecognisable when brought back to the Eastern camp for viewing. Considering that both Shima Sakon and Gamo Bitchu commanded only 1,000 samurai each and that they faced an attacking force of 16,000, it is evident they must have put up an extraordinarily valiant fight.

Oda Yuraku had courageously led his men deep into the conflict where he aggressively took on Toda (Katsushige) Shigemasa.[12] Shigemasa and the remainder of his 1,500 troops were already hemmed in by the Eastern forces before him and by the waves of Kobayakawa samurai crashing into his flank. One of the captains in the Oda army, Tsuda Nobunari, a cousin of both Nobunaga and Yuraku, was armed with a short spear, which he wielded with great skill. In the heat of the battle, he caught sight of his target, Toda Shigemasa, wildly directing his troops with his baton. Shigemasa was armed only with his favourite spear, his scabbard hung empty by his side. During an earlier encounter, Shigemasa had dropped his coveted weapon. Forced to draw and fight with his *tachi* sword, he continued until one of his lower-ranked samurai found the spear and returned it to him. Toda Shigemasa had never thought much of that samurai until that moment and in a flash of both gratitude and guilt, had given the man his sword and continued to fight on with only his treasured spear.

According to the *Bukou Gikki*,[13] Tsuda Nobunari advanced on his counterpart and challenged him directly. The two warriors had been on good

---

12.   Toda Shigemasa's actual birth date is unknown, but by 1582 he is recorded as being in the service of Niwa Nagahide, one of Oda Nobunaga's many trusted generals. Under Niwa Nagahide, he took part in the Battle of Yamazaki and the Battle of Shizugatake the following year. Toda led 1,000 men at the Battle of Komaki Nagakute in 1584. Due to an internal conflict within the Niwa clan, he left to serve Toyotomi Hideyoshi directly and was awarded Ago Castle in Echizen. He saw further action as part of the force sent by Hideyoshi to subjugate Kyushu in 1587 and was made captain of a 300-strong cavalry unit at the Siege of Odawara in 1590. Toda Shigemasa would fight in Korea before joining the Western forces at Sekigahara.

13.   The *Bukou Gikki* is a 17-volume manuscript compiled by the fourth lord of Hizen Hirado, Matsuura Shigenobu, in 1696. Despite being completed almost 100 years after the Battle of Sekigahara, the books contain a great deal of information regarding both Sekigahara and the Siege of Osaka in particular, along with many anecdotes regarding Oda Nobunaga, Toyotomi Hideyoshi, Tokugawa Ieyasu and other influential *daimyo* of the late Sengoku period. The books are considered to be mostly credible, with Lord Matsuura having spoken to samurai involved with the events directly when possible.

terms until the country had been divided. Still, old friendships having been cast aside, they circled each other on horseback, locked in mortal combat amid the mud and blood as men fought and died around them. Spear blows were exchanged at close proximity and, while the two concentrated on clashing with one another, Nobunari's samurai Yada Taibei came up along the left side of Toda's horse and released his stirrup. Grabbing the mounted Toda Shigemasa's left leg, he wrenched him from his horse, bringing him crashing to the ground. Yamazaki Gentaro, another of Tsuda's warriors struck at the prone Shigemasa. Although injured from both the fall and strike, the dazed Shigemasa attempted to struggle to his feet. Tsuda quickly dismounted with a shout, found his opportunity and struck again at Shigemasa with his spear.

Toda Shigemasa let out a short bloodcurdling shriek and then there was silence as he slumped to his knees, but fell no further. Tsuda Nobunari stood before him: he had impaled Shigemasa's head, the spear going clean through his face and out the other side. What's even more astounding is that Shigemasa was wearing his lacquered steel helmet and the spear had cleanly pierced that too. Tsuda took Toda Shigemasa's head as a trophy while still housed in its *kabuto* and left the spear sticking through both the head and helmet. Shigemasa, believed to have been aged around 43 at the time, was a much-respected *daimyo*, a fine warrior and an able administrator. His loss was lamented on both sides.

Until Sekigahara, Oda Yuraku was not known for his martial merits. Unlike his militaristic elder brother, the first of the eventual Three Unifiers of Japan, the warlord Oda Nobunaga, Yuraku was a peace-loving aesthete, a quiet man more interested in devoting himself to the development of the Way of Tea than the Way of the Warrior. A master and teacher of the tea ceremony, he had been used by Ieyasu on a number of occasions prior to Sekigahara as a spy. Oda would strike up a conversation with the lords he met as he visited various *daimyo* on the pretext of teaching the tea ceremony. The information he was able to gather in those moments of relaxation later proved invaluable to Ieyasu and his cause. Sekigahara transformed Oda Yuraku's standing within the samurai community, more so as he is also credited with having taken the head of Gamo Bitchu.

After Shima Sakon had been felled, Gamo Bitchu took charge of Mitsunari's forces and in taking command chose to attack Ieyasu's army directly. Gathering a small group of thirty hand-picked samurai, he set off for Ieyasu's camp. On the way, Bitchu's unit was intercepted by Oda Yuraku's equally small force. The twenty or so mounted Oda samurai with Yuraku in the lead raced ahead to stop Bitchu's troops. Halting in front of each other, the samurai announced themselves in the manner of battles of old. Gamo Bitchu offered his birth name of Yokoyama Kinai and asked if he was remembered by the Oda general. Yuraku answered in the affirmative and then offered to put in a good word with Ieyasu if his former friend would come across to the East. 'You're a younger brother of the great Oda Nobunaga!' replied Bitchu with a snarl. 'Where is your pride?' He then slashed at Yuraku, sinking his sword tip into his right thigh.

Slightly injured, Yuraku half fell, half jumped from his horse. Sawaii Hisazo, an Oda retainer, swiftly wheeled his spear around and with a war cry, slashed at Bitchu. Bitchu raised his *tachi* again to deflect the spear blow, but was caught by the weapon's force and was injured. Oda's foot soldiers had caught up by now and quickly gathered around the mounted samurai. As they did, Sawaii stabbed his spear again at the stunned general. Gamo Bitchu fell from his horse with a crash and lay winded for a second before the 52-year-old Oda Yuraku quickly pounced on him and cut off his head, the only one he ever took in battle.[14]

In the meantime, as Kobayakawa Hideaki's success was being realised, other Western troops had begun to defect. Kuchiki Mototsuna and Wakisaka Yasuharu, together with Akaza Naoyasu and Ogawa Suketada, also turned on their Otani 'allies', and in supporting the Kobayakawa troops, soon began to hem the Otani brigade in on two more flanks. The Otani had already lost a great many men in the intense fighting, repelling the Kobayakawa three times before being surrounded and overwhelmed by an estimated ten to one by enemy and turncoats alike. During the first of these repeated melees, Okudaira Sadaharu, the man sent by Ieyasu to keep a close eye on Kobayakawa at his camp, was killed, fatally shot from his horse as he charged the enemy lines. This brave warrior lies on the old battlefield, in one of the

---

14. Oda Yuraku is better remembered today for having given his name to the area known as Yurakucho south-east of Ieyasu's former Edo Castle, now the Imperial Palace and one stop south of Tokyo station where he maintained a residence. His teahouse, '*Joan*', long considered an architectural masterpiece, originally stood in Kyoto, but is now located in Inuyama, Aichi Prefecture, at the foot of his brother's former Inuyama Castle. Both structures have been designated as National Treasures.

very few graves dedicated to a single samurai at Sekigahara. When Ieyasu heard of his loyal samurai's death, he was saddened, knowing that he was responsible for having placed Sadaharu's life in danger from the start of his mission on Mount Matsuo. After Sekigahara, he provided for Sadaharu's mother by granting her lands in Omi Province worth 300 *koku*.

On the orders of Otani Yoshitsugu, Wakisaka Yasuharu had established his command post at the foot of Mount Matsuo below the Kobayakawa forces and east alongside the encampments of Akaza Naoyasu, Ogawa Suketada and Kutsuki Mototsuna. Along with the Kobayakawa, they had all defected to the East and attacked the Otani and other Western units, but of those four based below Matsuo, only Wakasaka Yasuharu had, like Kobayakawa Hideaki, earlier pledged his allegiance to Tokugawa Ieyasu and promised to turn. He had prepared his men to enable them to wheel left and pounce on his compatriots should the need arise. As such, following the battle, he was rewarded with lands, while the other three, Akaza, Ogawa and Kutsuki, had their fiefs reduced or confiscated.

The Death of the Leper Lord and the Collapse of the Western Army: 1 p.m.

With his close allies Hiratsuka Tamehiro and Toda Shigemasa now both dead and realising his part in the war was fast coming to an inglorious end, Otani Yoshitsugu instructed his retainers to assist him in committing ritual suicide. Carried in his open palanquin further up the hill from where his war camp had been set, he called for a felt mat to be spread on the ground. Quickly removing and discarding his armour, he ordered his retainer Yuasa Gosuke to take his head and hide it from the Eastern samurai.

With his *tanto* in hand, Yoshitsugu watched as his second crouched to his left and water was poured along Gosuke's blade for purification. Opening his robes, he muttered his final farewells before plunging the short blade into his left side. Having drawn the knife left to right across his stomach, he lowered his head slightly. Gosuke stood and with tears in his eyes, held his sword aloft for a moment then swiftly brought the blade down on his master's neck. Complying with his lord's wishes, he took the crippled man's head, dug a hole and buried it. Otani Yoshitsugu was the only *daimyo* to commit *seppuku* on the battlefield that day. His head was never found and remains hidden somewhere on Mount Tenma.[15] Yoshitsugu's two sons, having been dissuaded from following suit, quickly left the field and made their escape back to Echizen.

In the samurai rite of *seppuku*, it is interesting to note that unlike executions in Western countries where a professional executioner was employed, the removal of ones' head was performed by a kinsman, friend or trusted follower. Death from having cut open one's stomach was a slow and painful one and so in order to assist, the *kaishakunin*, as the second was termed, would quickly end the suffering with a swift, dedicated cut to the back of the neck, low enough not to hit the jawbone and while not quite severing the head completely, leaving a small section of skin to prevent the head from rolling away.

As Yuasa Gosuke was covering up the head, he was challenged by an Eastern forces' captain, Todo (Nizaemon) Takanori, a nephew of Todo Takatora, who had been a friend of his for many years. Now they faced each other not as friends, but as enemies. Takanori half suspected what his friend was doing, but promised he would not reveal where the head was hidden; however, as they were now opponents, they would have to fight to the death. Gosuke then stood, keeping his eyes on the warrior before him, wiped the dirt from his hands and drew his *tachi*. They faced each other for one last time, before a short, furious duel erupted.

Unlike modern portrayals of samurai combat, a true swordfight was usually over in a matter of moments. If one can imagine a kendo fencing match and one recognises that the moment of the initial clash would have brought death or, at the very least, injury serious enough to disable the first combatant struck, one can understand the brevity of a true swordfight. However, as the *tachi* was used when wearing armour, movement was somewhat restricted. Instead of a cutting, slashing style as employed when fighting with *katana*, the *tachi* was used more as a stabbing weapon. The stabbing motion allowed a warrior to attack his opponent in the vulnerable openings between his armour before cutting. As has been mentioned, the vulnerable points in the

---

15. While Otani Yoshitsugu's head is often believed to have been buried somewhere towards the top of Mount Tenma, a rare picture scroll depicting the Battle of Sekigahara in the possession of the Gifu Museum and viewed by the author in 2018 suggests that Yuasa Gosuke buried it at the base of the mountain in the softer soil along the riverbank.

armour were around the face and neck areas, also the shoulder and armpit sections. The inside of the wrists were also targets. The gap between the *do*, the breastplate, and the *kusazuri* plates below the waist, protected only by a cloth *uwa-obi* waistband, was a target for spears, as were the backs of the legs behind the knees and between the *haidate* thigh protectors and *kusazuri* into the groin area. Cuts to the neck, armpits or groin where major arteries can be found could result in death within between 8 to 12 seconds. As the fighting samurai closed in on each other, the duel would often become an aggressive judo-like grappling match,[16] with each man trying to topple his opponent. Once down, short swords or knives would be used to stab or cut the throat and dispatch the opposition.

The two clashed briefly before Yuasa Gosuke's spirit seemed to desert him. He began to weaken and retire. With a wistful look on his face, he stepped back, lowered his sword and allowed Todo Takanori to take both his life and head. Whether it was from not wanting to kill his friend, or the understanding that now his lord was dead he was no longer assured of a future, either way Gosuke seems to have allowed himself to be sacrificed.

When the news that the head of Otani Yoshitsugu's loyal retainer Yuasa Gosuke had been taken, Ieyasu himself asked to inspect it. Ieyasu knew the man to be hare-lipped and this defect confirmed the head's identity. When Ieyasu enquired about Otani Yoshitsugu's head, Todo Takanori refused to divulge its whereabouts out of loyalty to his friend Gosuke. Despite not getting the information he desired, Ieyasu is said to have been impressed with Takanori's sense of loyalty and character. A five-tiered gravestone dedicated to Otani Yoshitsugu was erected and paid for by the Todo clan shortly after the battle and remains on the mountain to this day. Beside it is the grave marker of his loyal vassal, Yuasa Gosuke, erected by the Yuasa family in 1916.

---

16. As an apprentice armour craftsman in the early 1990s I had always wondered why the *tousei gusoku*-style armour's clamshell-like cuirass rear piece while hinged on the left, overlapped the front piece to the right. It seemed that the slight forward-facing gap on the right side of the armour where the overlapping parts were tied closed could possibly catch and trap a spear. It appeared safer to have the gap facing backwards so spear thrusts could glide off the main plate. However, after years of working with and wearing samurai armour, the author came to understand that this was to prevent the opposition from gaining a grip when grappling in hand-to-hand combat.

Morale in the Western ranks had fallen dramatically with the news of Kobayakawa's defection. The subsequent loss of the Otani troops led to the fall of the southernmost flank of the Western forces, further compounding the dread. The remaining top-ranking allies began to have doubts as to the leadership ability and future of Ishida Mitsunari. Fear and confusion reigned, but by now it seemed too late to organise a counter-attack. The Eastern troops had again gathered and were set to attack Mitsunari's centre of strength.

Meanwhile, in the middle of the battlefield, in his effort to appease Lord Ieyasu and gain his trust, Togawa Michiyasu was continuing to inflict destruction on the enemy. He had once been a loyal retainer of Ukita Hideie, but had sided with the Tokugawa forces just prior to the battle and had joined Terasawa Hirotaka earlier that morning in attacking the Konishi, before deciding to follow the brilliant general Honda Tadakatsu for much of the day. Togawa Michiyasu had a number of men still able to fight and fight they did, deliberately passing the ranks of the embattled Konishi troops in order to lay into their former masters, the Ukita. By about 1:15 p.m., Michiyasu's army had dented the Ukita's new front line.

With the armies of the Furuta, Terasawa and Oda directly ahead of them, the samurai of Konishi Yukinaga and the remaining Ukita troops continued to suffer more attacks to their right quarters from the still fresh soldiers of the Kobayakawa. The deputy chief of the Western forces Ukita Hideie was naturally furious with Kobayakawa Hideaki for his defection and fully intended to take the young man's head for his treachery; however, bending to the advice of his retainers, he retreated to the rear as the assault drew closer. As the fighting intensified further and his troops were repelled yet again, Ukita Hideie, fearing for his life, fled the battlefield with two of his most senior retainers to the mountains surrounding Sekigahara, leaving his remaining men to decide for themselves whether to fight to the death or flee for their lives.

Konishi Yukinaga now looked out over the battlefield. His tall white banners, sporting two sets of three zig-zag line patterns, were scattered and the bulk of his men lay littered across the muddy plain in pools of blood. With waves of Kobayakawa warriors coming in from his right flank and realising all was lost, Yukinaga ordered the *nokigane*, the retreat bells, to be sounded and he too hastily turned and escaped to the hills west of Sekigahara. Yukinaga would most probably have wanted to die like a samurai in such a time of disgrace, but since having become a practising Christian, he could not take his own life. Instead, fleeing to a small village on the lower slopes of Mount Ibuki, the tallest peak overlooking the valley, he identified himself to the villagers and ordered them to take him to Ieyasu. This they did and were well rewarded by the Tokugawa.

Akashi Morishige, or *Kamon no Suke* as he was rightfully titled, was a high-ranking vassal and chief strategist of the Ukita and had fought valiantly from the very beginning against the Fukushima army. His men had also soundly defeated the small corps of samurai under Nakamura Tadakazu, the 10-year-old son of Nakamura Kazuuji who had been ambushed at Akasaka near Ogaki just days before. When his force as a whole was vanquished and Ukita Hideie had fled to the mountains, the war-weary Morishige surrendered to Kuroda Nagamasa, who offered him refuge in his private mansion. Akashi Morishige would later return to action fighting in and escaping from the fall of Osaka. Following Osaka, he went into hiding, never to be caught. He is believed to have died a pauper's death in 1618, three years after the Osaka campaign.

Flight of the Loyalists: 1:30 p.m.

Ishida Mitsunari began to panic. What had happened to the Mori on Mount Nangu? Why hadn't they attacked the Tokugawa from behind as planned? And what of the others making up that force, the Kikkawa, Ankokuji, Natsuka and Chosokabe? Concluding that the bulk of the battle was over and that Ieyasu would soon claim victory, Mitsunari then ordered his men to retreat and he himself fled from Sekigahara through the thick forests to the foothills of Mount Ibuki.

This left only Shimazu Yoshihiro and his nephew Toyohisa on the battlefield, with just 200 of their samurai still standing. Some accounts suggest Yoshihiro considered committing *seppuku* there and then, but was dissuaded by his nephew. Yoshihiro was a proud man. For a man of his stature, to die gloriously in battle was a far more appealing option than *seppuku*. Refusing to show his back to the enemy, instead of about-facing, a daring plan was hatched with the Shimazu men and their contingent making their escape directly ahead of them, straight through the middle of over 30,000 Tokugawa troops! The Shimazu charged with all the bravado they could muster. The various Tokugawa units looked on in bemusement, some even moving aside and taking up defensive positions before the Shimazu veered off to the south-east. The plan almost worked, except Ii Naomasa quickly roused his battle-weary troops and set off after the Shimazu as they slipped through the Eastern positions.

Leading the Shimazu escape was Kinowaki Kyusaku, one of the bravest and most loyal of the Shimazu men. Kyusaku had saved his master's life during a naval battle on the Korean coast and had always been at his lord's side. When Lord Yoshiharu died aged 85 in August 1619, thirteen of his vassals who had accompanied him at Sekigahara committed *junshi*, a form of suicide to follow one's master in death. Seven of these men chose to commit *seppuku* as a group, with Kyusaku acting as *kaishakunin*, or second, for all seven, cutting off their heads to alleviate their pain before ending his own life. His spirit is enshrined in the Tokushige Jinja Shrine in Kyushu.

With the Ii troops hot on their trail, the Shimazu then adopted a desperate form of retreat known as *sutegamari*, by which small groups of lower-ranked samurai and *ashigaru*, supported by a band of ninja from Koka, would stop and remain in position behind the fleeing main party as expendable decoys, sacrificed in order to allow their masters to escape. As they fled, the lower-ranking men would take turns to stop and assume defensive positions to affect a pause in the pursuit. They would inevitably be wiped out, but every minute they could hold the Ii troops back would be to the benefit of Lord Yoshihiro.

The Ii samurai finally closed in on the fleeing Shimazu near Utouzaka, south-east of the main battlefield, where another small band of the remaining Shimazu matchlockmen again stopped, turned and waited nervously for the red-armoured Ii warriors to approach. The Ii cavalry and foot soldiers thundered on, the gap between them closed, closer and closer they came and on the screamed order of '*Utte!*', 'Fire!', in unison the Shimazu men unleashed their firearms at the pursuing samurai. It was a shot from the arquebus of one Matsui Saburobee at a range of less than 15m that badly wounded Ii Naomasa in the right arm and shoulder. His son-in-law beside him, Tadayoshi, was also hit by another marksman.

Naomasa reeled and fell from his horse close to where the Shimazu army were making their stand. His red-plated samurai quickly surrounded their now vulnerable lord. Meanwhile the Shimazu turned continued their retreat as Naomasa and Tadayoshi were carefully tended to and carried back to the main camp at Sekigahara.

The escape continued and the two Shimazu lords and their men managed to make it to the road to Ise, where they split up. Shimazu Toyohisa held the rear, gallantly standing up to the still following Eastern troops with just thirteen other mounted samurai and managed to slow his pursuers, diverting them by wearing his uncle's *jinbaori* over his own armour in order to fool the opposing army into chasing him, enabling Yoshihiro to get away. Armed with a spear at first, Toyohisa and his brave band of thirteen samurai attempted to hold off the Ii soldiers. Dismounting, they crouched *yaribusuma* style and, as the Ii troops moved in closer, the Shimazu raised their spears against them. Bitter hand-to-hand fighting took place and when Toyohisa's spear broke, he drew his sword and continued to fight.

Eight samurai from the retinue of Honda Tadakatsu had also caught up and joined the Ii troops in their pursuit of the Shimazu. Armed with 3m-long spears, the Honda men surrounded the younger Shimazu and together they charged, impaling Toyohisa and lifting him into the air a number of times and dashing his 30-year-old body to the ground. When the Honda warriors withdrew their polearms from his lifeless body, his head was hacked off and brought back to the main camp in Sekigahara for the perusal of Ieyasu. The Tokugawa's *hatamoto*, Yamaguchi Naoto (1544–1622) a close friend of Toyohisa and who kept detailed records including names and incidents during the battle, was brought in to identify the head. The heroism of the Shimazu warriors, their actions and dedication to their lord remains highly acclaimed across Japan to this day.

At about 3 p.m., as the other Shimazu stragglers were making their escape to the south-east of the battlefield via Mount Nangu, they suddenly came across the tail end of the Chosokabe troops stationed there. The rearguard of Chosokabe Morichika's army at first believed they were being attacked and a great cry went up; however, upon recognising the Shimazu banners they soon realised their mistake. Taking temporary refuge, the Shimazu samurai told their allies about the outcome of the battle, of the defections and how the battle had been lost, before they continued with their urgent flight.

Another episode regarding the Shimazu clan escape involves a lowly ranked foot soldier serving Yoshihisa, named Hisanaga. Barely 16 years of age at the time of the conflict, Hisanaga was left behind when his straw sandals broke and the barefooted boy became lost. Seeing the army of Kato Yoshiaki making their way out of the Sekigahara basin, he approached and begged them to kill him. Taking pity on the boy, Kato Yoshiaki spared his life and cared for him for three years before sending him safely home to Kagoshima.

As has been mentioned, Shimazu Yoshihiro had initially planned to support the Tokugawa and despite bearing the many insults afforded by his Western 'allies', it appears there was another reason for the Shimazu to support the Western forces at Sekigahara; his elder brother Yoshihisa, the lord of Kagoshima's, third daughter Kameju. Kameju's mother had died when she was two years old. Her first husband had been killed in action during the Korean campaign. She had long been kept a hostage in Kyoto and during her time in the capital, Kameju had been secretly sending information home to Kyushu, which had greatly assisted the Shimazu clan in advancing their political and financial interests. It appears that Yoshihisa may have supported the West in an effort to save his niece's life.

The battle was over too for the forces on Mount Nangu. Situated in the easternmost part of the Sekigahara area, the army of Mori Hidemoto, Kikkawa Hiroie, Chosokabe Morichika and Ankokuji Ekei, aside from Natsuka Masaie's skirmish with Asano Yoshinaga, had failed to enter the battle, as had been Kikkawa Hiroie's plan all along. He had secretly allied himself with the Tokugawa the day before the war broke out, having strong family ties with the Mori and had wanted to protect the clan as much as possible. Although nominally in charge of the combined Western efforts, Mori Terumoto had sat out the battle in Osaka Castle and had Kikkawa Hiroie represent him in the field. Hiroie's agreement with Ieyasu was that he would not move against the Eastern forces, nor would he move against the West. Further, should Ieyasu win, he was not to confiscate the lands held by the Mori clan. Cunningly, Ieyasu had temporarily consented, thus averting an attack from the rear.

The armies waiting on Mount Nangu behind the lines of the Tokugawa, had wanted to move their troops when the noise of the battle reached them, but had waited for Kikkawa Hiroie to lead and in waiting, missed the battle. Had this combined Western force of over 28,000 entered the battle, it is most likely that Ieyasu would have been routed, as the Eastern troops would have been caught between two forces.

The nearly 30,000-strong Mori army had been merely spectators to six hours of the bloodiest samurai battle in history. Without a single significant engagement, the Mori contingent began their withdrawal back to Kyushu. Conscious of how the battle would end, Natsuka Masaie nervously gathered his remaining troops. Noting Chosokabe Morichika's withdrawal, he too quickly gathered his men and retreated to his Minakuchi Castle. He would be dead two weeks later. Not long after arriving home, he set fire to his fortress and in the conflagration, committed suicide along with his leading retainers. Another among those on Nangu that day, the schemer priest Ankokuji Ekei was not a true samurai and was no doubt very much afraid of the consequences of having initially sided against Ieyasu. For that reason, he too made a hasty retreat towards the perceived safety of Kyoto.

Shimazu Yoshihiro was able to successfully escape and with just eighty men remaining, returned to Satsuma in Kyushu, taking 19 days to do so during which time the stragglers were involved in a minor skirmish at Iga Ueno before reaching the coast and then faced attack by a Kuroda warship en route to Kagoshima. Although relieved to have him home, on his return his older brother, Yoshihisa, promptly had him arrested and confined to the mansion of the Fujizaka family, trusted retainers of the Shimazu. Soon, with the assistance of Fukushima Masanori, they requested and received a pardon from Ieyasu on the condition that Yoshihiro become a monk, ceding his domains to his son Tadatsune. The son, in gratitude, took a written character from the Tokugawa general's name, changing his own to Shimazu Iehisa. Some three years after the battle, the clan dared to send a small group to the Sekigahara region to discover the fate of and pay their respects to Toyohisa, whose sacrifice had allowed his uncle to return home alive. The Shimazu continued to serve throughout the Edo period and their well-preserved properties and museums in Kagoshima are today a popular tourist destination.

The Battle Ends: 2 p.m.

By 2 p.m. on Saturday, 21 October, 1600, though minor skirmishes continued to break out as mopping-up operations and the occasional last-ditch stand occurred, most of the fighting was over. Cries of '*Ei!*, *Ei!*' From the commanders and responses of '*Ooh!*', from the warriors could be heard across the battlefield as claims of victory began to ring out. Just over six hours had passed since hostilities had broken out on the plain. The Battle of Sekigahara was over, Tokugawa Ieyasu had won and a new era in Japanese history was about to begin. The bloodied, shattered remains of approximately 30,000 samurai littered the small battlefield. Including the associated battles that had led up to Sekigahara, an estimated 70,000 samurai had been killed in action. Until this moment, Ieyasu had shunned his helmet in favour of a brown crepe silk cap. The helmet was of similar manufacture to his armour. Known as the *Daikoku Zukin Nari*, it was lacquered steel, shaped like the cloth cap of the god of wealth and prosperity and also the God of Great Darkness, Daikoku. In front was a large upward-pointing golden wreath of ferns and a small, black, frowning horned-demon face device. With victory secured, the great warrior Ieyasu finally donned this helmet, from where the Japanese proverb 'After victory, tighten your helmet strings', is said to have arisen. By this he meant that despite being victorious, the end of a battle was a time to remain fully alert.

The Head-Viewing Ceremony: 2:30 p.m.

At about 2:30 p.m. that afternoon, Tokugawa Ieyasu then began the *Kubi Jikken*, or head-viewing ceremony, whereby he inspected a selection of the many hundreds of heads of senior-ranked enemy samurai taken by the allied soldiers.

For this grisly ceremony, the lord would be seated on a *shogi*, a folding stool covered with a bear or tiger skin. Surrounding him were his close personal bodyguards, all fully armed, some with swords at the ready, others with arrows notched on their bowstrings and half drawn, while spears were held in the fighting position. This was all due to a belief that the severed heads of samurai could, in a last-ditch attempt at revenge, fly up and bite the victors and so the lord would have his hand on his sword or steel-ribbed war fan at the ready too. One by one the heads would be presented at a distance of 4 to 5m, as a final precaution. Lower-ranked samurai heads would be displayed in bulk, tied by strings through the hair and around the head and hung from a 'washing-line' arrangement, made of chestnut or pear tree stakes. Any bald heads, or those offering little to tie cords to, were pierced from just above the ear, through to the forehead, through which a string could be threaded for display.

The heads of the lower-ranked samurai were displayed for viewing first, followed in order of rank the heads of the more important personages. When possible, the more prominent heads were displayed while still housed in their helmets and were known as *Kabuto-kubi*. If not taken while wearing *kabuto*, the severed heads of higher-ranked samurai and heads deemed to be of interest to the victor were mounted on a low tray or a thin square plank with a wooden spike through the middle. Either way, the presenter would hold the base while he kept his thumbs in the ears of the head. In some instances, a *kozuke*, a steel skewer half a length longer than a modern-day ballpoint pen and carried with the sword in a slot within the scabbard, would be inserted into an ear with which to hold the head steady. The head would be displayed to the lord right side first, then rotated slowly while an explanation of whose head it was, which samurai took it and any other relevant details were reported.

The expressions on the faces of the heads were closely scrutinised in the belief they could foretell the fortunes of the victors. If the eyes of the taken head were closed, or the eyes were open but looking down, then this was a lucky sign for the triumphant forces. If the eyes were open and looking up, then that was seen as being unlucky. Heads with the eyes open but looking to the right were understood to have been an auspicious sign for the conquerors, while eyes open but looking left was thought to bring future fortune to the vanquished. Some samurai families or regions had their own ways of interpreting the various facial expressions of their victims.

One type of expression believed to have brought great misfortune was a head with one eye open looking left, while biting its lip. Heads displaying this kind of expression were never presented to a lord. Instead they were taken away for a special *kubi-kuyo* or 'head service' performed by Buddhist monks to remove the bad omens.

While the heads were being viewed, the troops of Takenaka Shigekado busied themselves digging great pits in which to bury the gruesome trophies. The Eastern *kubizuka* or head mound was built near where Ii Naomasa and Matsudaira Tadayoshi had made their base. In 1900, when excavations for the nearby Sekigahara train station were being carried out, the bones of hundreds of headless bodies were unearthed. Another smaller head mound, the Western *kubizuka* on the other side of town in what is now a residential area, also contain the heads of samurai from both sides. Memorial services for those killed in battle and interred in the head mounds were held after the battle without discrimination between East and West, as was the custom of the time. Such services are still performed regularly to this day.

Chapter 4

The Aftermath

By around 2 p.m., the Battle of Sekigahara had been fought and won. Following the head-viewing ceremony came the ritual in which the commander expressed his appreciation to his subordinates and their armies for a job well done. First to be called was Kuroda Nagamasa. Ieyasu thanked him, saying that the day's victory was entirely due to the loyalty and bravery of the Kuroda clan and army. Ieyasu, taking Nagamasa's right hand in his own, also promised to patronise the Kuroda family as long as the Tokugawa house should last. As a further honour, Ieyasu presented him with a short sword made by the highly-regarded swordsmith Yoshimitsu.

Interestingly enough, the house of Kuroda was initially anti-Tokugawa. Although his son had fought valiantly, had survived and had been praised personally by the great lord Ieyasu, Kuroda Nagamasa's father, Josui, was unimpressed. When Josui heard how Ieyasu had personally thanked Nagamasa and had even shaken the man's hand, the father asked the son 'With which hand did he greet you?' 'With the right hand', replied Nagamasa. 'And what were you doing with the left hand?' asked Josui. 'Nothing', came Nagamasa's confused response. 'Well, why didn't you use it to stab Ieyasu there and then, when you had the chance?' commented the father.

Honda Tadakatsu and Fukushima Masanori were called up next and also received praise for their loyalty and for the expert handling of their troops during the action. The wounded Ii Naomasa and his son-in-law, Ieyasu's fourth son Matsudaira Tadayoshi, were next to be presented before the victorious Ieyasu who personally applied a bandage and medicine to Naomasa's wounded arm.[1] When Naomasa died two years later, his premature death was attributed to these wounds. During his greeting to Ieyasu, Ii was said to have very much complimented his son-in-law's actions in the campaign, saying, 'Hawks of

---

1. The medicine Ieyasu used on his close friend and ally was kept by the Ii family and still exists in the clan museum's vaults in Hikone.

fine breed always sport well'. Ieyasu, much pleased, answered that 'Only fine trainers produce fine hawks and they deserve acknowledgement too'.

News had reached Ieyasu of the remarkable feat of Tsuda Nobunari having taken Toda Shigemasa's head in battle, impaling the man's skull and *kabuto* clean through without damaging the spear blade. The great lord wished to see such an incredible accomplishment and so the speared head and helmet were brought before him as one. While admiring the spear blade, Ieyasu cut his little finger. The wound, although slight, greatly angered Ieyasu and sent him into a foul mood.

Upon inspection it was found the spear blade had been forged by the Muramasa, a famed family of blacksmiths once active in modern-day Kuwana, Mie Prefecture, long believed to be shunned by the Tokugawa and banned from their armoury as it was deemed bad luck to possess one of their blades. As a child, Ieyasu injured himself, cutting his hand badly with a sword made by Muramasa. His grandfather, Kiyoyasu, was killed in an unfortunate misunderstanding by Abe Yashichi wielding a Muramasa-forged sword. Ieyasu's father too apparently died from wounds sustained from a Muramasa-manufactured spear, while one of Ieyasu's sons, Nobuyasu, had been executed with a Muramasa blade.[2]

Tsuda's cousin and leader, Oda Yuraku, fearing this incident had offended his lord, took the spear blade and promptly broke it before Ieyasu's assembled generals, prompting one to remark that, 'Times have indeed changed. Not so long ago, it was the Oda family who struck fear into us all, now it is the Tokugawa who strikes fear in the Oda.'

Light rain had begun to fall as the Eastern-allied *daimyo* began arriving at Ieyasu's camp to offer congratulations and receive thanks, all except for Kobayakawa Hideaki who was still concerned that he had angered Ieyasu by not having entered the battle earlier. Ieyasu realised the position the young

2. While the story of the deaths and injuries attributed to Muramasa blades is true, the legend of the Tokugawa clan's fear of Muramasa did not evolve until the later peaceful days of the Edo period. It must be remembered that the brave Sengoku-period warriors of Ieyasu's homeland in Mikawa were particularly fond of the extremely sharp Muramasa weapons and so whenever an incident occurred within Tokugawa circles, a Muramasa blade could be expected to be involved, not because they were cursed, or desired Tokugawa blood, but because they were so commonly carried.

lord was facing and so Murakoshi Shigesuke, a Tokugawa retainer, was sent to call the young lord before Ieyasu. Hideaki was much comforted to discover Ieyasu had summoned him in friendship. He gave the messenger 100 pieces of gold in thanks, quickly put his armour back on, mounted his beautiful white horse *Shiranami* (literally 'White Wave') and rode to Ieyasu's camp.

Meekly, Hideaki came before Ieyasu, knelt formerly and lowering his head and pressing his hands to the earth before him, expressed his apologies for first having assisted the attack on Fushimi Castle and then for delaying his entrance on the Sekigahara battlefield. To his great relief, he was warmly received by Ieyasu who accepted his apologies and thanked him for his efforts during the battle. He also granted his wish of being allowed to fully redeem himself by leading the attack on Mitsunari's Sawayama Castle, which was dutifully carried out the following day.

Ieyasu himself spent the night of the 21st at Yamanaka, to the west of Sekigahara overlooking the important Nakasendo highway, where Otani Yoshitsugu had set up his command post. The following night he rested at the *Honjin* inn in the Nakasendo highway's post town of Imasu.[3] Ieyasu arrived at Sawayama on 25 October, in time to witness the destruction of Ishida's castle and family. Mitsunari's son Ishida Masazumi and his family were killed and the castle razed.

Meanwhile the Eastern troops besieging Ogaki Castle had set fire to the houses surrounding it at the onset of the battle. The fires raged for three days before the castle's keeper, Fukuhara Nagataka, knowing he would be defeated, surrendered the castle to the Eastern forces on condition that the remaining 7,500 troops inside would be spared. He then put an end to himself. Ogaki Castle itself survived intact and 350 years later became a National Treasure until it was destroyed by American air raids during the Second World War. It was reconstructed, albeit in concrete, and now serves as a fine museum dedicated mostly to the local region and its part in the Battle of Sekigahara.

---

3.   Located on the border between southern Gifu and Shiga Prefectures, Imasu-juku was the third largest of Gifu's sixteen post towns and flourished in the Myouou-ji Temple area. Ieyasu is said to have rested on a large rock in front of the inn and from that day on, the rock was preserved and revered by generations of the Ito family, owners of the inn. The *Honjin* was closed and relocated in 1870 and so the stone is now kept in the temple grounds.

Tokugawa Hidetada, who had been delayed by his attack on Ueda Castle, was still at Tsumago Castle, 127km away from Sekigahara, a good 26 hours by foot along the Nakasendo route when the battle took place. When Hidetada finally arrived at his father's side, the battle had been over for almost two whole days. His father, in great anger, at first refused to receive him. It appeared as though Ieyasu was about to disinherit his son when Honda Masazumi reported that it was *his* father, Honda Masanobu, who was to be blamed for Hidetada's failure to participate at Sekigahara.[4] Masazumi, in a gallant effort to repair the falling-out between Tokugawa father and son, even went as far as to offer the life of his own father in recompense for it. This seemed to placate Ieyasu and the following day he had an audience with his son, who again profusely apologised for his conduct. Ieyasu is said to have replied that Hidetada was not to worry about the matter any more and that the messenger sent to Utsunomiya may have made a mistake about the dates set for the campaign.

Ieyasu told him 'War is like a game of Go. If you take the essential pieces, the non-vital pieces will fall in the end anyway and so it is important to concentrate on the essential pieces'. He queried whether any of Hidetada's staff had not pointed this out to him during his siege of Ueda. Hidetada admitted that his vassal, Toda Issei, had mentioned it. Issei was summoned and Ieyasu personally presented him with *manju* sweet-bean cakes, saying it was doubtless Issei's lowly position meant his advice went unheeded. He promised to rectify that problem. Toda Issei was later made commander of Zeze Castle, built in 1601 in Omi, raising his 3,000 *koku* revenue tenfold.

Meanwhile, upon receiving word of the Western defeat at Sekigahara, Mori Terumoto, who was left in command of Osaka Castle during the campaign, wrote out his surrender terms to the Tokugawa forces. Then, in an effort to appease Ieyasu, Terumoto then summoned the son of Konishi Yukinaga, who had been left in his care at Osaka, and had him beheaded.

---

4.   One theory suggests that Ieyasu's vassal, Honda Masanobu, had indeed deliber-
     ately kept Hidetada from arriving at Sekigahara on time in an effort to preserve
     the Tokugawa clan. Had Ieyasu been overrun and lost, his son and heir being
     far away from the scene would remain alive to continue the family line. Other
     sources cite Masanobu as being one of the few advising Hidetada against laying
     siege to Ueda.

On 23 October, two days after the bloody battle at Sekigahara, 15,000 samurai attacked the castle at Sawayama, Mitsunari's personal fief, which at the time was in the care of his elder brother, Masazumi. The injured Ii Naomasa was the attacking force's commander-in-chief, with Kobayakawa Hideaki leading the actual attack. Included were the former supporters of the Toyotomi, Kutsuki Mototsuna, Wakizaka Yasuharu and Ogawa Suketada, all of who were now attempting to prove their loyalty to the Tokugawa. This group stormed the castle from the front, while Tanaka Yoshimasa and Miyabe Nagahiro attacked from the rear. It was agreed that the lives of those in the castle would be spared on the condition that Masazumi commit *seppuku*; however, some samurai of the garrison opposed to the surrender set fire to the castle. Masazumi, his wife, children and other members of the Ishida family ended their lives in the burning keep. Mitsunari's eldest son fled to the sanctuary of Mount Koya, his second son, who had been acting as an attendant to Hideyori in Osaka, escaped to Tsugaru in modern-day Aomori Prefecture and his third son to a temple in Yamanashi.

Instead of going directly to his fief or even Osaka as would have been expected, Ishida Mitsunari attempted to throw off his pursuers by taking a northerly route through the mountains. Unaware of the fate of his family and castle, he had escaped to the north-west of Sekigahara in an attempt to eventually reach Osaka via a westerly arc to Lake Biwa and later to Satsuma in Kyushu where he planned to raise another army.

As has been mentioned previously, Tanaka Yoshimasa was a former friend of Mitsunari and much indebted to the man. He had therefore spent most of the battle as an onlooker sandwiched between Fukushima on his left and the other front-line allies on his right. His central position on the battlefield had been overtaken by Tokugawa Ieyasu when the great lord advanced his command post from Mount Momokubari in the battle's second hour, forcing him to take action. However, he had now been ordered directly by Ieyasu to hunt for the Western leader and after two days of searching, Yoshimasa captured Mitsunari in his mother's home-town, the village of Furuhashi just outside of Inokuchi Mura in present-day northern Shiga Prefecture. Mitsunari had immediately fled to a temple where the head priest had been one of his childhood teachers.

'What is it that you need?' asked the kindly priest when confronted by an exhausted and frightened Mitsunari, expecting an answer of food, water and shelter. Instead, Mitsunari, belligerent as ever answered 'Ieyasu's head!' The priest then helped his former pupil hide in a rock cave behind the temple and instructed a villager by the name of Yojiro to take him food. When Tanaka Yoshimasa finally found him, Mitsunari was hiding in the cave which was no bigger than a modern-day Japanese eight-mat room, about 3m by 5m in size. He had abandoned the clothes he'd worn under his armour at the battle for those of a bedraggled peasant. Although most dishevelled and with a torn and battered straw rain hat covering his now unkempt head, hidden in the back of his sash was a farmer's sickle. Despite the disguise, one of Tanaka's men recognised him immediately. Yoshimasa was expecting resistance and was dreading having to take on Mitsunari, whom he had secretly expected would win at Sekigahara. Much to his relief, his erstwhile friend gave in quietly, handing the *wakizashi* short sword that had been presented to him personally by Hideyoshi to Yoshimasa as a sign of surrender. Mitsunari was tired, stressed, wet, cold and afraid. He had not eaten properly for days and was suffering from diarrhoea. The usually proud and arrogant *daimyo* was captured and turned over to the Eastern allies in a sad and sorry state.

Brought before Ieyasu, who had by now left Sekigahara for the ruined remains of Otsu Castle, Ishida Mitsunari was chided for having been the cause of so much bloodshed. Mitsunari retorted angrily that it was Ieyasu who had caused the war by turning against the Toyotomi. Fukushima Masanori, who was beside Ieyasu, then took his turn at insulting Mitsunari for making a fool of himself and asked him why he hadn't committed *seppuku* on fleeing the battlefield. Mitsunari retorted violently, calling him a traitor to those who had formerly united the nation, saying that Masanori could only say such things since Mitsunari had been defeated. He went on to explain that he had resisted the temptation to take his own life as he wanted to have his death be an extra burden on Ieyasu.

In the middle of this argument, Kuroda Nagamasa removed his coat, stepped up to Mitsunari and placed it around his shoulders. Touched by this display of kindness, Mitsunari genuinely thanked him. However, Nagamasa later revealed it was not so much a matter of kindness, but done because he did not want to hear Mitsunari claim that he too had been a traitor. During his time as a captive of the Eastern forces, Tokugawa Hidetada's trusted advisor Honda Masazumi was entrusted with guarding Ishida Mitsunari.

After the battle had ended, one of Ankokuji Ekei's leading retainers asked his master if it were not better to die like a samurai now than be captured. The cowardly Ekei refused to either take his own life or be killed and instead fled via Ise to Ohara, near Kyoto, with about sixty samurai. From there he escaped to the Kurama Gessho-in Temple about 20km north of Kyoto. On the way, his remaining samurai stole the last of his gold and they themselves fled. He arrived in Kurama with just six retainers remaining.

Ankokuji Ekei was discovered eight days later on 29 October following a tip-off from a *ronin*, a masterless samurai, whose former lord had suffered at his hands. His whereabouts were revealed as being near the Toufuku-ji Temple. The *ronin* then refused the handsome reward offered by Ieyasu on the grounds that it was not necessary, as it was the duty of a samurai to avenge his lord. By having helped capture a wanted fugitive who was bound to be executed, the *ronin* felt he had done that duty. Instead the reward is said to have been given by the *ronin* to the people of his home village.

Konishi Yukinaga had escaped to Mount Ibuki prior to his camp being overrun, but he was soon captured by Takenaka Shigekado. A certificate issued by Tokugawa Ieyasu to Shigekado thanking him for this excellent military service and the capture of Konishi Yukinaga remains.

The captured trio of Ishida Mitsunari, Ankokuji Ekei and Konishi Yukinaga were publicly exhibited around the Sakai area of Osaka with metal rings placed around their necks and, in Mitsunari's case, dressed in an embarrassing red and white short-sleeved kimono and carried through the city streets in a large open crate. In Osaka, Mitsunari was made to shout out his alleged crimes in a loud voice and describe the troubles he had caused as a further embarrassment. The three of them were further exposed to public ridicule in Kyoto on 5 November 1600. The very next day, 6 November, they were executed at Rokujo-ga-hara, the dry riverbed of the Kamo River in Kyoto. They were not permitted the honour of *seppuku*, but were simply decapitated, a most humiliating form of death for a samurai. Their heads were then put on display beside the city's Sanjo Bridge. Mitsunari's head mysteriously disappeared a few days later.[5]

---

5.   Ishida Mitsunari's skull was discovered in 1907 in Kyoto's Sangen-in temple. Somehow, his head had been removed from display on Sanjo Bridge and secreted in the temple for safekeeping. Using the skull as a base, Mitsunari's facial features were recreated by Dr Nagayasu Shuichi, former chief of engineering of the Tokyo National Research Institute of Police Sciences at the request of photographer and descendent of Mitsunari, Mr Ishida Takayuki. It appears Mitsunari had an elongated head and a pronounced defect in his teeth that caused them to bow

The fact that Mitsunari never gave up hope is interesting to observe. A well-known story is that on his way to the execution grounds, Mitsunari was offered a persimmon, but refused it on the grounds that it would be bad for his digestion. Konishi Yukinaga, his partner in death, is said to have remarked that as they were about to be executed, it was hardly necessary to consider his digestion. Mitsunari replied that, 'As one can never tell how things are going to turn out, one must at all times take care of one's health'.

Another interesting story with an ironic end is that of Mitsunari's treasured tea bowl. Before the battle at Sekigahara, Mitsunari had a final meeting with his childhood friend, the tea master Mozuya Soan. Soan was married to the daughter of the great tea master Sen no Rikyu under whom Mitsunari and Soan had studied. Together they performed the tea ceremony one last time using a famous tea bowl titled 'Yoshino'. The implement had once belonged to Soan, who had more than once regretted having sold it to Mitsunari for just 300 pieces of gold.

During the course of the ceremony, Mozuya Soan gave his friend advice: he warned Mitsunari that, 'The enemy are all around and that sometimes it is difficult to see who the real enemy is'. Well aware of how true his friend's advice was, Mitsunari took the tea bowl, Yoshino. and said, 'I may be killed in this coming battle and so I want you to look after this for me. If I win, I'll buy it back from you again', and handed the precious bowl to Soan.

After their final farewell, Soan put the *chawan* in a special bag that he then hung around his neck. Sometime after the battle Soan came across Kuroda Nagamasa in Hakata, Kyushu. Nagamasa asked what it was he always carried around his neck and Soan explained that it was the tea bowl Yoshino and of its connection to Mitsunari. 'Now that Mitsunari is lost', he stated, 'there is no need to keep this', and in saying so, gave the tea bowl to Nagamasa. He too felt guilty about having the tea bowl and in turn he presented it to Ieyasu. Yoshino then became a much-admired treasure of the Tokugawa.

On the day that Ishida Mitsunari was decapitated, the Uesugi troops fighting in the northern regions of Japan finally learned of the Western defeat at Sekigahara, retired from fighting and began to return home. During the retreat, they were confronted by the troops of Date Masamune and Mogami

---

outwards. The rest of his skeleton was later studied by Dr Ishida Tetsuro, no relation, of the Kansai Idai Medical University.

Yoshimitsu. Further fighting ensued before the Uesugi capitulated and sur-rendered completely.

With Mitsunari gone, Mashita Nagamori, who had escaped to Osaka Castle to protect the young Hideyori, then came forward and provided Ieyasu with information regarding the locations of various Western *daimyo* and wanted samurai. Nagamori was then spared, providing he retire to a religious life on Mount Koya. His reward for supplying the information and for obeying Ieyasu was 1,900 pieces of gold and 5,000 pieces of silver.

The former Western base of Ogaki Castle had remained under siege during the time of the battle. A final push to end the Western resistance inside was determined, but before the all-out attack was launched, a special rescue mis-sion was carried out. Ishida Mitsunari's retainer, Yamada Kyoreki, was trapped inside the castle with his family, two sons and teenage daughter Oamu,[6] who had accompanied her father from Sawayama Castle to Ogaki, where she would assist in casting bullets and as a *kubi kessho* artist, cleaning, perfuming and adding makeup to taken enemy heads preparing them for inspection.

Yamada Kyoreki had been the reading and writing instructor to a young Ieyasu, who held the man in very high regard. Because of this, a message from the Eastern forces offering to arrange an escape was smuggled into the besieged fortress. Following the plan, Kyoreki and his family are said to have tied a rope to the large pine tree directly west of the castle's keep and under-cover of darkness used it to lower themselves into the moat, where a waiting boat whisked them to safety. Since that story became popular, the pine tree at Ogaki Castle came to be known as 'Oamu's Pine'. The original tree died just prior to the Pacific War and a second-generation pine remains to this day. Ogaki Castle would surrender peacefully a week after the battle had ended.

Meanwhile, after having taken refuge at Asagumayama in Ise, Mitsunari's son-in-law, Fukuhara Naotaka, who had held Ogaki Castle, killed himself on 7 November. A day later, as has been mentioned, Natsuka Masaie, upon his

---

6. The girl's actual name is lost to history. Long after Sekigahara, when the girl had grown to become an elderly woman living in a nunnery, she had told her story to some local children, one of whom later became a writer and published the old woman's memoirs as *Oamu Monogatari*, the 'Tales of Oamu', which also records such details as a woman's role during samurai battles. The books became best sellers in the Edo period and Ogaki City commissioned an animated movie version of the story which was released around 2018.

return to Okayama Minakuchi Castle in Settsu, received written orders from the Tokugawa demanding his self-destruction. Unable to appeal and far from able to fight, he set the castle alight and committed suicide in the burning keep.

Ukita's Fate

Ukita Hideie had fled with his two most senior followers in the closing hours of the battle of Sekigahara, leaving the remainder of his samurai to do or die. The trio fled to the surrounding mountains and hid on Mount Aikawa for three days without food or water. There they were befriended by a local warrior, Yano Goemon, who, not realising who they were, helped them hide in a small cave near his hut. Hideie and the other men stayed on the mountain for three months, with Goemon bringing food and water.

After some time had passed, Ukita Hideie's retainer, Shindo Mizaemon, left the cave and went home, where he made contact with Hideie's wife, Go-Hime, and mother to tell them that not only was he alive and well, but Mizaemon himself had a plan to keep him safe. With 25 pieces of gold from Hideie's mother, Mizaemon then turned himself in to the Tokugawa authorities. Presenting himself to Honda Tadakatsu, he said that Hideie had killed himself on Ibuki Mountain and that he, Shindo Mizaemon, had burned and buried the remains. As a further ruse to aid this story, Mizaemon had taken his master's much-prized *wakizashi* short sword, which he handed over as proof.

Honda Tadakatsu then reported this to Ieyasu, putting forward his theory that the story of the death of Ukita Hideie was a cover-up. Ieyasu also thought it might be a lie and so he sent a contingent of soldiers up to Mount Ibuki for three days to look for proof. Nothing was found, but either way, Ieyasu was pleased to have Hideie's valuable *wakizashi* all the same. From there, Shindo Mizaemon made his way back to Hideie, who gave 20 pieces of gold to Yano Goemon for feeding and sheltering them. The remaining five pieces were kept by Ukita, who had since built and begun living in a small simple shack-like *yashiro* shrine on the other side of the mountain from Yano's hut, which still stands on Mount Aikawa to this day.

Ukita Hideie then made his way to Maeda Toshimasa's house in Kyoto, where he met up with his wife who had taken up residence in a nunnery. From there he went to Osaka and then to Satsuma where he lodged with the Shimazu. When he finally gave up life on the run over three years later, Hideie asked for mercy and was not treated so severely. He and his sons were exiled to the prison island of Hachijo-Jima in Izu, a volcanic island almost

287km south of Tokyo. His wife, who had fled to sanctuary with the Maeda clan, would continue to send rice, saké and clothing to her family. Ukita passed away in 1655 at the ripe old age of 84, the last of all the *daimyo* to have fought at Sekigahara to die.

Rewards and Punishments

Many of those who had supported Ieyasu were rewarded with land and an increase in stipend. For his fine services, Fukushima Masanori was made *daimyo* of Hiroshima, receiving the lands formerly held by Mori Terumoto together with a stipend of 498,000 *koku*. However, in 1610 Ieyasu called upon him to assist in the construction work on Nagoya Castle alongside twenty other *daimyo* formerly loyal to the Toyotomi including Kato Kiyomasa, Kuroda Nagamasa, Ikeda Terumasa, Kato Yoshiaki, Terasawa Hirotaka, Nabeshima Katsushige and others. Knowing it to be a financially ruinous order, Masanori unsuccessfully attempted to evade the demand, severely straining relations with Ieyasu.

Fukushima Masanori was expecting to play a lead role in the Osaka campaign of 1614, but Ieyasu had him confined to Edo. Four years later in 1619, for having rebuilt some typhoon-damaged walls of his Hiroshima Castle without permission from Edo, Masanori was charged with poor administration, demoted and transferred to Kawanakajima in modern-day Nagano Prefecture with an income of just 45,000 *koku*. He died at the age of 63 in 1624.

Kobayakawa Hideaki was allocated Ukita Hideie's former fief in Bizen and Mimasaka, modern-day Okayama Prefecture, with 574,000 *koku*, but died heirless two years later, at the age of 26 on 18 October 1602 and his properties were returned to the shogun. It is believed that the stress due to the Sekigahara campaign, in particular his guilty conscience at having betrayed his erstwhile allies, caused him heart problems. Rumours at the time had it that his illness and untimely death had been caused by the returning spirits of Ishida Mitsunari, Otani Yoshitsugu and others seeking revenge for his betrayal.

His former fief, Chikuzen, was awarded to Kuroda Nagamasa with 523,000 *koku*, while Kuroda's lands at Buzen went to Hosokawa Tadaoki. Tadaoki left his domain outside of Kyoto and took up residence in Kokura at Buzen. He also received smaller allocations, bringing his income up to 369,000 *koku* from 230,000. In 1614 and again in 1615, Hosokawa Tadaoki played a vital role in the Osaka campaigns, which led to the complete downfall of the Toyotomi. He retired from public life in 1619, handing his domains to his son, Tadatoshi. The elder Hosokawa died in 1645 at the age of 81, half a year after his vassal, Miyamoto Musashi, a man who is believed to have fought under the Ukita at Sekigahara and is now celebrated for his having become one of the finest swordsmen in all of Japan and famed for his books on strategy, in particular the *Go Rin No Sho*, the 'Book of Five Rings'.

Asano Yoshinaga received 395,000 *koku* and land in Wakayama, Kishu, as a reward, while Todo Takatora was offered an income of 203,000 *koku* and land at Imabari. Yamauchi Katsutoyo, who did little more than advise other lords to cooperate with the Tokugawa and in some cases managed to talk the masters of various castles into surrendering to Ieyasu, was given the lands vacated by Chosokabe Motochika along with 202,000 *koku* when he retired to Kyoto.

For his part in quelling the Kyushu *daimyo* loyal to the Toyotomi, Kato Kiyomasa received all of Kumamoto Province and a raise to 520,000 *koku*, while the other loyal retainers received strategically-important lands and administrative responsibilities, but little in the way of financial reward.

Ii Naosuke was given the Hikone region in Omi Province (Shiga Prefecture) overlooking Lake Biwa and a revenue of 180,000 *koku*. There he commenced work on Hikone Castle (now designated a National Treasure), completed by his sons after his premature death. Honda Tadakatsu took over the Tokaido station of Kuwana with 100,000 *koku* and the same amount went to the Okudaira family who were sent to Utsunomiya, where Uesugi Kagekatsu had begun building his castle. Sakai Ietsugu, the former lord of Yoshida Castle (Toyohashi, Aichi Prefecture) received 50,000 *koku* and a fief at Takasaki in Kosuke, modern-day Gunma Prefecture.

Terazawa Hirotaka received the Amakusa Islands, an increase of revenue to 120,000 *koku*, and Ikoma Kazumasa had his revenues raised to 170,000, while his son, Masatoshi, who had sided against Ieyasu, was pardoned in consideration of his father's services.

Due to his conduct during the battle, Mori Hidemoto had all his lands except the provinces of Suwa and Nagato (modern-day Yamaguchi Prefecture) confiscated. Hidemoto had been told that should he return to his castle quickly and quietly his property would not be further altered. In an afterthought, Ieyasu changed his mind and with the lands went Hidemoto's former income of 1,205,000 *koku*, reduced to just 369,000. He should, however, have counted himself lucky, as some ninety lesser *daimyo* lost everything. Nabeshima Naoshima and his wayward son, on the other hand, were lucky enough to be able to retain their family properties and 377,000-*koku* revenue at Saga.

Uesugi Kagekatsu was removed from his former lands at Aizu and was sent to Yonezawa as well as being deprived of 900,000 *koku*, leaving him with an income of just 300,000. Satake Yoshinobu, who had long been on good terms with the Ishida and the Uesugi, lost his property at Hitachi and was allocated the smaller domain of Akita with a reduction from 339,000 to 205,000 *koku*.

Strangely enough, Maeda Toshinaga, son of Toshiie, became the wealthiest of the feudal lords below Ieyasu with an increase in his stipend bringing him to 1,195,000 *koku*. Part of Toshinaga's new lands included those of his younger brother, Toshimasa, who had taken to the field against Ieyasu. Another recipient of a raise was Mogami Yoshiakira who had fought on Ieyasu's behalf alongside Maeda Toshinaga against the Uesugi. Yoshiakira rose from having revenue of 240,000 *koku* to receiving more than double at 570,000 *koku*. Date Masamune, the 'One-Eyed Dragon of the North', also received a raise of 25,000 to 605,000 *koku*.

The Sakihisa Letter

In late 2018 experts rediscovered an old manuscript in Kyoto's Youmei Library with new information regarding the Battle of Sekigahara. Known as the 'Sakihisa Letter', it was written just five days after the battle by Konoe Sakihisa (1536–1612), a court noble, active in political and military circles and having had close ties to Oda Nobunaga and later Toyotomi Hideyoshi, whom he officially adopted in 1585 in order to lend legitimacy to Hideyoshi's claim to the title of *Kampaku*.

Konoe Sakihisa had been visited three days after the great battle by a high-ranking warrior who had taken an active part at Sekigahara, but to avoid repercussions kept the man's name and affiliations secret. Upon hearing the warriors' tale, Sakihisa had gone in haste to see his son, Nobutada, who had left for Otsu the previous day, missing his father's visit. Konoe Sakihisa therefore hurriedly wrote the letter, informing his son of the details of the Battle of Sekigahara and left it in the care of a vassal. A rough translation of the letter is as follows:

Nobutada,

I came to see you yesterday but was informed you had departed for Otsu the previous day, so I have written this and left it in the care of a vassal and returned home.

Lord Ieyasu is slowly on the move with a large army and right now is in the Moriyama area of Omi. Yesterday my vassal, Mondo, arrived home.

How is your situation?

On the evening of the 18th day of the 9th month [24 October 1600] I was visited by a '*jin no hito*' [lit. an officer], who told me about what had taken place.

Lord Ieyasu had departed from Edo earlier this month and arrived on the 14th day [20 October] at the high grounds overlooking Ishida Mitsunari, Shimazu Yoshihiro, Konishi Yukinaga and the others inside Ogaki Castle.

Lord Ieyasu had an army of 50,000 separated into various camps. Fukushima Masanori was in the van, Hosokawa Tadaoki was second and Kanamori Nagachika was positioned third. Tanaka Yoshimasa and others had come from Edo with around 40,000 more and setting their battle-camps at Aonogahara, fought a fierce battle.

The Eastern forces had attacked early and claimed a great victory.

Kobayakawa Hideaki had turned during the battle, attacking his ally, the Otani troops and Otani Yoshitsugu was killed.

I have heard that of Lord Ieyasu's army of around 50,000, some 4,000–5,000 samurai were killed in action.

Lord Ieyasu's faction attacked Sawayama Castle on the 19th day [25 October] which soon fell. Mitsunari's son, Masazumi and all were killed.

Ishida Mitsunari and Shimazu Yoshihiro escaped towards the mountains and their whereabouts are unknown. According to my source, it is thought that they have fled to either Echizen, Etchu or Etchigo.

My contact tells me it is rumoured that these fugitives have come to me seeking refuge. This is a lie.

I am told Kikkawa Hiroie had used his position of influence to make a pact with Lord Ieyasu, but of this we cannot be sure. When Ankokuji Ekei fled, he was given chase to by Kikkawa's men, but he was able to elude them. His whereabouts are also unknown, but there is a rumour he has been captured. My source tells me that he believes Ukita Hideie was killed in action. It appears the Ukita forces were not so effective in battle.

Uesugi Kagekatsu and Lord Ieyasu have not yet reconciled their differences. Date Masamune had assumed Ieyasu's point of view and has taken back his former castle, Shiroishi Castle, from the Uesugi in battle.

Satake Yoshinobu had allied himself with the Uesugi and Mitsunari.

Sanada Masayuki of Nagano has positioned himself as an enemy of Lord Ieyasu. Tokugawa Hidetada and Sakakibara Yasumasa had attacked Ueda Castle and taken some time over it. This was Lord Hidetada's mission.

Natsuka Masaie has returned to his Minakuchi Castle and Ieyasu has dispatched a force to bring him down. It is Ieyasu's plan to defeat the three *Bugyo*. This is what I heard yesterday, the 19th day.

Natsuka Masaie has tried to make communications with Lord Ieyasu, but Ieyasu has apparently told him he is to be judged the same as the three *Bugyo*. I heard this yesterday, but I am not too sure of the details.

Having heard a report directly from someone who witnessed the battle, I write this for your understanding.

Ninth month, 20th day [26 October], I have been informed that Lord Ieyasu arrived today in Otsu. My vassal, Mondo, has been dispatched to him.

Nobutada, will you be going to Lord Ieyasu today? You may have heard this news already, however, I send it in great haste.

When you have read this letter, please burn it.

The letter is not a new discovery, as a former professor had begun translating and editing the manuscript prior to the Second World War, before leaving it unfinished and his findings unpublished in the library. The rediscovered letter contains fourteen articles describing such details as the date and circumstances that Ieyasu departed Edo Castle and Kobayakawa Hideaki's betrayal of the Western forces.

According to the manuscript, the battle was not called Sekigahara, but possibly Aonokahara at first, after the small region about 8km east of Sekigahara called Aono, now part of modern-day Ogaki City. Another satirical poem penned by the Mori clan's leader at Sekigahara, Kikkawa Hiroie, also mentions the action having taken place near Aonokahara. Yet another existing letter written to Date Masamune by Tokugawa Ieyasu on the day of the battle mentioned that Ieyasu's forces had destroyed the Ukita, Shimazu, Konishi and Ishida forces, but failed to mark the location as Sekigahara by name, instead stating that Ieyasu was fighting in 'Yamanonaka', or literally, the middle of the mountains. Of interest are old maps showing that the rice-growing area below Mount Sasao, Ishida Mitsunari's command post, where the bulk of the fighting took place, is listed as Yamanonaka. Another letter penned by Ieyasu to Kobayakawa Hideaki thanking his for his fine efforts and dated nine days after the battle mentions the action as having taken place at Sekigahara, noted on antique maps as being the area south of Ieyasu's final command post and where the Kobayakawa saw action on and around the Nakasendo Highway. Another of the earliest mentions of the battle taking place around Sekigahara Village by name appears in the Shimazu account, recorded a month after the battle, when the Shimazu army had returned to Kyushu. It is now believed that although the area is known collectively as Sekigahara, Ieyasu and other early reports placed the action in the specific areas where it was fought.

Epilogue: Shogun!

The Eastern forces under Tokugawa Ieyasu had been outnumbered at Sekigahara, they were surrounded, they were the usurpers of national power and yet they still won. As the victor at Sekigahara, history has treated Ieyasu kindly and it has been the headstrong and arrogant Ishida Mitsunari, in his show of loyalty to the Toyotomi, who has been in some ways incorrectly identified as the villain of the piece. Ishida Mitsunari lost because of his inability to get along with others and lead effectively. The Western forces were handicapped by discord and incoherency, while the Eastern forces remained unified, disciplined and focused. Had Mori Terumoto, or better still Toyotomi Hideyori, taken to the field, things may well have been very different.

Tokugawa Ieyasu was invested with the title of shogun on 24 March 1603, a position he handed to his son Hidetada some two years later, with another thirteen of his descendants continuing the lineage. Although Ieyasu had won and had been made shogun, he still did not have complete control of the nation, as the Toyotomi clan remained in existence in Osaka and many *daimyo*, although conquered, still harboured anti-Tokugawa sentiments and extreme Toyotomi loyalties. Knowing that the nation could again flare up in civil strife, the next ten years saw a golden age of castle construction and renovations, with bigger, more formidable and magnificent fortresses springing up across the land. In 1614, Ieyasu found an excuse to attack Osaka. The Toyotomi were curtailed. A second major attack the following year saw the extinction of the Toyotomi clan and secured absolute control for the Tokugawa, meaning that peace had finally come to Japan. As shogun, Ieyasu worked hard to create a strong and stable central government that was to last for some 260 years of relative peace, until 1868.

A new era had begun and was to become known as the Tokugawa or Edo period, after Ieyasu's castle city from where the nation was to be governed, a castle that would one day become the Imperial Palace, in the city that would eventually become Tokyo.

Ieyasu himself died of what is now believed to have been stomach cancer on 1 June 1616, aged 73. During the early seventeenth century, the Tokugawa Shogunate suspected that the steady influx and influence of the many foreign traders and missionaries foreshadowed military conquest by these European powers. The rapid spread of Christianity also fuelled these fears: an insurrection at Shimabara of an estimated 37,000 Christians, peasants, merchants, craftsmen and even *ronin* who were dissatisfied with religious persecution and discontent from excessive taxation and famine occurred, but for the shogunate, it became a bitter, image-staining victory. Over 27,000 were beheaded and executed by the more than 125,000 samurai sent by the shogun.

In 1635 the shogunate set in motion a policy of seclusion from the outside world. By this law of isolation, known as *sakoku*, aside from limited numbers of licensed Dutch and Chinese traders confined to the island of Dejima in Nagasaki, all foreigners were denied access to Japan; likewise, no Japanese were permitted to leave the country. Both entering and leaving Japan were crimes punishable by death.

Likewise the *Sankin Kotai*, or 'Alternate Attendance', policy was also initiated. This required the *daimyo*, or nobility to spend alternate years between their home domains and residencies in Edo (Tokyo). In principal, it was for them to provide military and administrative services to the shogun. A set number of the *daimyo's* samurai would remain at the lord's castle attending to their duties there, while the rest would accompany him to Edo and while stationed there would perform castle and town guard duties and so on. In reality, it was a way to impoverish the *daimyo*, making them spend twice as much to maintain two households and the expense of the *Daimyo gyoretsu*, the lavish processions in and out of the city would prohibit them from being able to afford weapons, armour and extra samurai. As their wives and heirs were to remain in Edo as representatives (read, hostages), any thoughts of staging an insurrection were soon quashed. It has been estimated that as much as 25 per cent of a *daimyo's* net revenues were allocated to the *Sankin Kotai* system to maintain the Edo state as well as fund the elaborate ceremonial processions.

Retinue numbers were decided by the government. *Daimyo* of 100,000 *koku* value would have to furnish at least 250 samurai, including 10 mounted samurai, 80 *ashigaru* and another assorted 150 personnel to make up these *Daimyo gyoretsu*. As the processions were also a show of status, extra staff would be included (the *daimyo* of Kaga, valued at 1,000,000 *koku*, once employed some 4,000 people in his procession!) and suitable splendour was expected, with fancy clothes worn by all and the required amount of samurai guards, administrative staff, servants, porters and horses. All had to be fed and lodged during the procession, thus creating a further financial burden on the *daimyo*, but a stimulus to the national economy.

During these processions, the *daimyo* would use one of the many highways, the kaido, with the five main routes being those of the Tokaido, Nakasendo, Koshu-kaido, Oshu-Kaido and the Nikko-Kaido. Another twenty-five minor routes were also used. Along each of the highways were designated stops, post towns, featuring special inns reserved for the *daimyo* and nobility called *Honjin* and *Waki-honjin*. The *Hatago* were lodging establishments for commoners and merchants. The processions encouraged cultural and economic growth along the highways. Road maintenance also aided local industry. They improved communication systems across the nation. The system was also imitated by the *daimyo* within their own domains ensuring peace through the subservience of their retainers. The *Sankin Kotai* system was virtually abolished in 1862 near the end of the Edo period, when the Tokugawa Shogunate was in danger of collapse. Within six months, the population of Edo had halved as the daimyo and their retinues returned to their provinces.

The 260 years following Sekigahara in which Japan was in isolation, cut off from the advances of the West, was a period of great cultural achievement for Japanese visual and performing arts and handcrafts. It was during this time that woodblock printing, *sumi-e* ink painting, and the performing arts of Kabuki, Noh and Bunraku theatre flourished. The tea ceremony and bon-sai cultivation were refined. It was during this time of peace that the samurai refined their own culture, which would later become defined by the word *bushido*, a moral code influenced by Shinto, Zen Buddhism and Confucian thought. *Bushido* stressed the virtues of mastery of the martial arts, loyalty, duty and honour unto death, an understanding of literature and the arts, frugality, benevolence and respect. Much of the Western World's modern understanding of the samurai and the ideals and images portrayed in many books and movies were originally formed in the seventeenth century, yet not codified until the late nineteenth century, long after the glory days of the samurai had ended.

Had Ieyasu lost the Battle of Sekigahara, Japan would not be the cultural and historical treasure trove that it remains today. Instead, the country may well have gone the way of many of the surrounding Asian nations, colonised by Western foreign powers, stripped of its traditions, its culture discarded or contaminated and weakened with Western thought and beliefs imposed upon it.

Peace was forged from the efforts of Oda Nobunaga and Toyotomi Hideyoshi and completed by Tokugawa Ieyasu with victory at the greatest of all samurai field battles, the decisive Battle of Sekigahara. This whole saga can be summed up in an old Japanese poem that states; 'Oda Nobunaga made the rice cakes, Toyotomi Hideyoshi cooked the rice cakes and Tokugawa Ieyasu ate them all'.

Sekigahara Timeline

In many cases it is difficult to pinpoint accurate dates, as, while most dates are remembered by the Japanese lunar calendar, some incidences recorded by foreign visitors at the time used the Julian calendar and others the Gregorian. Where possible, the Gregorian calendar dates have been used here.

18 August 1598
Toyotomi Hideyoshi dies.

Late 1599
Ishida Mitsunari's attempt on Tokugawa Ieyasu's life fails.

January 1600
Tokugawa Ieyasu commences his stay with Toyotomi Hideyori in Osaka Castle.

February
Uesugi Kagekatsu commences construction of Kazashigahara Castle in Aizu.

13 March
Uesugi Kagekatsu's retainer Fujita Nobuyoshi visits Tokugawa Hidetada in Edo Castle and tells him that the Uesugi have intentions to turn.

15 March
Ieyasu presents Mori with various gifts in appreciation for his assistance in Ieyasu's move into Fushimi Castle.

16 March
William Adams arrives at Bungo aboard the *Leifde*.

24 March
Horii Hideharu of Echigo Province confirms reports to Ieyasu that castle construction is going on in the Uesugi domains. On the same day, Ieyasu secretly orders fifteen cannon from the gunsmiths of Kunitomo Village, Omi.

1 April
Ieyasu sends an envoy to Aizu, who conveys his concerns about recent construction works to the Uesugi.

27 April
From Fushimi, Ieyasu starts to recruit an army to attack the Uesugi and communicates with Kyushu *daimyo* Shimazu Yoshihiro.

3 May
Ieyasu announces he is heading to Aizu to attack the Uesugi. Ieyasu orders Fukushima Masanori, Hosokawa Tadaoki and Kato Yoshiaki to advance to Aizu.

12 May
William Adams is presented to Ieyasu.

2 June
Ishida Mitsunari meets with Otani Yoshitsugu who is bound for Aizu. Mitsunari invites Yoshitsugu to Sawayama Castle and persuades him to join in the fight against Ieyasu. On the same day, Ieyasu arrives at Edo Castle.

5 June
Ukita Hideie visits the Toyokuni Yashiro Shrine and prays for victory against the Tokugawa.

6 June
Maeda Toshinaga's mother is sent as a hostage to Edo.

7 June
Ieyasu calls his retainers together at Edo Castle and announces the attack on Aizu will commence on 21 June. On the same day, on the orders of Ishida Mitsunari, Otani Yoshitsugu arrives at Tarui, just outside Sekigahara.

10 June
Uesugi Kagekatsu rallies his troops and allies.

11 June
Ishida Mitsunari, Otani Yoshitsugu, Mashita Nagamori and Ankokuji Ekei plan an attempt to topple the Tokugawa. Mashita Nagamori then informs Ieyasu of the proceedings.

12 June
Western troops set up border checkpoints at Echigawa. Nabeshima Katsushige defects from the Eastern forces.

15 June
Toyotomi Hideyori presents money, arms and provisions to Ieyasu to assist in his campaign against the Uesugi.

16 June
Ieyasu departs Osaka Castle.

18 June
Ieyasu leaves Fushimi castle for the northern districts.

20 June
Ishida Mitsunari informs Naoe Kanatsugu of Ieyasu's departure from Fushimi.

23 June
Ieyasu arrives in Hamamatsu Castle.

15 July
Mori Terumoto leaves Hiroshima by ship.

16 July
Mori Terumoto arrives in Osaka. Nagatsuka Masaie, Mashita Nagamori and Maeda Gen'i write letters encouraging other *daimyo* to oppose Ieyasu. Ieyasu arrives in Kamakura and prays at the Tsuruoka Shrine for victory.

6 August
Ishida Mitsunari's army of 6,700 pass through Sekigahara en route to Tarui.

10 August
Ishida Mitsunari arrives at Ogaki Castle.

22 August
Fukushima Masanori and Ikeda Terumasa leave Kiyosu for Gifu Castle. Ieyasu orders Date Masamune to abandon the attack against the Uesugi. Masamune receives 500,000 *koku* as a reward from Ieyasu. On the same day, Fukushima Masanori attacks Tatehana Castle. Ishida Mitsunari forbids the families of *daimyo* in Osaka from returning to their homes. Kato Kiyomasa and Kuroda Nagamasa's wives manage to escape.

23 August
Fukushima Masanori attacks Gifu Castle. It falls and Oda Hidenobu surrenders. Meanwhile at Godogawa, Kuroda Nagamasa and Tanaka Yoshimasa engage Mai Hyogo.

24 August
Eastern forces' samurai gather at Akasaka, overlooking Ogaki. Tokugawa Hidetada's troops leave Utsunomiya and follow the Nakasendo route to Mino. Mori Hidemoto and 30,000 troops attack Anotsu Castle in Tsu, Ise. The Hosokawa mansion in Osaka is attacked by Ishida Mitsunari's samurai. Hosokawa Tadaoki's wife Gracia and his retainers kill themselves.

25 August
Anotsu Castle surrenders.

26 August
Hosokawa Yusai enters Tanabe Castle and prepares for a siege. Ishida Mitsunari returns to Sawayama Castle to prepare for battle.

27 August
In Edo, Ieyasu receives news of the fall of Gifu Castle. Hachitsuka Iemasa surrenders his lands at Awa to Toyotomi Hideyori, leaves Osaka and retires to the sacred Mount Koya. Ukita Hidiei, Kobayakawa Hideaki and Shimazu

Yoshihiro lay siege to Fushimi Castle. On the same day Tokugawa Hidetada leaves Edo for Aizu.

29 August
The Western-allied Onogi Shigemasa and others lay siege to Hosokawa Yusai in Tanabe Castle. On the same day, Ieyasu leaves Edo Castle for Aizu

30 August
Ishida Mitsunari pens and distributes his list of thirteen grievances against Ieyasu to various *daimyo*. Mori Terumoto is announced as Grand Leader of the Western campaign, although Ishida Mitsunari retains full control. Date Masamune attacks the Uesugis' Shiroishi Castle.

1 September
Ieyasu arrives in Oyama, modern-day Tochigi Prefecture. There he receives word Fushimi Castle is under siege.

2 September
Ieyasu gathers his troops and holds a council of war with his generals. The attack on the Uesugi is cancelled, instead an attack on Ishida Mitsunari and the Western forces is decided upon. On the same day the Uesugis' castle at Shiroishi fall to Date Masamune.

3 September
Maeda Toshinaga commences attacks on the Western forces in Kaga and Echizen, 25,000 troops depart Kanazawa Castle.

4 September
Satake Yoshinobu sends messages to other Western loyalist *daimyo* outlining his opposition to the Tokugawa and encouraging others to follow suit.

6 September
Ishida Mitsunari leaves Sawayama Castle, and visits the siege of Fushimi.

7 September
Fushimi Castle falls.

9 September
Maeda Toshinaga attacks and defeats Yamaguchi Munenaga of Kaga.

11 September
Ankokuji Eikei leaves for Owari, while Nagatska Masaie leaves for Ise. On this same day, Ishida Mitsunari, now in Ogaki Castle, demands Kiyosu Castle surrender. Mitsunari is refused by Kiyosu caretaker Osaki Gemba. Meanwhile Ieyasu returns to Edo Castle.

12 September
Ishida Mitsunari and 6,700 troops enter Tarui.

13 September
Ieyasu requests Date Masamune join Tokugawa Hidetada in fighting the Uesugi.

15 September
Maeda Toshinaga, en route to Mino, hears rumours of Western forces approaching and so he retreats back to Kanazawa. At Komatsu, Niwa Nagashige and Asai Nawate's forces clash with Maeda Toshinaga's army.

16 September
Ishida Mitsunari enters Ogaki Castle.

17 September
Fukushima Masanori returns to Kiyosu.

18 September
Eastern troops arrive in Kiyosu and are billeted in various temples and houses.

20 September
Eastern allies Fukushima Masanori and Ikeda Terumasa gather at the Fukushimas' stronghold, Kiyosu Castle.

22 September
Marumo Kanetoshi flees Mino's Fukutsuka Castle to Ogaki Castle.

24 September
Mogami Yoshiaki writes to the Uesugi samurai Naoe Kanetsugu and offers his son as a hostage.

25 September
Murakoshi Shigesuke arrives at Kiyosu Castle.

7 October
Ieyasu leaves Edo Castle with 30,000 men. On the same day his son Hidetada arrives at Karuizawa.

9 October
Otani Yoshitsugu leaves the Hokuriku region for Sekigahara, and arrives in Mino. That same day, Gujo Hachiman Castle is attacked by Endo Yoshitaka.

10 October
Western General Ukita Hidiei leaves Ise for Mino and arrives at Ogaki Castle. Kyogoku Takatasugu arrives at Otsu Castle, and changes loyalties from West to East. Ieyasu arrives at Odawara. Inaba Sadamichi leaves Inuyama to reclaim Gujo Hachiman.

11 October
Ieyasu arrives in Mishima, Izu. On the same day, Gujo Hachiman Castle falls and Endo Yoshitaka is ousted.

12 October
Ieyasu arrives at Kiyomi Seki, Shizuoka.

13 October
Tokugawa Hidetada's forces commence the siege of Ueda Castle and a stalemate ensues. Ieyasu arrives in Shimada, Shizuoka.

14 October
Western troops in Ise head for Mino. Mori Hidemoto, Kikkawa Hiroie and Ankokuji Eikei head for Mount Nangu at Sekigahara and set up camp. The same day Ieyasu arrives in Naka, Izumi, Shizuoka.

15 October
Tachibana Muneshige's 15,000 troops surround Otsu Castle. Just 3,000 defend the castle. Ieyasu arrives in Shirosuga. Kobayakawa Hideaki's messenger makes contact with Ieyasu there.

16 October
Ieyasu arrives in his hometown of Okazaki, while at the same time, in Kyushu, Kuroda Josui attacks castles and *daimyo* loyal to the West.

17 October
Ieyasu arrives at Atsuta Shrine. Meanwhile Tokugawa Hidetada receives news that Ieyasu has left Edo Castle and is heading to Mino. He disengages his troops from the Ueda campaign to join his father.

18 October
In Owari Ichinomiya, Ieyasu meets with Toda Takatora, and together they enter Kiyosu Castle. On the same day Maeda Toshinaga leaves Kanagawa Castle.

19 October
Uesugi retainer Naoe Kanetsugu lays siege to Hasedo Castle in modern-day Yamagata. Hosokawa Yusai surrenders Tanabe Castle to the West. On the same day, Ieyasu enters Gifu Castle and Hidetada reaches Suwa.

20 October
Ieyasu arrives at Okayama in Akasaka about noon and meets with his men. He announces his intention – real or otherwise – to attack Sawayama Castle and then Osaka. Shima Sakon makes his attack on Eastern troops at Kuisegawa. That night, Western forces depart Ogaki Castle for Sekigahara.

20/21 October
Overnight and in heavy rain, Western and Eastern forces arrive in Sekigahara and commence preparations in darkness.

21 October
The Battle of Sekigahara is fought.

BATTLE HOUR BY HOUR

The following times are approximations, as accurate timekeeping was not recorded and as Japanese days and nights were divided into 12 hours. An ancient Japanese 'hour' is equivalent to two of our current hours.

1:30 a.m.

Ishida Mitsunari and 6,000 troops depart Ogaki Castle in heavy rains for Sekigahara, 14km away.

2 a.m.

The Shimazu troops pull out of Ogaki for Sekigahara.

Fukushima Masanori leads the Eastern army from Akasaka for Sekigahara.

4 a.m.

Fukushima's Eastern forces collide with the Ukita troops of the Western army.

4:30 a.m.

The Konishi and Ukita troops arrive and set up their battle camps in Sekigahara.

7 a.m.

Eastern army all in position.

8 a.m.

The fog lifts. Ii and Matsudaira make their reconnaissance mission.

8.10 a.m.

Ii and Matsudaira advance past the Fukushima headquarters and, attacking the Ukita front lines, are first into battle, followed by Fukushima Masanori.

8.30 a.m.

The Kuroda, Hosokawa, Kato, Tsutsui and Tanaka launch an attack on Ishida's front-line defences at Shima and Gamo

9.00 a.m.

Todo Takatora and Kyogoku Takatomo cross the battlefield to engage the Otani troops.

9.30 a.m.

The Furuta and Oda armies advance and confront the Konishi troops.

10.00 a.m.

Honda Tadakatsu crosses the battlefield in advance of Ieyasu's relocation.

10.30 a.m.

Ieyasu's main unit is moved closer to central Sekigahara.

11.00 a.m.

Otani again attacked by Todo and Kyogoku.

Ukita and Fukushima renew attacks, and Fukushima driven back 600m.

11.30 a.m.

Honda and Togawa troops engage Konishi.

Otani prepares for Kobayakawa's expected defection.

Terazawa attacks the Ukita army from the flank, as Ukita battles Fukushima head-on.

Ii and Matsudaira attack Shimazu.

12.00 p.m.

Shimazu counter-attacks Ii and Matsudaira.

Ieyasu himself moves into central Sekigahara.

12.10 p.m.

Ishida Mitsunari sends up a signal flare for Kobayakawa and the troops on Mount Nangu to commence an attack.

12.20 p.m.

Ieyasu fires upon Kobayakawa, Kobayakawa leaves Mount Matsuo and attacks the Otani, Kinoshita, Toda and Hiratsuka camps.

12.30 p.m.

Otani prepares for death.

With Gamo crushed and Shima injured or dead, the remaining men of both armies retreat.

12.40 p.m.

Kobayakawa troops vanquish the Otani forces before turning their attentions to the Ukita.

Akaza, Ogawa, Kuchiki, Wakizaka defect and turn on remaining Otani samurai.

1.15 p.m.

The Ukita, already embattled, now come under attack from Togawa, who passed by the Konishi camp in an effort to get Ukita.

1.25 p.m.

Ukita flees the battlefield.

1.30 p.m.

Konishi comes under attack from Kobayakawa, Konishi flees the field.

Shimazu commence their retreat, whereby they escape through the middle of the Eastern troops.

1.40 p.m.
Ii sees Shimazu escape, begins pursuit.
2.00 p.m.
Ii wounded by Shimazu matchlockmen.
Ishida Mitsunari, in fear of being overrun, makes good his escape to Ibuki.
2.10 p.m.
Ieyasu claims victory at Sekihgahara.
2.30 p.m.
Ieyasu and the Eastern forces commence their head viewing ceremony.
3.00 p.m.
Retreating Shimazu troops come into contact with Chosokabe troops south of Mount Nangu.
4.00 p.m.
Chosokabe and their allies retreat from Sekigahara.

Otsu Castle falls to the West. Kyogoku Takatsugu flees to Mount Koya having prevented 15,000 Western troops from participating at Sekigahara.

23 October
Sawayama Castle is attacked and falls. Ishida Mitsunari is captured by Tanaka Yoshimasa in Ibuki no Furuhashimura.

24 October
Shimazu Yoshiharu arrives in Sumiyoshi.

26 October
Ieyasu enters the remains of Otsu Castle. He holds a council of war to decide Ishida's fate and further plans.

27 October
Mori Terumoto informs Ieyasu he is leaving Osaka.

29 October
In Ogaki Castle, Fukuhara Naotaka apologises to Ieyasu, shaves his head and retires to Mount Koya. On the same day Ankokuji Eikei is captured in Kyoto.

1 November

Ieyasu and his son Hidetada enter Osaka Castle and meet with Toyotomi Hideyori.

3 November

While in Yonezawa Castle, Uesugi Kagekatsu discovers the Western forces were defeated and so he too concedes defeat.

6 November

Ishida Mitsunari, Konishi Yukinaga and Ankokuji Ekei are executed in Kyoto. On this same day Akamatsu Norihide kills himself in Kyoto. The Uesugi troops laying siege to Hasedo Castle learn of the Western defeat at Sekigahara, cease the attack and prepare to disengage. During the retreat, the Uesugi forces are confronted by troops of Date Masamune and Mogami Yoshimitsu and a battle ensues.

7 November

Mashita Nagamori provides Ieyasu information on whereabouts of wanted Western *daimyo* and samurai. He is rewarded with lands at Yamatokoriyama and 200,000 *koku*. This same day, Fukuhara Naotaka kills himself in Asagumayama, in Ise.

8 November?

In Omi, Nagatsuka Masaie commits *seppuku*.

10 November

Ieyasu gives Kobayakawa Hideaki 50,000 *koku*.

11 November

Kuroda Josui attacks Kawaradake Castle in Fukuoka.

11 November

The Mori army advances to near Kokura Castle in Bizen.

15 November
Ieyasu deprives Mori Terumoto of all but two of his seven existing fiefs. Suo and Nagato remain Mori lands. Ii Naomasa and his troops arrive in Satsuma, where Shimazu Iehisa apologises for his family's involvement at Sekigahara.

17 November
Kuki Yoshitaka, a Western *daimyo*, commits *seppuku*, just hours before his pardon arrives.

20 November
Maeda Gen'i is allowed to retain his lands at Tamba and Kameyama and stipend of 50,000 *koku*.

22 November
With permission from Ieyasu, Ii Naomasa sets off to take the castles belonging to Chosokabe Morichika. Maeda Toshinaga is presented with the former lands of Niwa Nagashige and Yamaguchi Munenaga, being Kaga, Noto and Etchu, a total of 1,200,000 *koku*.

23 November
Mogami Yoshimitsu attacks and takes the Uesugis' Oura Castle.

27 November
Terazawa Hirotaka offers an apology and pleads for mercy from Ieyasu on behalf of his friend, Shimazu Yoshihiru.

Sekigahara: Who's Who

Eastern Forces

Asano Yoshinaga (1576–9 October 1613)

Born at Odani Castle, Omi Province (modern-day Shiga Prefecture) to Asano Nagamasa, brother of Toyotomi Hideyoshi's wife Nene and therefore a nephew of the *Taiko*. Asano Yoshinaga first saw action during the Siege of Odawara in 1590. Yoshinaga and his father, Nagamasa, were awarded Fuchu in Kai Province (around modern-day Yamanashi Prefecture) before being accused of treason against Toyotomi Hidetsugu, another nephew and close retainer of Hideyoshi. Maeda Toshiie's intervention in the situation allowed the Asano clan to retain both their lives and their fief. Under the command of Kato Kiyomasa, Yoshinaga and his father showed their fighting skills at the Siege of Ulsan in Korea. Despite their once-strong Toyotomi connections, they joined the Eastern forces at Sekigahara. Yoshinaga's daughter, Haru, would later marry Tokugawa Ieyasu's ninth son, the first lord of Nagoya Castle, Tokugawa Yoshinao.

Date Masamune (5 September 1567–27 June 1636)

Known as the 'One-Eyed Dragon of the North', Date Masamune was born in Yonezawa Castle (Yamagata Prefecture). Masamune had lost an eye as a child to smallpox and so he wore a sword guard strapped over the empty socket. Because of this defect, his own mother openly favoured his younger brother, Kojiro, as heir of the Date clan. His relationship with his mother and brother would continue to decline and stories of her attempts to poison him and his slaying of his own brother in retaliation, are famous.

His support of the Tokugawa at Sekigahara and subsequent receiving of lands at Sendai would make Masamune one of the most powerful *daimyo* in Japan. Despite this, Ieyasu and the Tokugawa clan remained suspicious of the man and his policies to the very end.

Fukushima Masanori (1561–26 August 1624)
Born in Ama (Nagoya City), Masanori is believed to have been a cousin of
Toyotomi Hideyoshi. He first saw battle during the Siege of Miki Castle
(1578–80) fighting under Hideyoshi and again two years later at the Battle
of Yamazaki. Masanori distinguished himself at the Battle of Shizugatake
in 1583 when he claimed the honour of taking the first head in battle, that
of the enemy general Ogasato Ieyoshi, and became famous as one of the
'Seven Spears of Shizugatake'. (Those seven, Fukushima Masanori, Hirano
Nagayasu, Kasuya Takenori, Katagiri Katsumoto, Kato Kiyomasa, Kato
Yoshiaki and Wakizaka Yasuharu, would all betray the Toyotomi clan, at
the Battle of Sekigahara and again at the Sieges of Osaka 14 and 15 years
later, siding with the Tokugawa.) Masanori had loyally followed Hideyoshi
through his many campaigns and was made a *daimyo* for his efforts in the
Kyushu campaign. He was awarded Imabari Domain (Ehime in Shikoku)
with an income of 110,000 *koku*. Masanori once again proved his worth in
Hideyoshi's ill-fated Korean Campaign in 1592, when he led a direct attack
on the city of Chungju.

In 1595 Masanori led 10,000 samurai to the temple of Seiganji on holy
Mount Koya where Toyotomi Hidetsugu, the nephew of Hideyoshi, had
escaped following accusations of having plotted a coup. On Hideyoshi's
orders, Hidetsugu was forced to commit *seppuku* and his family, including
wives, children and mistresses, thirty-nine people in all, were executed. This
brutality would alienate many *daimyo* from the Toyotomi cause five years later
during the Battle of Sekigahara. Masanori had been awarded Hidetsugu's fief
in Kiyosu, just outside of Nagoya City, along with a 90,000-*koku* increase in
revenue. Masanori's great dislike for Ishida Mitsunari drove him to join the
Tokugawa-led Eastern forces at the great battle in 1600.

Hachisuka Yoshishige (20 February 1586–29 March 1620)
The first of fourteen Hachisuka *daimyo* of Tokushima in Shikoku. The
Hachisuka clan were long associated with Toyotomi Hideyoshi and served
them well. After the death of Hideyoshi, Yoshishige was adopted by
Tokugawa Ieyasu's adopted daughter, Ujino-hime, in an effort to strengthen
ties between the two clans. As such, the then 14-year-old Yoshishige, tem-
porarily taking the place of his ill father, sided with the Tokugawa in 1600.
Yoshishige also participated in the Siege of Osaka in 1615, again in support

of Ieyasu. Following the Tokugawa victory at Osaka, he was awarded Awaji Island as part of his domain. He died of illness aged just 35 in Tokushima and was buried at the Kougen-ji Temple.

Honda Tadakatsu (17 March 1548–3 December 1610)

Honda Tadakatsu was regarded as one of the greatest of samurai by many of his peers, including Oda Nobunaga and Toyotomi Hideyoshi. Born in Mikawa Province (modern-day eastern Aichi Prefecture) Tadakatsu was a steadfast and loyal retainer of Tokugawa Ieyasu from childhood. Together with Ii Naomasa, Sakai Tadatsugu and Sakakibara Yasumasa, Honda Tadakatsu was recognised as one of the *Shitenno*, the 'Four Heavenly Guardians' of the Tokugawa. He distinguished himself at the Battle of Anegawa in 1570 and survived the disastrous Battle of Mikatagahara two years later. Naturally he was at Ieyasu's side at the battles of Nagashino, Komaki-Nagakute and Sekigahara. Despite having taken part in the forefront of over 100 battles, he was reportedly never once wounded in action.

Hosokawa Tadaoki (28 November 1563–18 January 1646)

Warrior, scholar, tea master, poet and statesman Hosokawa Tadaoki fought his first battle as a 15-year-old under the command of Oda Nobunaga. In 1580, he received the Tango domain in modern-day northern Kyoto Prefecture and was soon married to the daughter of Akechi Mitsuhide, another of Oda Nobunaga's trusted generals. The arranged marriage served to further strengthen ties between the Oda generals. After his father-in-law Akechi Mitsuhide turned traitor and killed Nobunaga in the Honnoji Incident, he sought the assistance of Hosokawa Tadaoki and his father, Fujitaka, who, shocked at the incident, both refused to help. Tadaoka fought alongside Toyotomi Hideyoshi against Tokugawa Ieyasu in the Battle of Komaki Nagakute in 1584 and was also present during the Toyotomis' Siege of Odawara against the Hojo Clan in 1590.

In 1600, both Tadaoki and his father sided with the Tokugawa. One of the major reasons being that Ishida Mitsunari, leader of the Western forces, had attempted to take Tadaoki's wife, Gracia, hostage and in attacking their mansion had caused her death. This act further drove Tadaoki to the Eastern camp. Tadaoki's father then entrenched himself in Tanabe Castle with 500 samurai and kept an attacking Western force of 15,000 from the battle at Sekigahara. Tadaoki commanded around 5,000 samurai at Sekigahara and was involved in some of the fiercest hand-to-hand combat on the field that day, clashing directly with the troops of Shima Sakon below the Loyalists' base on Mount Sasao. After Sekigahara, Tadaoki was awarded land in Kokura and retired in 1620.

Ii Naomasa (4 March 1560–24 March 1602)

Along with the generals Honda Tadakatsu, Sakakibara Yasumasa and Sakai Tadatsugu, Ii Naomasa was regarded as one of the 'Four Heavenly Guardians' of the Tokugawa. Famed for his blood-red armour, Naomasa was born in Hoda Village in Totomi Province (modern-day western Shizuoka Prefecture). His family served Imagawa Yoshimoto for many years until Yoshimoto's death at the Battle of Okehazama in 1560.

Naomasa's father was later to be falsely accused of treason and executed by Imagawa Yoshimoto's son. Naomasa was only a small child when his father was cut down and he was taken in by the Tokugawa family. Highly regarded by Ieyasu, a former hostage of the Imagawa himself, Naomasa commanded the initial attack that began the battle at Sekigahara.

Ikeda Terumasa (31 January 1565–16 March 1613)

The Ikeda clan were originally vassals of Oda Nobunaga. Terumasa had taken part in Nobunaga's last campaigns and fought under Hideyoshi at the Battle of Nagakute in 1584, in which his father and elder brother were killed. By order of Hideyoshi, Terumasa had married Ieyasu's second daughter in an attempt to strengthen political ties. This succeeded in doing so, but to the eventual detriment of the Toyotomi. In return for his services to Ieyasu at the Battle of Sekigahara, he was awarded Himeji Castle, which was greatly expanded under his control and remains to this day as one of the finest surviving examples of a Japanese castle. Himeji is a designated National Treasure and is a World Heritage site. By the time of his death in 1613, Ikeda Terumasa's power and influence was such that he was nicknamed *Saigoku no Shogun*, or 'The Shogun of the West'.

Ikoma Kazumasa (1555–11 May 1610)

Ikoma Kazumasa served with distinction under the Oda family and fought alongside the Toyotomi forces in Korea, taking an active part in the Battle of Ulsan Castle. While Kazumasa's father remained with the Toyotomi loyalists, he himself joined the Tokugawa ranks at Sekigahara. Through this dual allegiance, the Ikoma clan managed to retain their lands in Shikoku following the great battle.

Kanamori Nagachika (1524–20 September 1608)

Kanamori Nagachika first served the Saito clan of Mino (Gifu), later pledging loyalty to Oda Nobunaga, whereby he was made master of Takayama and Matsukura Castles in Mino. At the Battle of Nagashino in 1575 Nagachika joined Ieyasu's general Sakai Tadatsugu in a daring ambush on the rival Takeda armies, capturing a number of fortresses and killing the great Takeda Shingen's younger brother Nobuzane. Following Nobunaga's death, Nagachika became a retainer of the Oda general Shibata Katsuie and later Toyotomi Hideyoshi. Under Hideyoshi, Nagachika become a close follower of the tea master Sen no Rikyu. When Hideyoshi ordered the execution of the tea master, Nagachika risked his position within the Toyotomi administration by protecting Rikyu's son, sheltering the boy in his own home. Nagachika finally served Tokugawa Ieyasu.

Kato Yoshiaki (1563–7 October 1631)

Born in Mikawa (Aichi Prefecture) Kato Yoshiaki's father was a vassal of Tokugawa Ieyasu. He was sent as a page to Toyotomi Hideyoshi, eventually becoming one of the renowned 'Seven Spears of Shizugatake' and one of Hideyoshi's most highly regarded and trusted generals. Recognised for his seafaring abilities, Yoshiaki was at the forefront of the fierce naval battles that took part off the southern Korean coast during Hideyoshi's two invasions of Korea. He was responsible for constructing Iyo Matsuyama Castle (Ehime Prefecture) in 1603. When he was transferred to Aizu in 1627, the five-storey castle keep was dismantled and taken with him. He died in Edo at the age of 69.

Kuroda Nagamasa (3 December 1568–29 August 1623)

Kuroda Nagamasa's father was the famed Kuroda Kanbei (1 January 1547– 19 April 1604), a strategist for Toyotomi Hideyoshi. As a child he had been taken hostage and nearly put to death as his father had been accused of espionage by Oda Nobunaga and imprisoned.

Kuroda Nagamasa took part in his first major battle in 1584. He was said to have been a ferocious fighter and was cautioned by his generals for risking his life too many times by going deep into the enemies' formations when attacking. Nagamasa is said to have commented that his death should be 'Nothing to worry about while my father is still alive'. He was one of the few *daimyo* who turned to the Christian faith, being baptized as Damien. He would lead 6,000 samurai in the first Korean campaign. His loyalties shifted to the Tokugawa prior to hostilities at Sekigahara. His men were responsible for bringing down the great warrior Shima Sakon and for many well-planned attacks on the headquarters of the Western forces. Nagamasa also took part in both attacks on Osaka Castle in 1614 and 1615, again under Tokugawa colours.

Kyogoku Takatomo (1571–17 September 1621)
Having distinguished himself at a young age while in the services of Toyotomi Hideyoshi, Kyogoku Takatomo was granted the extremely high honour of being allowed the use the family name of Hashiba, Hideyoshi's original family name, and made the master of Ida Domain in Shinano Province (Nagano Prefecture). Just prior to 1600 Takatomo had allied himself with Tokugawa Ieyasu and would fight for the Eastern forces alongside another fine warrior, Todo Takatora, entrusted with the task of keeping the Western-allied Otani contingent at bay. Following Sekigahara, Takatomo was awarded Tanabe Castle in Tango Province, with a 125,000-*koku* stipend. He later built Miyazu Castle in Tamba, making it his base. The Kyogoku remained a highly respected *daimyo* clan to the end of the Edo period in 1868.

Matsudaira Tadayoshi (18 October 1580–1 April1607)
Fourth son of Tokugawa Ieyasu by his second and favourite wife, Lady Saigo. With his father-in-law, Ii Naomasa, the 20-year-old Tadayoshi was one of the first into battle on the bloody day at Sekigahara. Wounded late in the battle, he was awarded a 570,000-*koku* fief and Kiyosu Castle, but died heir-less at 27.

Mogami Yoshiaki (1 February 1546–29 November 1614)
Born the first son of the *daimyo* of Yamagata, Mogami Yoshimori, Yoshiaki was a staunch supporter of the Toyotomi clan. However in 1595, Hideyoshi's nephew, Hidetsugu, was accused of plotting a coup against his uncle and was forced to commit suicide. All thirty-nine members of Hidetsugu's family – children, wives and even mistresses – were executed. Among them was the 15-year-old daughter of Yoshiaki who had only just arrived in Kyoto

and had not yet even met her husband-to-be. Her death led Yoshiaki to form a deep hatred for the Toyotomi and to join the Tokugawa-led Eastern forces at Sekigahara. In 1600 he supported Ieyasu by fighting alongside his nephew Date Masamune against Uesugi Kagekatsu that summer and later that year on the battlefield at Sekigahara. Yoshiaki commenced non-military construction to control flooding of the Mogami River and damming and irrigation projects that led to improved rice yields in his domain, thus establishing the modern city of Yamagata. He died 14 years after Sekigahara at Yamagata Castle.

Oda Nagamasu (1548–24 January 1622)

Also known as Oda Yuraku, Nagamasu was the younger brother of the first national unifier, Oda Nobunaga and, as a disciple of Sen no Rikyu, was an accomplished practitioner of the tea ceremony, later creating his own tea-ceremony style, formulated to better suit the culture, tastes and aesthetics of the warrior class. That style, *Uraku Senke*, remains in use to this day. Nagamasa converted to Christianity in 1588 and was baptised as 'John'. Viewed as a weak man with effeminate airs, his efforts at the Battle of Sekigahara would change his standing among the samurai.

Takenaka Shigekado (1573–2 November 1631)

The son of the famed Toyotomi tactician Takenaka Hanbei, Shigekado was 12 years old in 1585 when he first saw action at the Battle of Komaki Nagakute. He served Hideyoshi, as had his father, later siding at the last minute with Tokugawa Ieyasu at Sekigahara. He was master of a nearby castle town and the Sekigahara region came under his jurisdiction. During the battle, Shigekado fought alongside Kuroda Nagamasa and saw some of the fiercest action of the day in their attempts on the Western base on Mount Sasao. Shigekado was highly regarded for his skills in calligraphy and poetry. He died aged 59 while in Edo.

Tanaka Yoshimasa (1548–23 March 1609)

Believed to have been born in Torahime, Omi (Shiga Prefecture), Tanaka Yoshimasa was another highly ranked samurai formerly serving under Toyotomi Hideyoshi and a close acquaintance of Ishida Mitsunari. He joined the Tokugawa upon the death of the *Taiko*, as Hideyoshi was titled. He was another *daimyo* introduced to Christianity by Kuroda Nagamasa and baptised under the name Bartholomew. Tanaka was later made lord of Okazaki Castle, Ieyasu's birthplace, and was responsible for the Twenty-Seven Bends of Okazaki, a series of turns on the Tokaido designed to hinder the progress of any potential invading forces. After the great battle, Tanaka Yoshimasa concerned himself with increasing commerce and improving urban conditions within his fief.

Terazawa Hirotaka (1563–18 May 1633)

Hailing from Owari Province, Hirotaka was also a former vassal of Toyotomi Hideyoshi and played a major role in organising the construction of Hizen Nagoya Castle and the transportation of troops from Hizen to the southern Korean peninsula as part of Hideyoshi's invasions of Korea. Following Hideyoshi's death, he severed his ties to the Toyotomi clan to lead his 2,400 men in the fight for the Tokugawa in 1600. He was later made Lord of Karatsu, but his mismanagement of local government and over-taxation in part led to the Shimabara Rebellion not long after his death.

Todo Takatora (16 February 1556–9 November 1630)

Famed for his 1.9m stature, his fighting prowess and mainly for his expertise in castle design, Todo Takatora was born in Todo, Koura Village, Omi Province. A veteran of the Battle of Anegawa, the sieges of Usayama, Tamba and Miki Castles, the battles of Yamazaki, Shizugatake and Komaki Nagakute amongst many others, including various skirmishes during the Korean Invasions, Takatora commenced his military career as a low-ranking samurai, working his way up to the position of *daimyo*. He changed his allegiance seven times, working for a record ten different warlords. Takatora developed from being a wild, headstrong youth into a wise, considerate statesman and talented engineer while serving under General Hashiba Hidenaga, the younger brother of Toyotomi Hideyoshi. He later changed his allegiance to Tokugawa Ieyasu, becoming one of Ieyasu's closest friends and trusted advisors. His legacy is having left over twenty of the most innovative and best designed castles across the country.

Tokugawa Ieyasu (31 January 1543–1 June 1616)

Born in Okazaki Castle, Mikawa (Aichi Prefecture), son of the *daimyo* of Mikawa, Matsudaira Hirotada. At the age of six, Ieyasu was sent as a hostage to the rival Imagawa clan in exchange for assistance in repelling the Oda clan.

The samurai tasked with taking the boy to the Imagawa believed that the interests of the Matsudaira were better served with an alliance with the Oda against the Imagawa and so the entourage was diverted to Oda Nobuhide, where the young Ieyasu was kept for three years in Nagoya. At the age of nine, Ieyasu was swapped for an Oda hostage of the Imagawa following an attack on the Oda and was sent to the Imagawa stronghold at Sumpu (Shizuoka). Ieyasu won his freedom in 1560, when Imagawa Yoshimoto was defeated in the Battle of Okehazama on the outskirts of Nagoya by Oda Nobunaga, and allied himself with the victor. In the following years Ieyasu took part in various battles, increasing his presence and power with almost each one, including Azukizaka, Anegawa, Tenmokuzan, Mikatagahara, Nagashino, Komaki and Nagakute and finally the battle that would bring him supreme power and the title of shogun, Sekigahara.

Tomita Nobutaka (????–7 April 1633)

Born in Omi Province to a vassal of Toyotomi Hideyoshi, Tomita Nobutaka also served Hideyoshi, becoming lord of Tsu Castle and later the first feudal lord of Uwajima Castle. Tomita Nobutaka and his wife would lead 1,700 samurai in defence of Tsu Castle against a Western combined force of 30,000 just three weeks prior to the battle at Sekigahara.

Tsutsui Sadatsugu (6 June 1562–2 April 1615)

Tsutsui Sadatsugu was the cousin and adopted son of the lord of Yamato Province, Tsutsui Junkei. He was adopted in order to be named as Junkei's heir and maintain family control of the fief. Upon his adopted father's death, Toyotomi Hideyoshi provided Sadatsugu with land at Iga in Mie Prefecture where he built the first version of Iga Ueno Castle. Despite offering his services and samurai to Ieyasu in 1600, he was removed from his position as lord of Iga Ueno and the Tsutsui clan was abolished eight years after the Battle of Sekigahara, having been charged with misgovernance.

Yamauchi Katsutoyo (1545/46?–1 November 1605)

Born in Owari Province, Yamauchi Katsutoyo served under Oda Nobunaga from the age of nine until Nobunaga's death in 1582. During that time, he participated in the battles of Anegawa (1570) and Nagashino (1575). Following the death of Nobunaga, Katsutoyo became a retainer of Toyotomi Hideyoshi.

He helped captured Gifu Castle and led 2,000 men into battle at Sekigahara for the Tokugawa cause, for which he was later rewarded with Tosa Domain (now Kochi Prefecture) where he built the surviving Kochi Castle. Katsutoyo worked his way up from being an ordinary man with little talent, to being the lord of an entire province thanks to his wise and beautiful wife.

Western Forces
Akaza Naoyasu (????–1606)
Akaza Naoyasu was the son of Akaza Naonori, a close retainer of Oda Nobunaga who perished along with his master in the attack on the temple of Honnoji. Naoyasu then served under Hideyoshi and fought in the capture of Iwatsuki and Oshi Castles and at the Siege of Odawara. During the Sekigahara campaign, Naoyasu was initially placed under the command of the Otani and was one of those who betrayed the West, turning to assist the Eastern cause at the last minute. Following the battle, he would lose his land and title, only to become a retainer of Maeda Toshinaga.

Naoyasu met an inglorious death in 1606. While inspecting the flooded Daimon River, he fell from his horse and was drowned. His son later changed the family name to Nagahara and they remained Maeda clan vassals for the rest of the Edo Period.

Ankokuji Ekei (1539–6 November 1600)
A Rinzai-sect Buddhist monk, the abbot of the Tofuku-ji Temple, one of Kyoto's five great Zen temples, and a diplomat serving the powerful Mori clan of south-western Japan, Ankokuji Ekei meddled in the affairs of the samurai. Although politically astute, he was also seen as both greedy and cowardly. He joined the forces sent to Korea by Hideyoshi and was subsequently awarded a fiefdom of 60,000 *koku* in Iyo Province (Ehime in Shikoku). Having fled from the field of Sekigahara and gone into hiding, Ankokuji Ekei was captured and later decapitated in Kyoto along with Ishida Mitsunari and Konishi Yukinaga.

Chosokabe Morichika (1575–11 May 1615)
Once the powerful ruler of Tosa Province (now Kochi in Shikoku), Chosokabe Morichika was a veteran of the 1590 Siege of Odawara and later saw action in Korea as part of the invasion forces. The Chosokabe chose to face off

against Ieyasu at Sekigahara, although they failed to take action. Morichika's army again supported the Toyotomi at the Siege of Osaka in 1614 and 1615. Morichika and his sons were all executed on 11 May 1615 following the Battle of Tennoji, the last skirmish of the Siege of Osaka, thus ending the clan.

Gamo Bitchu (Yorisato) (????–21 October 1600)
Believed to have been born with the name Yokoyama Kinai and despite his reputation and standing within the samurai community, along with his major role in the Battle of Sekigahara, very few reliable details regarding Gamo Bitchu-no-Kami Yorisato (Bitchu being his domain name, i.e, Lord of Bitchu Province) remain. He commanded just 1,000 samurai in his position below Ishida Mitsunari's base camp on Mount Sasao. Gamo Bitchu faced some of the fiercest fighting on the day and lost his head to Oda Yuraku during the battle.

Ishida Mitsunari (1560–6 November 1600)
Born in Nagahama, Shiga Prefecture, Ishida Mitsunari soon came to the attention of Toyotomi Hideyoshi, rising rapidly in the ranks to become one of the top five commissioners in Hideyoshi's administration. Although he had many friends in the bureaucracy, he was also prone to making enemies amongst the leading samurai warriors due to his brash, rigid character, particularly as he had been appointed the role of commissioner during Hideyoshi's invasion of the Korean Peninsula. Considered meddlesome by his contemporaries, Ishida Mitsunari had been the first to accuse Ieyasu of treachery against the child ruler Toyotomi Hideyori, sparking the conflict that caused the nation to split into two factions, East and West.

Kikkawa Hiroie (7 December 1561–22 October 1625)
A master of strategy and diplomacy, Kikkawa Hiroie made his battlefield debut aged nine alongside his father in 1570. Seventeen years and numerous battles later, he became head of the Kikkawa clan following the deaths of both his father and elder brother. He was highly praised by Hideyoshi, particularly for his loyalty to the Mori clan. It was this loyalty that led him to form a secret pact with the Tokugawa prior to Sekigahara, promising that the Mori forces would refrain from entering the battle on either side, providing Ieyasu allowed the clan to retain its land and titles. It was an effort to ensure the survival of the Mori clan. Apart from being the leading general of the huge Mori forces at Sekigahara, Kikkawa Hiroie is best remembered

for having written the *Kikawashi Hatto*, a set of laws with some 188 clauses created to further the prosperity of the domain.

Kobayakawa Hideaki (1582–1 December 1602)

Kobayakawa Hideaki was the fifth son of Toyotomi Hideyoshi's brother-in-law Kinoshita Iesada and therefore a nephew of the *Taiko*. He was adopted by his uncle and, a few years later, adopted again by Kobayakawa Takakage.

During the Korean campaign, at the Battle of Keicho, Hideaki personally captured an enemy general, breaking the siege of Ulsan Castle. Although his valour was heroic, Hideaki was known to have attacked innocent women and children during the campaign, which angered many of his contemporaries and estranged him from them.

Furthermore, in reports back to his uncle in Osaka, one of the commissioners, Ishida Mitsunari, had condemned the young man's actions as reckless, something Hideaki would be severely reprimanded for, and for that would come to permanently resent Mitsunari. Prior to the Battle of Sekigahara, Hideaki positioned himself on the Western side along with his relatives and associates, but his intentions seemed unclear until the final moment.

Konishi Yukinaga (1555–6 November 1600)

Konishi Yukinaga was born the son of a wealthy merchant. His wealth helped him obtain samurai status and under Hideyoshi, he was awarded the Province of Higo, around modern-day Kumamoto in Kyushu. He was among the leaders of Hideyoshi's war in Korea, gaining fame for his exploits in the capture of Pusan, Seoul and later Pyongyang. Exposed for a deception whereby he negotiated a truce with China's Ming Dynasty using Hideyoshi's name, he was censured by Hideyoshi, but permitted to retain his status and allowed to lead the second invasion.

Following the great battle at Sekigahara, he was captured on nearby Mount Ibuki. However, having converted to the foreign religion of Christianity, he refused to commit *seppuku* and instead was later executed.

Kutsuki Mototsuna (1549–12 October 1632)

A minor but key player in the outcome of Sekigahara. Mototsuna lost his father to war when he was two and from then on was head of his clan. Mototsuna served the Ashikaga Shogunate at first and from the age of 21 assisted Oda Nobunaga in an attack on the neighbouring Asakura clan. Like many of his contemporaries, Kutsuki joined the Toyotomi forces on the death of Nobunaga in 1582. In 1600, he fought alongside Otani Yoshitsugu's forces. His family, however, was spared and he retained his lands after the great battle for his services to Ieyasu.

Mashita Nagamori (1545–23 June 1615)

Hailing originally from Mashita Village in Owari (western Aichi Prefecture), Nagamori was a samurai under Hideyoshi from the days of Nobunaga and was recognised for his administrative and diplomatic abilities. For his services, he was later appointed one of the five senior commissioners in Hideyoshi's government.

Nagamori was forced to commit *seppuku* aged 71 in 1615 on account of his son, Moritsugu, absconding from his position under Tokugawa Yoshinao at the Siege of Osaka and joining the Toyotomi forces in defending the castle.

Mori Hidemoto (25 November 1579–26 November 1650)

A cousin of Mori Terumoto, Hidemoto was specifically chosen by Hideyoshi to lead the second Korean invasion and as such was placed in charge of seasoned warriors including Kato Kiyomasa, Kuroda Nagamasa, Nabeshima Naoshige, Ikeda Hideuji, Chosokabe Motochika and Nakagawa Hidenari. At Sekigahara, he would be positioned under Kikkawa Hiroie and as such would be prevented from entering the theatre of war. Although his income and power would be considerably curtailed by Ieyasu after the great battle, he was able to maintain a reasonable position under the Tokugawa shogunate. He died a day after turning 71, 50 years after the Battle of Sekigahara.

Mori Terumoto (22 January 1553–27 April 1625)

Born to the distinguished and influential Mori clan, Mori Terumoto's grandfather was Mori Motonari and his father was Mori Takamoto. Overcome by Toyotomi Hideyoshi, he submitted and joined the Toyotomi ranks, receiving the land around Hiroshima as his fief. He essentially founded Hiroshima with the construction of his castle there. Terumoto was appointed by Hideyoshi as one of the five members of the Council of Regents established to rule in the stead of Hideyoshi's five-year-old son following the *Taiko*'s death. Unlike his warlord grandfather and strategist father, Terumoto was believed to have been of below average ability as a warrior and governor.

At Sekigahara, although nominally appointed leader of the Western forces by Ishida Mitsunari, he remained in Osaka Castle with Toyotomi Hideyori, surrendering to Ieyasu soon after the battle. Had Terumoto been on the field that fateful day and had he brought Hideyori with him, it is possible that the eventual turncoats would not have betrayed the West, some Eastern supporters may have returned to their original loyalties and Ieyasu could well have been defeated.

Natsuka Masaie (1562–8 November 1600)

A native of Owari Province, Natsuka Masaie was appointed by Hideyoshi as one of the five commissioners along with Ishida Mitsunari in the Korean Campaign. He was recognised for his strong intellect and mathematical abilities. Prevented from entering the fray by Kikkawa Hiroie, he would spend the entire battle on Mount Nangu. At the end of the slaughter at Sekigahara, he fled to his fief in Minakuchi, set fire to his castle and committed *seppuku*.

Oda Hidenobu (1580–24 July 1605)

Oda Hidenobu was the son of Oda Nobutada and the grandson of Nobunaga. He was just two years old when they were both killed in the Honno-ji Incident. This led to a dispute as to who would head the Oda clan. Toyotomi Hideyoshi supported the infant Hidenobu, while his rival – and uncle – Nobutaka, was supported by Shibata Katsuie. Eventually, Hidenobu would become the head, under the close watch of Hideyoshi. Prior to Sekigahara, Hidenobu held Gifu Castle, considered an important element in Mitsunari's strategy. However, the castle was taken by Fukushima Masanori and Ikeda Terumasa in the weeks before the battle. After losing Gifu, in defeat, Hidenobu's samurai committed ritual suicide in the castle and the bloodstained floorboards were later used in the ceiling of the Sofuku-ji temple in Gifu. Hidenobu renounced the world and became a priest, but died almost five years after Sekigahara.

Ogawa Suketada (1549–1601)

Ogawa Suketada came to prominence serving under Akechi Mitsuhide, later Shibata Katsutoyo and finally Toyotomi Hideyoshi. He was made the *daimyo* of Imabari (Shikoku) and initially sided with Ishida Mitsunari's forces at Sekigahara. His actions during the battle would drastically change the outcome.

Otani Yoshitsugu (1559–21 October 1600)

Remembered today for two main aspects, his crippling leprosy and his loyalty, particularly his loyalty to and friendship with Ishida Mitsunari. It has been recorded that Yoshitsugu put friendship before anything else and that although he was inclined to have supported the Eastern forces at Sekigahara, joined his friend Mitsunari out of loyalty. Otani Yoshitsugu was the only *daimyo* to have committed *seppuku* on the battlefield at Sekigahara.

Shima Sakon (9 June 1540–21 October 1600)

Born in Heguri, Nara, Shima Sakon was in the service of the Tsutsui clan. The highly respected veteran warrior had retired from active service following the death of his master Tsutsui Junkei, but was enticed back into service by a generous offer from Ishida Mitsunari. Sakon would command just 1,000 samurai at Sekigahara and, in defending the Western headquarters, would bear the brunt of some of the fiercest fighting.

Shimazu Yoshihiro (21 August 1535–30 August 1619)

A skilled general born in Kagoshima, Kyushu, Shimazu Yoshihiro wielded great influence over his domain, despite his older brother being the legitimate head. Although a loyal general of the Toyotomi faction and having distinguished himself during Hideyoshi's Korean campaigns, in 1600 Yoshihiro decided to ally himself with the Tokugawa forces. However, he was slighted during the relief of Fushimi Castle prior to the main battle and he again changed allegiances, siding with the Western forces. He would prove to be pivotal to the outcome at Sekigahara.

Toda Shigemasa (1557–21 October 1600)

A brave and much-respected warrior, Toda Shigemasa served under Niwa Nagahide until Niwa's death in 1585 and after that pledged his loyalty to Hideyoshi. He participated in the Kyushu campaigns, the Siege of Odawara and the Korean campaigns. He was killed in action during the Battle of Sekigahara while under the command of Otani Yoshitsugu.

Ukita Hideie (1573–17 December 1655)

Ukita Hideie was the *daimyo* of Bizen and Mimasaka (now Okayama Prefecture) and one of the five-strong Council of Regents appointed by Hideyoshi. Hideie was married to Gohime, born a daughter of Maeda

Toshiie who had been adopted by Toyotomi Hideyoshi. The Ukita clan were at first against the Oda and Toyotomi, but capitulated to Nobunaga shortly before his death. Hideie took part in Hideyoshi's military campaigns in Shikoku (1585), Kyushu (1586), the Siege of Odawara (1590) and the Korean campaigns. One of the first to see action at Sekigahara, he was defeated as a number of former allies turned traitor. Following Sekigahara, Hideie was captured and sent into exile on the prison island of Hachijojima. He was the last of the lords who fought at Sekigahara to die.

Wakisaka Yasuharu (1554–26 September 1626)

As was typical of the *daimyo* of the late Sengoku period, Wakisaka Yasuharu served under a number of lords. Originally in the service of Akechi Mitsuhide under Oda Nobunaga, upon the death of Nobunaga and the subsequent killing of his assassin, Mitsuhide, Yasuharu joined the forces of Hideyoshi, achieving fame in becoming one of the 'Seven Spears of Shizugatake'. As one of Hideyoshi's most trusted generals and as commander of his maritime forces, he was awarded the fief of Awaji Island in the Inland Sea. He participated in Hideyoshi's campaign to quell Kyushu, the Siege of Odawara and both invasions of Korea, during which he annihilated the Korean fleet under Won Gyun in July 1597. Although initially expressing interest in being alongside Ieyasu in 1600, he sided with the West at the outset. Together with Kobayakawa Hideaki, Ogawa Suketada, Akaza Naoyasu and Kutsuki Mototsuna, their actions would turn the tide of the great battle at the last minute.

Glossary

A

Aijirushi – Identification tags worn by samurai during battle.

Ashigaru – Low-ranking foot soldiers.

Ashikaga – Noble family and former shoguns.

Atsuta – The nations' second most important shrine, located in Nagoya.

Awabi – Dried shellfish used in samurai ceremonies, particularly in the *Shutsujin-shiki*, the pre-battle ceremony.

Azuchi – Site of Nobunaga's most glorious castle near Lake Biwa

B

Bugyo – Rank: Commissioner.

C

Chawan – A tea ceremony bowl

D

Daimyo – Title: Refers to the powerful territorial feudal lords.

Do – Armour covering the torso, breast and back.

E

Edo – City. Tokugawa Ieyasu's seat of power. Currently known as Tokyo.

F

Fukigaeshi – The ear-like flanges peculiar to samurai helmets.

Fushimi – Castle and town south of Kyoto.

G

Gessan – Plates of steel or leather to protect the hips and thighs, found hanging below the *do* (body armour) on samurai armour. Also known as *kusazuri*.

Gifu – Town and site of a very strategic castle. Capital of modern-day Gifu Prefecture.

Go – A game of strategy. Played on a thick wooden table with small, round black and white stone pieces.

Gussoku – A suit of samurai armour.

H

Hachiman – The God of War.

Haidate – An apron-like piece of armour worn under the *do*, protecting the thighs.

Hamamatsu – Town in modern Shizuoka Prefecture and site of one of Ieyasu's strategically important castles and long-term residences.

Hanbo – Part of the lower face armour protecting the chin and jaw.

Hara ate – Lit. 'Stomach wrap'. Armour protecting the torso and upper chest.

Hara-kiri – Lit. 'Stomach cut'. Crude term for *seppuku* (q.v.).

Hiei San – Holy mountain north-east of Kyoto.

Hinawaju – Matchlock gun. Also known as *teppo*.

Horagai – Conch-shell horn.

Horo – A type of ballooning cape, often shaped with bamboo, worn by mounted samurai.

Hotoke do – A type of samurai armour, created to look smooth, like the stomach of the often-topless depicted God, Hotoke.

Hyorogan – Round, cake-like nutritious warrior rations.

I

Imokaranawa – A type of soup made by *ashigaru* from potato stalks boiled in thick miso paste.

Inuyama – Town and site of a castle now listed as a National Treasure.

J

Jibu-shousuke – Title: Responsible for court functions, genealogy and marriages.

Jin – Samurai battlefield camp, consisting of rudimentary furnishings, and surrounded by *jinmaku* (q.v.).

Jinbaori – Sleeveless samurai surcoat, worn over the armour.

Jingasa – A type of helmet, usually conical, usually worn by *ashigaru*.

Jinmaku – Cotton hemp curtains decorated with crests set up around a *jin* (q.v.).

Jumonji yari – a cross-shaped (*jumonji*) spear head.

Juzu – Buddhist rosary beads. Also the term given to the rice ration packs worn by *ashigaru* slung across their chests.

K

Kabuto – A samurai helmet.

Kachodoki – War cry performed in unison prior to battle.

Kachushi – Armour craftsman.

Kakuyoku – Crane Wing battle formation. Very effective against large armies.

Katana – The samurai sword.

Kendo – The Way of the Sword, a modern martial art.

Kimono – Robe-like upper clothing worn by the Japanese, held closed by an *obi* sash.

Kirisaki – Crest of paulownia leaves.

Kisouma – A type of short-legged, sturdy native horse used by the samurai.

Kiyosu – Town in modern-day Aichi Prefecture and site of a most strategic castle.

Koku – A measurement of rice, defined as the amount required to feed one person for a year, or about 180 litres. It was by this measurement that *daimyos*' wealth was assessed.

Kombu – Dried seaweed used in soups and in samurai ceremonies.

Kote – Sleeves on a suit of armour.

Koya San – Mount Koya. A holy mountain, long used as a place of exile for the nobility.

Kozuke – A small steel skewer carried tucked into the sword scabbard.

Kubi Jikken – A post-battle ceremony where the heads of enemy samurai were displayed and inspected

Kubizuka – A head burial mound.

Kuri – Chestnut. Important as a food source and used in certain ceremonies.

Kurihangetsu – A crescent moon-shaped war standard.

Kusazuri – Plates of steel or leather to protect the hips and thighs, found hanging below the *do* on samurai armour. Also called *gessan*.

Kuwagata – Antler-like flanges fitted to the front of samurai helmets.

M

Maedate – Crest-like device fitted to the front of samurai helmets.

Matsuo – Mountain to the south of Sekigahara where Kobayakawa set up camp.

Mikatagahara – Battlefield near Hamamatsu where Ieyasu lost to the Takeda in 1573.

Mikawa – Tokugawa-held domain, now western Aichi Prefecture.

Minamoto – Ancient and powerful noble warrior clan of Imperial descent.

Mino – Province. Modern-day Gifu Prefecture.

Miso – A long-lasting and nutritious paste-like food made from fermented soybeans.

Mogami Dou – A two-piece body armour of horizontal plates and hinged to the left in a clamshell fashion.

Momokubari – A small mountain east of Sekigahara where Ieyasu first set up camp.

Muramasa – Family of swordsmiths from Kuwana, Mie Prefecture, famed for their particularly fine blades.

N

Naginata – A glaive-like polearm.

Nagoya – Castle city in central Japan, capital of Aichi Prefecture.

Nakasendo – A strategically-important major highway running through the central mountainous regions of Japan between Kyoto and Edo.

Nanban gussoku – Armour incorporating foreign elements.

Ninja – Spies, agents and mercenaries.

Nuinobe do – A two-piece body armour of multiple horizontal plates, usually laced vertically, and hinged on the left.

Nurigasa – A type of wide rain hat.

O

Ogaki – City and site of a splendid castle in Gifu Prefecture.

Okazaki – Capital of Mikawa Province (Aichi Prefecture) birthplace of Ieyasu and site of his ancestral castle.

Okashi Gussoku – Lit. 'Borrowed armour', supplied by a lord to his *ashigaru*.

Okegawa do – Type of armour made with horizontal strips of steel resembling a barrel.

Omi – Province, north-east of Kyoto and containing Lake Biwa, currently Shiga Prefecture.

Onna Kubi – Lit. 'Women's heads'. Heads having been taken as a trophy found after a battle with the nose and upper lip missing.

Oni – Devil.

Osaka – City and site of Hideyoshi's most impressive castle.

Owari – Region now comprising western Aichi Prefecture.

R

Rokujogahara – The execution grounds on the Kamo River banks, Kyoto

Ronin – Lit. 'Wave man'. A masterless samurai.

Ryo – A feudal period gold coin. A pre-Yen unit.

S

Saihai – A short tasselled-paper or yak-hair whip used by commanders to direct troops in battle.

Sake – A traditional Japanese alcoholic drink made from fermented rice.

Samurai – Lit. 'One Who Serves'. The warrior class of feudal Japan.

Sashimono – The battle flag worn on the back of a samurai's armour.

Sasao (Sasaoyama) – Small mountain north-west of the Sekigahara battle-field where Ishida Mitsunari set up his headquarters.

Seppuku – A form of ritual suicide.

Shaku – A measurement of both length and weight. Approx 30cm or 400g.

Shikoro – Neck guard below and around the samurai helmet bowl.

Shogi – A foldable stool used in war camps.

Shogun – Grand General. Hereditary military dictator.

Shutsujin-shiki – Samurai pre-battle ceremony.

Sode – Shoulder armour.

Sou Taisho – Title: Commander-in-Chief.

Suji kabuto – Samurai helmet, the bowl of which is made from rounded triangular lames riveted together.

Suneate – Armoured shinpads.

T

Tachi – Sword worn with armour, slung with the edge of the blade facing downwards.

Taiko – Title awarded to a regent, closely matching that of Shogun. Used by Toyotomi Hideyoshi.

Tairo – Lit. 'Great Elder'. Title: Statesmen and high government official.

Taisho – Commander, general or captain.

Tanto – Small knife under 30cm in length carried by samurai.

Tatami gussoku – Lit. Foldable Armour. Type of armour consisting of steel plates connected by chain mail. Usually worn by lower-ranked samurai

Teppo – Japanese matchlock gun. Also called a *Hinawaju*.

Teppotai – Unit of matchlockmen.

Tokaido – The Eastern Sea Route. A strategically important major highway running over 514km between the capital, Kyoto, and Edo.

Toryu Gunpo Koushasho – Book on the winning ways of strategy.

Tosando – A major highway traversing the eastern mountain ranges,

Tousei gussoku – Lit. 'Modern Armour', being an armour style created from the mid-1500s to the end of the samurai period.

Tsuba – Hand guard of a sword.

U

Ueda – Town and castle in modern-day Nagano Prefecture.

Utsugatana – A type of sword usually worn by samurai with the edge of the blade uppermost and when not in armour.

W

Wakizashi – A short companion blade to the *tachi* or *katana*.

Washi – Strong traditional Japanese paper.

Y

Yari – A spear.

Yaribusuma   An effective battle formation consisting of a wall of spearmen.

Yoroi – Suit of armour, also known as *kachu*.

Yoroibakama – Baggy trouser-like clothing tied at the shins, worn under a suit of armour.

Z

Zohyo Monogatari – A handbook for foot soldiers.

Zunari kabuto – A type of samurai helmet, popular for its low cost, simple construction and high protective qualities.

Select Bibliography

E de Shiru Nihonshi, Sekigahara Kassen Byoubu (Shueisha, 2011).

Frederic, Louis, *Japan Encyclopaedia* (Cambridge, Massachusetts: Harvard University Press, 2002).

Ietada Nikki ('Diary of Ietada'). Waseda University collection.

Iisawa Shoji, *Zusetsu, Sengoku Kachu Shu* (Gakken, 2003).

Ikkojin, edition 136 (September 2011).

Keicho Nenjuki ('Diary of the Keicho Period'). Waseda University collection.

Kessen Sekigahara, Sengoku no Mottomo Nagai Hi, Rekishi Gunzo Series, *Sengoku* Selection (Gakken. 2000).

Morimoto Masahiro, *Matsudaira Ietada Nikki* (Kadokawa Sensho, 1999).

Mu Rekishi Series 4, *Sekigahara no Tatakai* (Gakken Mook, 1987).

Murdoch, James, *A History Of Japan During the Century of Early Foreign Intercourse (1542-1651)* (Kobe Chronicle, 1903).

Nakanishi Ritta, *The History of Japanese Armor, Vol. 2* (Dainippon Kaiga Co. Ltd, 2009).

Naramoto Tatsuya, *Nihon no kassen: monoshiri jiten* (Tokyo: Shufu to Seikatsusha, 1994).

NHK (Nippon Hōsō Kyōkai), 'Sono Toki Rekishi ga Ugoita' (315th broadcast).

NHK Shuzai Han, *DoDo Nihonshi*, Vol. 12 (Chuo Shuppan, 1998).

Ogaki-Haku Tokubetsu Ten, *Kassen Sekigahara* (Studio Bega, 2000).

Owada Tetsuo, *Sekigahara Kassen no Subute* (Shinjin Butsu Orai-sha, 1984).

Owada Tetsuo, *Shousha no Kenkyu, Haisha no Kenkyu, Sekigahara no Tatakai* (Mikasa Shobou, 1993)

Owada Testuo, *Sekigahara no Tatakai, Shosha no Kenkyu* (Mikasa Shobo, 1999).

Owada Tetsuo and Chris Glenn, *Must See Sekigahara* (Sunrise Publishing, 2018).

Papinot, E., *Historical and Geographical Dictionary of Japan* (Tuttle, 1972).

Rekishijin, editions 1 (2010), 5, 7 (2011), 17, 23, 25 (2012), 32, 34, 39 (2013), 40 (2104), 73 (2016). Special editions: *Sengoku Busho no Shi* (2012), *Sengoku Busho Saikyo Ranking* (2013).

Rekishi Kaido, June 2010, May 2013 editions.

Sadler, A.L., *The Maker Of Modern Japan; The Life of Shogun Tokugawa Ieyasu* (Tuttle, 1937).

Sansom, George, *A History of Japan: 1334-1615* (Stanford University Press, 1961).

Sekigahara Dai Kessen (Shinjinbutsu Oraisha, 2000).

Sekigahara Gunki, 1713.

Sekigahara Kassen Zu (Chuo Koronsha, 1980).

Sekigahara no Tatakai, Shosha no Kenkyu, Haisha no Kenkyu (Mikasa Shobo, 1993).

Sekigahara Tatakai no Subete (Shinjin Butsuo Raiisha, 1984).

Sekigahara Tourist Association, *Sekigahara Guide Book* (2005).

Senran No Nihonshi 3, *Sekigahara 1600* (Shogakukan, 2008).

Shiramine Jun, *Sekigahara Tairan, Hontou no Shousha* (Asahi Shinsho, 2020).

Shukan Time Travel, *Sekigahara no Shitou Hachi Jikan. Saigen Nihonshi*, Vol. 10 (Kodansha, May 2001).

Toudaiki ('Chronicle of the Times'), 1623-1644 (excerpts).

Tougou Ryu, *Sengoku Kassen Manual* (Kodansha, 2001).

Taniguchi Gyokuten, *Sekigahara Kassen ni Manabu* (Sanmesse Co., 1983).

Taniguchi Katsuhiro, Iisawa Shoji and Ono Nobunaga, *Zusetsu, Sengoku Busho* 118 (Gakken, 2001).

Turnbull, Stephen, *The Samurai, A Military History* (Japan Library, 1996).

Index